The Politically Incorrect Guide® to the American Revolution

Be sure to check out

The Politically Incorrect Guides® to...

The Politically Incorrect Guide® to
The American Revolution

Larry Schweikart
Dave Dougherty

REGNERY
PUBLISHING
A Division of Salem Media Group

Regnery® is a registered trademark of Salem Communications Holding Corporation

Cataloging-in-Publication data on file with the Library of Congress

First e-book edition 2017: ISBN 978-1-62157-650-1
Originally published in paperback, 2017: ISBN 978-1-62157-625-9

Published in the United States by
Regnery Publishing
A Division of Salem Media Group
300 New Jersey Ave NW
Washington, DC 20001
www.Regnery.com

Manufactured in the United States of America

10 9 8 7 6 5 4 3 2 1

Books are available in quantity for promotional or premium use. For information on discounts and terms, please visit our website: www.Regnery.com.

Distributed to the trade by
www.perseusdistribution.com

To the Sons and Daughters of America's Revolution

Contents

The Great Revolution

Revolutions come and go. One could not even begin to calculate the number of revolts and revolutions in world history, or even in the modern era. So what's another revolution?

In any case, was America's War of Independence a revolution at all?

To listen to the leftist writers (the term "scholars" doesn't seem applicable) whose interpretations dominate the teaching of American history, the Revolution was contrived by the wealthy. Howard Zinn asked, "Did ordinary white farmers have the same interest in the revolution as John Hancock... or the slaveholders or the bondholders? Not really." Another Marxist writer, John Peterson, has praised the American Revolution, but only because "the Americans carried through the bourgeois democratic revolution on a scale never before seen in history." A website called Knowledgenuts claims, "America's Revolution Was Fought by the Poor, Not the Citizens."

The Marxists can't seem to make up their minds: was the Revolution fought by the poor or by the wealthy landowners for their own interests? But let's not let logic stand in the way of a good Marxist rant. Not only are the leftist writers wrong, they can't even tell a consistent story!

A Book You're Not Supposed to Read

The Anatomy of a Revolution by Crane Brinton (New York: Vintage, 1965) is a solid comparison and contrast of the American, French, English, and Russian revolutions.

Other scholars—the ones who don't hate America—have referred to the Declaration of Independence as "The Great Declaration." We submit that it's time to change the name of the American Revolution to "The Great Revolution," for it, unlike any other, changed all of history for the good. America's revolution was the first in history to assert that ordinary people could tell their leaders what to do, and not the reverse.

Our revolution immediately became the model for many other revolutions—beginning with the flawed French Revolution. Yet America's stuck and France's did not. The American Revolution resulted in the foundation of a stable and prosperous republic. Elsewhere, revolutions were followed by countless other revolutions, coups, and wars. The only major issue the American Revolution left unresolved—the full application of the phrase "all men are created equal" to slaves in America—was resolved in the Civil War. As bloody as that was, the U.S. government never stopped functioning, and the U.S. Constitution never ceased operating. Indeed, the ultimate result of that Civil War was to apply the rights guaranteed by the Constitution and the Declaration's bold statement that "all men are created equal" to all.

America's revolution was different from the outset. America supplied the world with the blueprint for a citizen revolution, but non-Americans were lacking the necessary traditions and foundations for such a revolution to succeed.

France needed five tries—interspersed with a restoration of the monarchy and two dictatorships—to get a functioning republic without fatal flaws. Germany had its republic fail grotesquely and completely. Many other "republics" in Latin America and Africa did not even get off the ground. So-called "democracies" and "republics" in Africa are as distant from the rule of the people—the basis of a republic, or *res publica*—as one can get.

Exceptional

What made the American Revolution different? In *The Anatomy of a Revolution* Crane Brinton tried to find a common thread among the American, French, English, and Russian revolutions, but he had to admit that the American Revolution was different—it never went through a truly violent stage like those that infected all the others—leading him to conclude that the American Revolution wasn't a revolution at all! In fact, it was, but it differs dramatically from all of the other revolutions because *America* differs dramatically from all other nations.

The United States is unique, exceptional. Many today shy away from the phrase "American exceptionalism," finding it jingoistic, but it is the reality. American exceptionalism rests on four pillars found nowhere else—at least not going back to the origin of any other country: 1) a Protestant religious foundation; 2) the common law; 3) private property with written titles and deeds; and 4) a free market economy. England had the last three traits, but not true Protestantism. England was originally Catholic, and even when the Church of England broke away from Rome it was still a copy of the Catholic Church, with top-down governance. Germany had common law under the Germanic tribes, but not after Napoleon conquered Europe and installed civil law (if they had not lost it before then). Many of the Asian Tigers have free markets (more or less) and private property rights, but they

A Book You're Not Supposed to Read

A Vigorous Spirit of Enterprise by Thomas Doerflinger (Chapel Hill: University of North Carolina Press, 1986) documents the economic mobility in colonial Philadelphia.

have never had common law or the Christian religion. And on and on. Only America, from her inception, has had all four.

So from the beginning the American people had both a religious and a political philosophy of bottom-up governance. That explains why British attempts to regulate trade and introduce new taxes and laws that even *potentially* threatened to allow top-down control of the American colonies were viewed with sheer terror and united the colonists immediately.

A Rich Man's War? A Poor Man's Fight?

A failure to appreciate the uniqueness of American origins leads to misunderstanding of the Great Revolution itself. Modern-day Marxists have blatantly distorted the events of 1776, portraying the American revolutionaries as driven by wealth and race. In their view, the Revolution was an attempt by the rich white guys at the top to protect their wealth. But colonial society was not as stratified as the leftists make out. A number of studies on colonial wealth have found that while inequalities did exist, movement between income levels was common and often rapid. People fell out of the top ranks routinely, and just as frequently others climbed up into them. So the concern about x percent of the population owning y percent of the wealth is misplaced—because the actual individuals who made up the x percent were constantly changing.

To claim, on the other hand, that the brunt of the sacrifices of the Revolution was borne by the poor pretty much disregards the life stories of the fifty-six signers of the Declaration, all of whom were men of substance, and all of whom put their "Fortunes" as well as their "Lives" and "Sacred

Honor" on the line when they signed the document. Virtually all of them paid a heavy price for their signatures: almost all lost land, many were forced to run for their lives during the war, many lost children or wives, and several ended up in desperate economic circumstances, even in debtors' prison.

The impact of the American Revolution was immediate and worldwide. French intellectuals began to apply the concepts that had animated the American Revolution to their own situation immediately, and within forty years, Latin American republics would seek to copy the Americans' experience. But none of these other revolutionaries understood the fundamental underlying basis for the long-term success of our revolution, and consequently it was inevitable that their own revolutions would not produce similar results.

France's revolution was almost entirely class-based, and it involved a hefty dose of anti-clericalism. Whereas in the American Revolution it was the Presbyterian Church (more or less) vs. the Anglican Church, in the French Revolution it was the secularists vs. the Catholic Church. And lacking any long-standing constitutional framework, such as existed in the Americans' 150 years of practicing common law and limited government, France quickly disintegrated into mobs and the guillotine. Likewise, Russia's revolution pitted the secular communists against a monarchy—supported by a hodgepodge of not-communists—again, all without any experience of self-government (other than a short time in the ineffective Duma). But the original English revolution—popularly known as the English Civil Wars—which predated America's, while involving its own share of bloodshed, nevertheless never saw the abandonment of the common law. The priority of the rule of law over the "divine right of kings" was finally ratified in the Glorious Revolution that installed William and Mary in 1688.

In the nineteenth and, more frequently, the twentieth centuries, revolutions repeatedly unseated monarchs, dictators, or colonial regimes, only to give birth to new dictatorships. In the first thirty years after de-colonization, sub-Saharan Africa saw sixty-four military coups. Were not many of these countries one-time colonies of England, like the United States? What happened? Unlike Britain's American colonies, her African colonies were tightly controlled by colonial administrators and developed no practice of self-government. And few were Christian nations.

Even closer to home, however, the result was the same. Mexico, having kicked out the Spanish in 1821, first had an emperor, then a dictator (Santa Anna) who was ousted, then returned, then was overthrown and exiled, then returned again during the Mexican War, then was removed yet again. Mexico only remained "independent" for nine years until the French placed a puppet government in charge for a failure to repay debts. That government was in turn booted out in 1865. And on and on. Mexico saw constant turmoil until well into the twentieth century. The question, again, is why? And the answer, again, is obvious: Mexico, under the Spanish monarchy, had no history or habit of self-government. America had over 150 years' worth of "benign neglect" from England under which to hone democratic skills. Nor did Mexico have the common law, or a Protestant tradition that supported the idea that the people were sovereign rather than a pope, king, emperor, or dictator.

None of the hundreds of revolts, coups, and overthrows in the African states has ever been called great. Not one inspired other peoples to seek their rights, nor did any serve as a model for anything other than corruption and failure. But America's revolution did. What others pointed to, and attempted to emulate, was not the separation from England, but the aftermath—a stable, relatively peaceful country with regular exchanges of power not just between individuals who shared a similar worldview, but between factions and parties with substantially different ideas on how the American founding should be perpetuated.

What made all this possible began at Lexington in darkness, when a few shots "heard 'round the world" gave British regulars a seemingly easy victory over their colonial cousins. Within hours, though, the British troops realized they had poked the bear, and hastily retreated back to Boston. From that point on, the War for American Independence became a struggle not just between two sides differing over who should be in authority, but between two different military strategies. For the Americans under General George Washington, the objective was simple: keep the army together and keep it alive. As long as Washington still had an army, the United States of America had hope. Thus Washington endured defeat after defeat, nearly losing the army entirely at Long Island; yet through the force of his will and the commitment of patriots he maintained its existence long enough to strike a surprise blow at Trenton on Christmas in 1776. Trenton became the revolutionary equivalent of Tet, the Viet Cong–North Vietnamese attack in 1968 that convinced the American media that the U.S. had lost the Vietnam War. It was perceptions that Trenton changed, not battlefield realities. Washington survived the winter, and while he lost Philadelphia, the following fall an American force largely consisting of militia cut off and defeated General John Burgoyne's column at Saratoga, persuading the French to join the war effort on the side of the Americans.

In the American South, the British capture of Charleston in 1780 marked a low point, but was hardly a fatal blow. Nathanael Greene maintained a Patriot military presence in the South until Americans could crush a Tory army (made up of colonists loyal to Britain) at the Battle of King's Mountain (1780) then, under Daniel Morgan, defeat a mixed British-Tory force at the Battle of Cowpens (1781). These victories led up to the Yorktown campaign, where, with the assistance of the French navy, the Patriot forces surrounded Lord Cornwallis and forced his surrender.

Leading up to and alongside these victories, though, Patriot forces took a consistent beating. After the first battles in Massachusetts the war went through five major campaign phases—though several of them overlapped: 1) The unsuccessful American invasion of Canada; 2) the American defeats at Long Island and New York; 3) the pursuit of the Americans by the British through the "middle colonies" and American victories at Trenton and Princeton, followed by Washington's stalking the British around Philadelphia, and the great American victory at Saratoga; 4) the Southern campaign; and 5) the climactic Yorktown campaign. Each of these phases involved profound misperceptions and underestimations by both sides: the Americans badly misunderstood their Canadian cousins as being willing allies. While the Americans were losing, the British underestimated the ability of the colonial forces not only to survive, but to "train on the run"; they underestimated Washington's forces and their resilience and determination. The British also grossly overestimated the support of the Southern Tories and their ability to fight, or both. And Charles Cornwallis overestimated the ability of the Royal Navy to maintain a supply line and escape route out of Yorktown. Overall, the Americans were able to correct their misperceptions, while the British were not.

Washington had been flanked at the Battle of Long Island and lost two-thirds of his troops. He and his men constantly ran from larger British forces and had to winter in outdoor locations while the British lounged in Philadelphia and New York. (One joke ran that General Howe had not so much as captured Philadelphia as Philadelphia had captured Howe.) At Valley Forge, cold, starvation, and disease ravaged Washington's small army. Yet he again kept it together. In the South, Greene's army was defeated by Cornwallis at Guilford Courthouse, but dealt such heavy casualties to the British that it was a strategic victory.

Despite the critically important gains in the South, ultimately the war was about Washington and his army. Washington (the "indispensable man," as biographer James Thomas Flexner called him) was the glue that held the Revolution together. Not only was he commander of the armies—though not without petty resentments from other generals—but he was the icon, the symbol of American resistance. If James Otis, Samuel Adams, and the

Articles of Association drafted at the First Continental Congress were the sparks that ignited the Revolution—making possible Jefferson's Great Declaration—and if John Adams and Benjamin Franklin were the kindling that gave it legal and philosophical sustenance at its beginning, Washington was the wood. And as long as the fuel remained, the fire burned.

A Book You're Not Supposed to Read

Washington: The Indispensable Man by James Thomas Flexner (New York: Mentor, 1974).

Holy Fire

The Patriot troops came overwhelmingly from the ranks of Scotch-Irish, with perhaps as many as half the American forces at a given time being of Scotch-Irish stock. One cannot overemphasize the importance of the Presbyterian, Scotch-Irish backbone of the Revolution against not just the English, but the English of the Anglican Church. Many scholars have commented on the religious nature of the American Revolution, while often at the same time downplaying Washington's own faith. But works by Peter Lilleback and William J. Johnson have shown beyond doubt that Washington himself was a devout Christian. That was yet another reason he was so necessary to the success of the "Glorious Cause." If the American Revolution was not primarily about the kingdom of heaven, there is no doubt that religious faith—and religious tensions—played a central role in the motivations of the Americans.

In 1776, most Patriots believed that the Hand of God was creating America's constitutional republic, and that the result would be a first in human history. Its creation would fulfill the Almighty's design to establish Christian liberty, protected by civil government and formed by biblical principles. This belief was the fusion of two thousand years' worth of Judeo-Christian religious and philosophical principles combined with Greco-Roman concepts

A Book You're Not Supposed to Read

American Scripture: Making the Declaration of Independence by Pauline Maier (New York: Alfred E. Knopf, 1998).

of democracy and government. The American republic was to be something different, "something new upon the face of the earth," in the words of historian Pauline Maier—an inspiration and challenge to the whole world. If the American republic failed, it would be because its people had failed God and rejected His government. The world would plunge back into darkness. It was all or nothing, and the Patriots must not fail. At least, that's how Americans felt.

Given the precarious position in which the Patriot troops found themselves after the first defeats in New York, it was natural for Washington to complain about the militia. The difference between colonial militia and trained professionals was substantial, and had nothing to do with courage, but rather with tactics. The fighting style of professional British Redcoats involved staying in rank and moving to within range of the enemy before delivering a volley of concentrated fire (or sometimes two), then charging the weak spot of the enemy's line with the bayonet. Colonial flintlock rifles or muskets—even when they outranged the reliable "Brown Bess" musket of the British Army—did not have an attachment for a bayonet, and thus after discharge at a rapidly approaching enemy the flintlock was at best a club. Moreover, colonial troops were not trained in using muskets for close combat, so that many abandoned the weapon altogether in favor of the tomahawk or the knife. Needless to say, the Redcoats were at an advantage in such a situation.

And there were other factors that limited the militia's effectiveness. American units tended to elect their own officers. That meant that the officer had the support of his men, but often for reasons other than military acumen. Indeed, someone known to be economical with the lives of his troops might be quite popular, but a failure on the battlefield because of his unwillingness to take a difficult position and risk high casualties. Worse, militiamen were homebodies, extremely effective when fighting for their home turf, but completely unreliable on long-distance campaigns.

For these and other reasons, the militia—to Washington's disgust—repeatedly broke and ran when placed in open fields facing solid lines of British bayonets. In fortifications, where they were not likely to be wounded in the legs (so that they could still count on getting away if they had to), they generally fought extremely well—at Bunker Hill, for example. But neither the militia nor the state troops assigned to the Continental Army were trained in European fighting maneuvers. So on top of evading a head-on conflict that could result in the army's death or capture, Washington had to train his regular troops in basic military maneuvers as time and resources permitted between battles, and he had few drill instructors who knew their stuff. After the arrival of several Europeans, including Tadeusz Kościuszko and Friedrich von Steuben, training took on added vigor and began to show results. Even with the improvement of the Continental Army, however, the militia played a critical role in the war effort, especially at the victories over the Hessians at Bennington, Vermont, and Cornwallis's energetic cavalry leader Banastre Tarleton at Cowpens.

What Are the Odds?

Contrary to some traditional patriotic American histories, the Revolution was a close-run thing. Patriot forces suffered extensive losses in numerous battles, and for every victory it seems there were often two or three equally disastrous losses. Even after the Patriot success at Saratoga in 1777, the chances of ultimate victory remained extremely slim.

Despite the extraordinary efforts of Washington, the sacrifices of his Northern troops, and the stunning victories in the South, the knockout blow required the assistance of the French: one can search history long and hard

A Book You're Not Supposed to Read

Logistics and the Failure of the British Army in America, 1775 –1783 by Arthur Bowler (Princeton: Princeton University Press, 2016).

for French naval victories, and their defeats (Aboukir Bay, Trafalgar, and so forth) are well known. Yet the arrival of the French fleet under Admiral Francois Joseph de Grasse and his running fight with the Royal Navy culminating in the victory at the Virginia Capes damaged British prestige; and by preventing the British from reaching Cornwallis at Yorktown by sea, de Grasse allowed Washington and the French troops to force Cornwallis's surrender, and put a nearly immediate end to British hopes for victory. In addition, French money and arms kept the Continental Army paid (irregularly) and supplied.

With the loss of Cornwallis's entire army at Yorktown, the British government came to the realization that it could not win the war. Despite still having four intact armies in North America, England had seen three of its brightest professionals humiliated and two entire armies (plus the Hessian mercenaries) surrendered. And despite still holding major cities such as New York, Charleston, and Savannah, the British had not pacified enough of the countryside to venture out except in large numbers or with their Tory and Indian allies. Most of all, as new research by Arthur Bowler demonstrates, the Redcoats were simply ill-equipped to maintain a major effort in North America over such a long period of time: the British did not even have an organization capable of supplying the army until the war was nearly over, if then.

All these factors—Washington's crucial role as a rallying point, timely victories by the Americans, the vast space that the British had to pacify, the assistance of the French, and poor British logistics—contributed to American independence. But then there was one more element that cannot be measured or proven: Divine Providence. Whether it was Washington's escape from Long Island under a sudden fog, or his miraculous uninjured ride between two armies volleying at each other in broad daylight, or the brilliant timing of Thomas Paine's immortal words, or France's sudden change of heart, the United States had what has to be described by a secularist as extraordinary good luck—and by a believer as divine intervention.

The result was something the world had never seen: a nation of laws, with power surging from the bottom to the top, dedicated (as Abraham Lincoln would later say) to the proposition—for the first time in human history—that "all men are created equal." Leftists and critics of America gleefully point to the fact that those words were not a reality, but paradoxically that is the point. Up to that point, no other people had ever uttered them, even as a desired goal. The Judeo-Christian tradition in which almost all of the founders were immersed emphasized the role of the covenant, a divine contract sealed by blood that could not be broken by man. America's founding, and its Great Declaration, were in the minds of those founders part of that covenant, and while the promises of the contract were not fulfilled in 1776 or even 1876, they nevertheless were there all along to be seized by every American.

CHAPTER 1

Revolutionary Road

When did the American Revolution start? Many people—at least if they haven't spent too much time in public school—would still say "in 1775 at Lexington and Concord." Americans all used to know that on the morning of April 19, 1775, a column of seven hundred British soldiers marched on Lexington and Concord, Massachusetts. At Lexington Green, the van of about three hundred encountered about seventy militia, and shots were exchanged. No one has yet proven who fired first. The British, of course, claimed the colonials started it. But according to the colonial accounts, someone on the British side fired first. Since dawn was still a half-hour away when the first shot rang out, it's no wonder that the accounts are in conflict.

This was the famous "Shot Heard 'Round the World," the shot that began the American Revolution. But when did the Revolution really *start*?

It would not be unreasonable to claim that the American Revolution began almost the moment English colonists arrived in the New World. The British exploration program, to save money for the government, utilized "joint-stock" companies to settle America. English shareholders in London and other English cities purchased speculative interests in companies that

Did you know?

★ Even before 1700, local insurgencies in America had seized control of colonial governments

★ One of the causes of the American Revolution was a tax *cut*

★ The Battle of Alamance, North Carolina, over British taxes, preceded Lexington and Concord by four years

they hoped would find gold or other sources of wealth in the New World. Especially at first, the stockholders did not make the trip themselves. Nor did British government officials. The English government issued charters that gave companies exclusive rights (monopolies) to settle, develop, and conduct trade with and within specific regions. Company officers and managers became the colonial government under the policy *rex in abstentia* ("the king in his absence").

Colonial governors, even those later appointed directly by the king, were extremely limited in their powers. The policies they decreed could be and often were overridden by Parliament. In addition, the governors were thousands of miles away from Parliament and the king—and often even from regular British troops. Communication with Great Britain took months, even assuming that Parliament or the king's ministers supported the governors' policies and acted without delays. To deal with pressing issues, colonists quickly became accustomed to having councils—even representatives—that advised the governors. These colonial "assemblies" soon gained a great deal of autonomy.

The Rights of Englishmen

In 1619, Sir George Yeardley, the royally appointed governor of Virginia, met with his council and assembly according to the Royal Charter of Virginia (1606) that had guaranteed the colonists full rights as Englishmen identical to those of Englishmen residing in England. This term had a clear significance: "the rights of Englishmen" had evolved and developed, been fought over and refined at great cost to English patriots over four hundred years, ever since the Magna Carta. In the London Company document creating the "general Assemblie"—with the consent of Parliament—there was a promise that after the colony and its government had been securely established, "No orders of our Court afterward shall bind [the] colony unless they be ratified in like manner in their general Assemblie." This was nothing less than the elevation of the "general Assemblie" over the governor and even (although this would be tested) the Parliament itself!

While the Virginia colonists, though often religious, had not come to the New World primarily for religious freedom, the Pilgrims (Puritan separatists from Scrooby) had. Having been blown off course and arrived much farther north than their charter allowed, the Pilgrims agreed to the Mayflower Compact before they left the ship. This document pledged loyalty to the king, but the colony elected its own governor. The compact marked another step toward independence.

With both the Pilgrims and the Massachusetts Bay Puritans, another element of self-rule and representative government was built into the American system. The Puritans were religious reformers who strongly believed in "congregationalism," in which local churches—not a larger church body or an individual like the archbishop of Canterbury or the pope—set doctrine. It was another instance of bottom-up governance in America, whereas England and Canada were both still either Anglican (England) or Catholic (Canada).

As the English colonists spread out from Virginia and Massachusetts, they took self-government with them. The 1639 *Fundamental Orders of Connecticut*, for example, has been called the world's first written constitution. Almost all the colonies developed something similar.

Moreover, from an extremely early date, these largely self-governing colonies began communicating with each other and even forming early multi-colony governments. In 1643, the New England Confederation of

A Book You're Not Supposed to Read

Under the Cope of Heaven: Religion, Society, and Politics in Colonial America by Patricia Bonomi (New York: Oxford, 2003) shows that religion was as fundamental to the average life of colonial Americans as politics or finances were.

★ ★ ★

What Was So "Glorious" about the Revolution of 1688?

Did you ever wonder how events get their names? The Revolution of 1688 placed a king (and queen) on the throne of England: William of Orange and his wife Mary. What was so revolutionary—not to mention glorious—about that?

In the Glorious Revolution common people— the representatives in Parliament, where most were not aristocrats—officially endowed a leader with power. Until that time, emperors, kings, and queens had been "ordained" to rule by birthright, reigning by "the divine right of kings." Now commoners were in essence placing the crowns on the heads of William and Mary. It was bottom-up, not top-down governance.

William and Mary re-established English control over the American colonies, but the notion of unified colonies acting apart from England did not go away. In 1697 William Penn introduced a "Plan of Union" for the American colonies, citing Indian attacks and the inability of the British government to provide effective defense. (A number of wars pitting the English against the French and their Indian allies followed, culminating in the French and Indian War of 1754–63 that evicted France from North America until Napoleon recovered Louisiana from Spain.) Penn's plan called for Boston, Rhode Island, Connecticut, New York, New Jersey, Pennsylvania, Maryland, Virginia, and Carolina to send two representatives each to a council meeting each year. The king's commissioner would preside over the meeting, but this constituted an attempt to form a North American legislative body equal to Parliament.

Massachusetts, Connecticut, Plymouth, and New Haven was created to defend against Indian attacks and incursions by the Dutch in New York. Although this confederation dissolved in 1686 when King James II revoked the colonial charters and established the Dominion of New England, the precedent for cooperation had been set. In England's Glorious Revolution of 1688, citizens in Massachusetts rose up to overthrow King James's governor, Edmund Andros, and temporarily restored self-government.

Pulpit of Democracy

By 1700, local insurgencies had already seized control of colonial governments a number of times. Occasionally—as with Leisler's Rebellion in 1689–91—the instigator paid with his life, but in other instances the perpetrators were pardoned. Governing English Anglicans and Puritans (plus a good number of Quakers) was proving difficult enough, and then, from 1710 to 1775, some two hundred fifty thousand Presbyterians from Ulster and other parts of Ireland arrived in America seeking to escape political, religious, and economic persecution. These Scotch-Irish had a much different worldview from the Anglican English, and it colored everything, from how they farmed to how they fought.

★ ★ ★
Fiercely Independent

The Hearts of Steel, or Steelboys, was a movement active in Ulster (Northern Ireland) from 1769 to 1773 against steeply rising rents and the resulting evictions that were causing families great suffering. Composed almost exclusively of Presbyterians, the Steelboys won a preliminary battle at Gilford, County Armagh, where they had mustered an army of almost five thousand men. But soon they faced veteran British troops, who hunted them down unmercifully, triggering the final large Scotch-Irish wave of emigration to America from 1772 to 1775, estimated to have been as high as forty thousand people. To call these Scotch-Irish anti-English would be a massive understatement, and they had large families. Two of these Scotch-Irish immigrants were James Dougherty and his wife Jane, whose marriage in the Presbyterian Church was not recognized by British authorities. James went with Arnold to Quebec in 1775, was captured, ultimately enlisted in the Twelfth Pennsylvania Regiment, fought at Trenton and Princeton, was transferred to the artillery for other battles, then became one of Washington's Lifeguards. He served in the Continental Army until it disbanded in 1783. Dougherty was the great-great-great-grandfather of author Dave Dougherty.

A Book You're Not Supposed to Read

The Pulpit of the American Revolution, or the Political Sermons of the Period of 1776. With a Historical Introduction, Notes, and Illustrations, 2nd ed., John Wingate Thornton ed. (Boston: D. Lothrop & Co., 1876) covers important and influential sermons from 1750 to 1783, attesting to the role of religion in the Revolution.

These Scotch-Irish proved to be the backbone of the Revolution, and especially of the Continental Army, including such generals as Hugh Mercer, "Mad" Anthony Wayne, Richard Montgomery, John Stark, Daniel Morgan, and Henry Knox, to name just a few. A third or even as many as half of the Continental troops were Scotch-Irish—going by the estimates of British General James Robertson and Joseph Galloway, who served in the Continental Congress. On the other side, up to one-third of the British forces may have been *Catholic* Irish and Scots. Many English saw the rebellion as little more than a Scotch-Irish revolt: Horace Walpole jibed that "our American cousin has run away with a Scotch-Irish parson." George Washington attested to the high number of Scotch-Irish in his ranks.

Scotch-Irish, unlike many of their colonial brethren, were not fighting for "the rights of Englishmen." They were motivated by the same hatred of England that would later inspire the Irish to rebel against English rule. In fact, revolutionary ideals crossed back to Ireland from America rather than coming here from Ireland. In America, the fusion of hatred for England and the love of revolutionary ideas led the Scotch-Irish to emphasize allegiance to church more than to any secular government. And the Presbyterian Church was stridently for American independence, more so than any other denomination.

Then there were the Germans, who mostly settled in the Shenandoah Valley and Pennsylvania, where by 1775 they made up a third of the population. Many were members of pacifist sects such as the Dunkers or Mennonites, but the majority were Lutherans. One thing they had in common with each other—and their Protestant neighbors—was that they were familiar with both persecution from government-supported churches and congregational governance.

In short, the religious and ethnic origins of most colonial Americans meant that they had no trouble bucking authority, speaking their minds, and exercising self-government in both political and religious spheres. Historian Robert Middlekauff put it this way: "Religion shaped culture [and] the churches in the colonies differed from one another. But beneath the surface their similarities were even more striking—a governance so dominated by laymen as to constitute a congregational democracy...." They began to connect the dots between their faith and their politics, feeling that both should begin with the individual, not the state.

Egged on by these new arrivals, British Americans began exercising a growing level of home rule. The Albany Congress of 1754 debated Benjamin Franklin's Albany Plan of Union, which would have created an association of eleven colonies, headed by a colonial assembly and a president appointed by the crown. But the individual colonies were too independent for that step, and rejected it. Nevertheless, the Albany Plan reveals that Americans were already thinking in terms of a united America under the rule of their own representatives—twenty years before the Revolution.

Most British Americans, including even many of the "low church" Anglicans, also held an abiding belief in providential order and progress and saw themselves as a growing, prosperous, self-governing people. This represented yet

★ ★ ★
Fun Fact

The "Pennsylvania Dutch" were not from Holland, but Germany. The word Dutch is really an Americanization of "Deutsch," the German word for German.

A Book You're Not Supposed to Read

The Glorious Cause: The American Revolution, 1763–1789 by Robert Middlekauff (New York: Oxford University Press, 2007) emphasizing the long build-up to the Revolution, is one of the fairest and most comprehensive one-volume treatments of the American War of Independence.

★ ★ ★

Wait, Is That a Whig?

In the wake of the English Civil Wars, the restoration of the monarchy, and the Glorious Revolution of 1688, England had seen the rise of a political theory called "Whiggism." Whig theory was well developed in the writings of John Locke. Whigs believed in individual liberty and limitations on the monarchy (and later, on Parliament as well). They believed that "balanced" government—in which the king and his ministers were checked by the Parliament's power of the purse—was necessary to maintain liberty. Whigs saw corruption and despotism as inevitable results of an overactive state, which would necessarily begin to restrict men's liberty.

Most Americans were Whigs (in the original English sense, not to be confused with the Whig Party of the 1830s). They sought limitations or "checks" on the executive *and* legislative powers, but thought the legislature was less prone to tyranny since it was more easily controlled through elections.

another major element of the Americans' character: they brought with them—and greatly developed and expanded—the Whig view of history as a progress from authoritarianism and ignorance to enlightenment and self-rule. They not only hoped but confidently expected that the future would see increasing limitations on the state's power over its citizens.

So America was primed for a revolution. But what events actually sparked the War of Independence? The first causes long pre-dated the Revolution, including the Navigation Acts, first passed in 1651. These laws were regulatory, designed to maintain economic balance (and dependence) within the empire. The most onerous feature of the acts for colonial Americans was that all trade to and from the colonies was restricted to Great Britain and her dominions. Trade between Boston and the nearby Dutch colony of New Amsterdam (New York), for example, was forbidden. The British monopoly led to high prices. To add insult to injury, colonists paid taxes on those overpriced goods as determined by the House of Commons although the colonists had no representation in Parliament.

In addition, the Navigation Acts, destined to be in force throughout the British dominions until the 1840s, contained various subsidies (often called bounties) and taxes on all colonies, each specific bounty or tax intended to encourage or discourage production of certain goods or crops. For example, England wanted the West Indies producing sugar, so West Indian sugar was subsidized. England did *not* want the West Indies growing cotton or tobacco (even if those crops could grow in the West Indies), but rather than outright prohibiting such activities, Parliament taxed them. Meanwhile the American South was prompted to grow rice and ship indigo, both of which received bounties, but to refrain from growing sugar, which was taxed. According to historian Bernard Bailyn, for over a century the response from the Americans (and everyone else) was to willingly comply. But in light of the other main event that converged with the Navigation Acts to cause the American Revolution, that would soon change.

> ## A Book You're Not Supposed to Read
>
> *The New England Merchants in the Seventeenth Century*, revised ed., by Bernard Bailyn (Cambridge: Harvard University Press, 1979).

That other cause was the French and Indian War, which saddled England with both a huge war debt and also the continuing costs to garrison North America. Britain would need to build forts and furnish troops in this new territory to hold the Indians in check and protect settlers. But except for a few garrisons in the northwest and at Fort Ticonderoga, England procrastinated, as such installations would cost money England did not have.

Pay Your Own Way!

Parliament's solution was to make the American colonists pay for the cost of the French and Indian War and their own continuing defense. Accordingly, the American colonies would be subject to new taxes that did not apply to any other colonies. Even worse, the soldiers to watch the western borders and protect American settlers were generally furnished by the American colonists themselves through their militia organizations. British

★ ★ ★

Did a Tax *Cut* Cause the American Revolution?

In February 1767, Parliament reduced the taxes on land by 25 percent. This came to a revenue loss of five hundred thousand English pounds—all of which had to be made up somewhere. (Or, of course, services could have been cut, but governments never like to do that.) These tax cuts added even more pressure on Parliament to look to the American colonies for revenue, to make up the difference.

troops were held in reserve, mostly in a few isolated forts and major cities.

Americans felt, and quite rightly so, that they had provided their own security from the very beginning of colonial history, and even furnished substantial numbers of troops during the French and Indian War. England had suffered relatively few casualties other than through the military stupidity of British commanders, while colonist settlements and farms had paid a high price in blood in their own defense.

When Parliament first tried to make the colonies pay England for their defense, it was a disaster. The Stamp Act of 1765 required a stamp (accompanied by a tax) on documents for all business transactions (as well as for births, deaths, marriages, divorces, and even playing cards). This act affected every American colony equally, and the outrage was instantaneous. Below the surface was a concern that with taxing paper transactions as a first step, Bibles might be controlled and taxed next, and that this might lead to the imposition of Anglicanism on all the colonies. So there was a powerful religious component to the resistance to the act. Americans' outrage was so great that a Stamp Act Congress was called, and representatives of nine colonies showed up. And even those colonies that did not send representatives were sympathetic: some had governors that forbade attendance, others lacked the money to send representatives.

The Stamp Act Congress proceedings were secret, and only sketchy journal information about the goings-on remains. Neither the House of Lords nor the House of Commons received the colonies' petitions containing all the grievances, but both heard the message loud and clear, and Parliament repealed the Stamp Act. But standing on its authority, Parliament passed the Declaratory Act in which it reasserted its power to issue such acts "in all cases whatsoever." Nevertheless, the colonists had forced Parliament to back down.

But a huge issue still remained. With the French gone, the west beyond the Alleghenies lay open for settlement, except there were Indians inhabiting much of the land. (The French had deliberately maintained a very light footprint with low population to perpetuate their fur-trading operations.) Any attempt at English settlement there would be resisted. In October 1763, therefore, King George issued a proclamation prohibiting colonists from settling in these new territories, and further prohibited any molestation of Indians in those lands. Theoretically, England was now in the position of having to protect the Indians against the American colonists.

Worse than the Indian issue, however, was the fact that the king's governor in Quebec had been given authority to administer the western lands—an indicator to American Protestants that England was seeking to expand the power of Catholicism. In the Treaty of Paris that ended the French and Indian War in 1763, England had guaranteed the free exercise of Roman Catholicism in Quebec and the western lands—and done nothing to favor Protestantism.

Protests were immediate, especially by George Washington and other Virginians who had been promised western land for their military service. Parliament had to back down, adjusting the line westward through a number of treaties that opened much of Kentucky, West Virginia, and western Pennsylvania to settlement. But Protestant suspicions of British religious intentions continued to linger, and those suspicions would be confirmed in 1774 with the passage of the Quebec Act.

A Book You're Not Supposed to Read

Origins of the American Revolution by John C. Miller (Boston: Little, Brown and Co., 1943) remains the classic non-progressive work covering the time from 1760 to 1776.

★ ★ ★

It's NOT the Economy, Stupid

Although it's pretty much a dead issue among scholars now, just fifty years ago a number of Marxist and leftist academics claimed the American Revolution was all about the money—that the burden of the Navigation Acts was so heavy that the "rich white guys" who made up the merchant and planter class in the American British colonies had to fight or go broke.

This has been handily debunked. A bevy of scholars including Douglass North, Peter McClelland, and Robert Thomas have demonstrated that the Navigation Acts had negligible effects on the colonies' economy. Thomas pointed out, for example, that while there were some burdens in the form of taxes and limitations on exports, there were also many benefits, especially from the presence of the Royal Navy to protect shipping and of the British regular forces to guard the colonists against Indian attacks and infringements on their territories by the Spanish. Moreover, American producers also received a number of subsidies from England for producing desired goods.

Thomas found that the tax burden of the Navigation Acts amounted to forty-one cents per colonist in 1770, but averaged over ten years it was even lower than that, possibly averaging twenty-five cents a year. Total burdens on *all* Americans were under $900,000 in 1770, or less than 1 percent of the colonial GNP. These numbers have been confirmed by other studies.

Who goes to war over a quarter? It's abundantly clear that the Americans were not in revolt against the impact of British policies on their wallets, at least in the short term. What concerned them was the unrelenting nature and direction of the imperial policies, all enacted without any input from the colonists themselves.

Even before the French and Indian War, Parliament had already imposed a number of onerous taxes and regulations on the American colonists, including the Wool Act, the Molasses Act, and the Iron Act (the latter sharply increased American iron ore exports to England and limited American iron production). But those were regulatory taxes, meant primarily to shape patterns of trade in the British Empire. The Sugar Act of 1764 was for raising revenue. It attempted to achieve that goal by three different mechanisms: increasing customs enforcement, levying new taxes on many items that were widely consumed in America, and increasing old duties already in place. None of this was done with the consent of the Americans, leading James Otis to publish *The Rights of the British Colonies Asserted and Proved*, in which he claimed the "natural, essential, inherent, and inseparable rights of our fellow subjects in Great Britain." Or, to put it more succinctly, "the rights of Englishmen."

A War of Ideas

Otis, who had already spoken out against the abuses of the Navigation Acts, now argued against the Sugar Act, claiming several principles concerning the rights of citizens. In his words:

- "The supreme and subordinate powers of legislation should be free and sacred in the hands where the community have once rightfully placed them...."
- "The supreme national legislature cannot be altered justly till the Commonwealth is dissolved, nor a subordinate legislature taken away without forfeiture or other good cause...."
- "No legislative [body]...has a right to make itself arbitrary...."
- "The supreme legislature cannot justly assume a power of ruling by...arbitrary decrees, but it is bound to dispense justice by known settled rules and by duly authorized independent judges...."
- "The supreme power cannot take from any man part of his property, without his consent in person or by representation...."

Otis also argued that taxes could not be laid on the colonists without their consent.

A Book You're Not Supposed to Read

James Otis: The Pre-Revolutionist by John Clark Ridpath (Chicago: Union School Furnishing Co., 1898) is a good sketch of America's forgotten "pre-founder."

Already low-level violence, such as the beating, tarring, and feathering of customs collectors, had been occurring for some time. Customs commissioners feared for their lives, several resigned, and many others did their jobs half-heartedly. In February 1770, a boy named Christopher Seider was killed by a customs agent. Mass protests with Boston meetings of up to five thousand people at a time ensued, and violence seemed inevitable.

It's a Massacre!

In March 1770, an incident over an officer's private debt to a wigmaker's apprentice led to a soldier striking the boy, and a crowd gathered quickly. Another officer with a half-dozen Redcoats arrived, muskets at the ready. The officers were pelted with rocks and snowballs, and one of the soldiers slipped, fell down, then stood and fired. Others then fired as well. Five civilians were killed. The pamphleteers went into action, decrying the "Boston Massacre." Seeing the potential for a full-scale revolution, the British government wanted a trial, and after several Tories turned down the job, the Patriot John Adams took up the defense of the soldiers. Six were acquitted. Two were found guilty of manslaughter, but they were given a series of sentence reductions that finally reduced the sentence to the branding of their thumbs.

In North Carolina, the "Regulator" movement led to violence in May 1771. The Regulators were mostly Scotch-Irish who resented arbitrary property seizures for non-payment of taxes by officials of the crown as much in America as they had in Northern Ireland. Royal governor William Tryon dispatched a force of a thousand men to march into Orange County, where they found a Regulator army double their size. At the Battle of Alamance, Governor Tryon himself started the hostilities by shooting one of the Regulators who was negotiating for peace. After a two-hour battle they ran out of ammunition and melted away. Tryon hanged seven prisoners without a trial, and became the archetypal bloodthirsty British oppressor. Later he was appointed governor of New York

Fun Fact

Many North Carolinians consider the Battle of Alamance, rather than Lexington and Concord, to be the opening shot of the American Revolution, as the Regulator rebellion was triggered by British taxation policy.

and made a major general during the war. Tryon plotted to kidnap George Washington in 1776, carried on brutal raiding against women and children until 1780, and died peacefully in his bed in 1788.

In May of 1773 British Prime Minister Lord Grenville persuaded Parliament to pass the Tea Act. It eliminated the taxes paid by the British East India Company on tea transshipped through England and allowed the company to ship tea directly to America. The law was primarily intended to help bail out the struggling company. But undergirding the act was Parliament's putative right to tax the colonists, who had no representation. If the colonists acceded to the Tea Act, they would be accepting the principle that Parliament could impose any taxes on them at any time without any say on their part.

Tea constituted a critical part of Englishmen's diets, especially in America, where the surface water was mostly unfit to drink. People were consigned to drink ale, rum, or tea. Indeed, in America tea was not replaced by coffee until the 1850s. Thus the British government was meddling with *everyone's* way of life. Excepting only Bible sales or printing, Parliament could not have picked a more unifying item to regulate.

American resistance was as swift and almost as widespread as with the Stamp Act. In New York and Philadelphia, tea was forced to be shipped back to England, and in Charleston, it was unloaded but left to rot on the docks. But in Boston, when no one would unload the tea, the royal governor refused to allow the ships to leave port with the tea still on board. What ensued was the famous Boston Tea Party in December 1773, organized by the resistance group the Sons of Liberty, who dressed like Mohawk Indians, boarded three East India Ships, and tossed some 342 chests of tea into the water. This was all prearranged: the captain of the *Dartmouth* allowed the "Mohawks" to board, open the chests—one lock was broken, and the captain was reimbursed—and dump the tea.

The Great Greenwich Tea Party

Following the Boston Tea Party, a number of other similar raids took place across the colonies—in York, Maine; in Philadelphia, Pennsylvania; and in Greenwich, New Jersey, at Cohansey Creek. There, the captain of the *Greyhound*, deciding it was too dangerous to unload cargo in the Delaware Bay of Philadelphia, had docked elsewhere, unloaded his tea, and put it in the cellar of Tory Daniel Bowen. Bowen expected to carry it overland to Philadelphia, but on the night of December 22, 1774, forty patriots dressed as "Mohicans" broke into Bowen's house, took the tea to an open field, and set it on fire. Although many of the instigators were arrested, none was convicted. Few know of the "Great Greenwich Tea Party" because Sam Adams was not around to publicize it.

British reaction to the Boston Tea Party in particular was immediate and severe, partly because that was where England already had troops (and had experienced trouble) but also because there was a major pocket of the Sons of Liberty located in Boston. Parliament passed the Coercive Acts (known in America as the Intolerable Acts) that closed the port of Boston, limited assemblies, and allowed the governor to move trials for offenses committed in Massachusetts to England.

The Limits of Toleration

The British had, as modern Americans say, "stepped in it." At every turn, they had ignored the concerns of the Americans, imposed laws without their consent that had the maximum negative impact anyone could imagine, and were even suspected of reigniting a religious war. It should have come as no surprise when a "gun grab" finally brought this simmer to a boil. Unfortunately, the British had decided to pick on colonists who were armed to the teeth.

CHAPTER 2

From Simmer to Boil

By 1774, agitation throughout the thirteen American colonies had reached the point where many colonists were openly defying the British government. Their grievances were many, but primarily the colonists felt that they had built their towns, cities, and colonies by their own hard work, sweat, money, and in many cases, blood. More than a few grievances originated in their lives back in the British Isles. Tyranny by the crown, rent racking, and religious persecution had driven many poor souls to America. Braving all the New World's risks, trials, and dangers, these immigrants had built a new life for themselves and their families in liberty, under a type of self-government unseen in most of the world. They had tamed the wilderness, fought off Indians, cleared the land, built their homes, farms, and churches, and raised their children—all with little or no help from the royal government.

What Was "Benign" about "Benign Neglect"?

Historians have frequently used the phrase "benign neglect" to describe England's relationship with the American colonies. By that, they mean that England governed loosely, providing only a minimum of oversight.

Did you know?

★ Not wanting to jeopardize British assistance against Indian attacks, Georgia sent no delegates to the First Continental Congress

★ British literary giant Dr. Samuel Johnson urged arming the Indians against the American Patriots

★ A Hessian diarist saw "very few churches and most of them in ruins" in America because their ministers had all joined the Revolution

A Book You're Not Supposed to Read

A History of the American Revolution by John Alden (New York: Knopf, 1969). Though dated, John Alden's simple and straightforward book remains a classic, perfect for high school and college students.

But how was this benign?

In 1770 the British were providing the Americans with some military protection against Indians with the limited numbers of troops they had, which amounted to about ten thousand total soldiers in all of North America, maintained at a cost of about two hundred thousand pounds annually. This was entirely in keeping with British Imperial strategy well into the 1800s, when England governed her entire world empire with as few as one hundred fifty thousand regulars, relying on local forces to fill the gap. After protests against British taxes related to the (by then repealed) Stamp Act, however, four British regiments, totaling roughly four thousand men, had been stationed in Boston. Although some were removed in 1769, about half that number remained, and it was those troops who engaged in the clashes with colonists that would result in the attempt to seize Patriot military supplies in Lexington and Concord.

Whether Redcoats were protection—British police enforcing law and order—or an occupying force depended on one's perspective. And the same was true of the Royal Navy. American merchant trade was indeed protected at sea, in a sense: pirates knew that British warships would attack and sink them if they were caught. But every merchant ship could not possibly be protected by the Royal Navy any more than every speeder can be caught by the Highway Patrol. Thus, estimates of the benefits of belonging to the empire were in the eye of the beholder.

As the eighteenth century progressed, British rule was becoming less neglectful—and, in the colonists' eyes, less benign. One sore spot was the actions of some colonial governors—such as Massachusetts's Thomas Hutchinson, who served as acting governor in 1760 and then was appointed by the new governor to be chief justice of the Massachusetts Superior Court. He issued "writs of assistance" in 1761 permitting arbitrary searches by customs officials anywhere they desired. Hutchinson—who just happened to have a nice house with good stuff in it—was a convenient whipping boy. When it came time to protest, what better location?

Although Hutchinson actually opposed the Sugar Act and agreed with James Otis on "no taxation without representation," Hutchinson nevertheless consistently supported Parliament. When his brother-in-law Andrew Oliver was appointed "stamp master" to collect the hated Stamp Tax, mobs ransacked both Oliver's and Hutchinson's houses. Once again the acting governor, Hutchinson was also faced with having to quell fiery tempers among the citizenry after the Boston Massacre. He had the British soldiers involved in the incident arrested and then attempted to cool the unrest by postponing the trial for six months.

Hutchinson was a classic example of a well-meaning colonial administrator trying to persuade Parliament to address local concerns while keeping the peace. Yet it was easy for Sam Adams to portray him as a puppet of the king. Under "benign neglect" the colonists had been allowed extensive independence when it suited the crown, but they were slapped back into line when it didn't. In that respect, "benign neglect" was unsatisfactory—it constituted little more than repeatedly teasing the colonists with self-government before reminding them who was boss.

Please, Mr. Postman

That was the colonial viewpoint. Parliament and the royal governors saw the situation quite differently. From their point of view, Great Britain had financed the war against the French and Indians at great expense, with little contribution from the colonies. Now they wanted the colonies not only to pay for the troops quartered in America for frontier defense, but to make good on the debt from England's war with the French. Up to 1773, the variety of parliamentary acts designed to produce revenue from the colonies had yielded less than satisfactory results. Then, with the Tea Act of 1773, the fat was really in the fire. Both sides had run out of patience—as the Boston Tea Party and the closing of the Port of Boston made clear.

Patriot "committees of correspondence" were keeping the colonies in constant communication with each other; and people throughout the colonies feared that what the British had done in Massachusetts could happen in any colony. The First Continental Congress was called in September of 1774 at the instigation of Virginia to coordinate the colonists' response. Attended by fifty-six delegates from twelve colonies (Georgia—still hoping for assistance from Britain against Indians—did not send delegates), the Congress's main concern was a response to the "Intolerable Acts" of 1774, which in turn sprang from the Boston Tea Party and other responses to the Tea Act of 1773.

The First Continental Congress in Philadelphia was a meeting of eagles. The attendees included George Washington, Samuel and John Adams, Patrick Henry, John and Edward Rutledge, John Jay, and many other notables. (James Otis was there only in spirit, having developed a mental illness, exacerbated by a blow to the head from a British tax collector in 1769, shortly after which he had been forced to retire from public life.) Peyton Randolph from Virginia presided.

Yet from the British point of view, the Congress was a meeting of traitors. It possessed no authority from the mother country to make laws or function as a government, and meeting to specifically resist English laws flirted with treason. A rumor—later proven false—that Boston had been fired upon by British ships initially ignited the delegates' passions to make a petition to the king. So in October 1774 Congress sent King George a "Declaration and Resolves" enumerating the rights of Americans and asking for the repeal of the "Intolerable" Coercive Acts. The Declaration and Resolves cited the "immutable laws of nature" and claimed the rights to "life, liberty and property." Keeping a standing army in the colonies in a time of peace was "against the law," and the right to assembly could not be legally infringed. These rights, the delegates asserted, were the rights of all Englishmen—not forfeited, surrendered, or lost by settling in America. And fundamental to those rights—"the foundation of English liberty, and of all free government"—was having a voice in the legislature that governed them.

These Resolves were a bombshell in London. King George, reacting in kneejerk fashion, concluded that the Americans needed discipline and responded by sending additional troops to the colonies.

But even before learning the results of its petition, Congress moved on to take effective action against the British government. Earlier lobbying and petitions had proven ineffective; American complaints had been heard only when they were backed up by boycotts of British goods. Two

★ ★ ★
Terminus a Quo?

If deciding when the American Revolution actually started is difficult, so is pinpointing the time and place that the first government of the United States of America was established. But there is a good argument for putting it at the convention of the First Continental Congress on September 5, 1774 in Philadelphia.

A Book You're Not Supposed to Read

England in the Age of the American Revolution by Lewis Namier (London: Palgrave, 1961) presents the "British side" of things.

★ ★ ★

Say It Ain't So, Joe!

The first item on the agenda at the First Continental Congress was the Plan for Union with Great Britain by Joseph Galloway, a man much conflicted. A dedicated Tory who never dreamed America could become independent, Galloway was later considered a traitor by the Patriots and sought refuge with the British in New York City before emigrating to England in 1778. Yet his plan, which failed by only a single vote, advocated an American legislature at a time when many Americans were still living in a fantasy world in which the king would treat Americans with respect.

such boycotts had already proven at least partially successful in reducing British trade and changing British policy: the first in 1765 following the Sugar and Stamp Acts, which Parliament had then repealed; and the second in 1768 that caused Parliament to repeal all of the Townshend duties except the one on tea. The idea of a total boycott gained ground steadily in the First Continental Congress, until the Articles of Association, commonly called only "the Association," was passed.

On October 6, after the Congress had been sitting for a month, Paul Revere arrived from Boston with the Suffolk Resolves, written by Dr. Joseph Warren; they were adopted on September 9. These radical declarations urged withholding all trade from England, Ireland, and the West Indies, and an immediate boycott of all "British merchandise and manufactures." After Joseph Galloway's Plan of Union failed by a single vote, other delegates drafted the Articles of Association, based on the Virginia Association that George Mason had drafted in 1769, and called for a complete embargo on trade between the British Empire and the colonies.

"The Enemies of American Liberty"

After reciting a list of grievances against the crown, the Articles of Association put into action measures that would wreak havoc on the British mercantile system that ruled the colonies. It said, in part, "To obtain redress of these grievances, which threaten destruction to the lives, liberty, and property of his majesty's subjects…we are of opinion, that a non-importation, non-consumption, and non-exportation agreement, faithfully adhered to, will prove the most speedy, effectual, and peaceable measure.…"

The Association contained a pledge to neither import nor consume British goods. It encouraged sheep farming in America to provide wool for clothing, which had previously been imported—yet another step toward economic independence.

But the key provision of the Association was Article Eleven, which created the mechanism by which the boycott would be implemented:

> That a committee be chosen in every county, city, and town, by those who are qualified to vote for representatives in the legislature, whose business it shall be attentively to observe the conduct of all persons touching this association; and when…any person…has violated this association, that such majority do forthwith cause the truth of the case to be published in the gazette; to the end, that all such foes to the rights of British-America may be publicly known, and universally condemned as the enemies of American liberty; and thenceforth we respectively will break off all dealings with him or her.

In essence, the Association had started a national legislative body for America, and new local government, as well, in the form of the committees throughout the colonies that enforced the "no trade with England" policy. The local committees wrote their own articles of association, often vying with one another in radicalism, particularly in reciting the offenses by King George or Parliament. Many pledged to take military action to secure the rights of the people, yet they were readily signed by ordinary citizens, openly and with confidence in the righteousness of their cause.

★ ★ ★
Guilt by Association

The committees were patently illegal, as neither the Continental Congress nor the Articles of Association had been authorized by royal governors, Parliament, or the crown. No authority had been given to the colonists to form a Congress, and its decrees had no legal status. Nor did the colonies enjoy sovereignty—that resided in the King of England, George III. Thus the Association was truly revolutionary, something that could have put every member of the Constitutional Congress on the scaffold in the Tower of London if apprehended by British authorities.

This was no minor commitment. Signing an Association agreement, as tens of thousands did, was an act that put the committee members' names on record as supporting treason—which could be punished by death at the end of a British rope. With everything to lose, the committee members worked constantly and vigorously stoked the revolutionary spirit—which in the end would need to see the country through eight long years of ruinous war. Although the colonists themselves suffered greatly from this policy—exports from the American colonies declined by 95 percent—the value of English imports plunged by 93 percent. In a single year, the Patriots had established themselves as economically independent of Great Britain, and enraged King George and his supporting aristocrats, who were seeing their profits from the colonies vanish.

The committees in every county, city, and town were instructed to operate as though no British government even existed in America. They not only inspected customs books and published the names of offenders but raised

★ ★ ★
The Association Was Not a Rock Band

The Declaration of Independence almost two years later was hardly more treasonous than the Articles of Association, yet the Association has been overlooked by writers of history texts. Sometimes they comment on extra-legal "patriot committees," but most fail to mention the Articles of Association even once.

★ ★ ★

Loyalists and Rebels, or Tories and Patriots?

From 1775 to 1783, the British House of Commons consisted of two parties, Whigs and Tories. The Whigs were liberal, pressing for the sovereignty of man, while Tories were the traditional conservative party. In the American colonies, supporters of the crown were called Tories after the British party in Parliament. "Loyalist" was used only by the Tories themselves, as opposed to "Rebel," which is what the British called the Americans fighting for independence. Individuals supporting the Revolution (and the independence of the thirteen colonies, after the Declaration of Independence) generally called themselves "Patriots," although others sometimes called them "Whigs" and referred to them as holding "Whiggish views." Patriots never called anyone supporting the crown anything but a Tory.

But since 1960 it has become the fashion in progressive educational circles to use the term "Loyalist" as the politically correct term, suggesting that being loyal to the crown was as honorable as being for American independence. Many recent history books use "Loyalist" and "Rebel," inadvertently betraying their authors' politics—a Marxism so hostile to American freedom that it is willing to wear the colors of eighteenth-century monarchists in opposition to American patriotism. ("Politically correct" is a term that originated in Stalin's USSR to describe a stance completely consistent with the Communist Party line.) The authors of this book use Patriot and Tory throughout, proudly proclaiming our Patriot and politically incorrect orientation.

troops locally. The Association demonstrated a new unification of purpose and of sentiment to resist British rule. It put the American Revolution on the path of no return, and eventually all the colonies except New York and Georgia formally approved it.

The Articles forced the common people in every locality to take a stand: Patriots for an independent nation and Tories for the crown. Neutrals supposedly took neither side, but their neutrality greatly benefitted the British—and now they were suspected by both sides. There was no turning back: individuals had to choose, as the result would clearly be civil war.

★ ★ ★

What Were the Militias?

Generally speaking, the militia was defined as "the Body of the People"; it consisted of all military-age men (roughly ages sixteen to fifty) in a community. George Washington, in a letter to Alexander Hamilton in 1783, wrote that he wanted all male citizens from eighteen to fifty to be carried on militia rolls, provided with uniform arms, and be accustomed to use those arms—so that they would be immediately proficient in case of an emergency call-up. He recommended limiting the standing regular army to only a few thousand enlisted men, but with an oversized officer corps, so the militia could be supplied quickly with trained officers in time of need.

Militia in colonial times were part-time organizations, officered by prominent men in the communities where they were mustered. The smallest unit was usually a company, consisting of forty to ninety men, commanded by a captain. These were strictly local units, organized and drilled by the town or county in which the members lived. Sometimes militia units refused to leave their state and fight in other states, desiring to act only as a home guard. More often, the militia call-ups were affected by the time of year. Spring planting and fall harvesting limited both the initial response and the duration of service.

Militia also fought Indian incursions and Tory raiding parties—service often resulting in heavy casualties not counted in Revolutionary War casualties. But this was valuable duty by the militia, freeing up regular Continental Army units to concentrate on the British. Some battles, such as Bennington and Kings Mountain, (both Patriot victories), were fought solely by short-term militia units.

This militia system continued up to 1903, when the Militia Act of 1903 went into effect, creating an active militia of state National Guard units, and the unorganized militia of all able-bodied male citizens from the ages of seventeen to forty-five.

The colonists believed that the right to arm oneself to defend one's life and liberties was an individual right. Virginia's first constitution said, "A well-regulated militia, *composed of the body of the people*, trained to arms, is the proper, natural, and safe defense of a free State [emphasis added]." It further stated, "The people have a right to keep and to bear arms for the common defense." This was without restriction.

(Prior to the adoption of the U.S. Constitution, all of the states except Rhode Island had enacted state constitutions. These have been practically expunged from our history by progressive politicians and historians since they not only represent revolutionary fervor but also give the U.S. Constitution its context. The original state constitutions of Massachusetts, Georgia, Maryland, New York, North Carolina, Pennsylvania, and Virginia, for example, definitively stated that all power resided, originated, was vested in the people, or was derived from them, and several of them asserted that all government functionaries were at all times accountable to the people.)

As British authority simply ceased to be recognized by many towns and localities where Association committees were established, the committees' decrees and actions became the de facto law of the land. Patriots seized control of localities, sometimes by force. Kangaroo courts were set up to try people for trading with the British, and offenders who staunchly defended the king or showed Tory tendencies were often run out of town or the county. This was not a pretty period in American history, as the Patriots were denying the Tories the very liberties the Patriots said they were fighting for. The best that can be said is that women and children were rarely harmed. But men were tarred and feathered, businesses destroyed, contraband confiscated, and heavy fines imposed. Tories fled to cities on the coast or found safe havens with relatives in quieter areas. Boston lost all traces of British authority except for the military garrison there.

Ethnic Cleansing

As the population divided itself into three distinct political groups, towns and areas took on political orientations: some became hotbeds for Patriotism, some were Tory, and some were unable to be roused by either side. Country of origin and religion played major roles, as towns and areas had often been settled by relatively homogenous groups, so that there were Puritan-Congregational towns, Quaker-Dunkard-Mennonite-Baptist neighborhoods, and Scotch-Irish areas. This pattern was borne out in the formation of the militia:

often full companies were Scotch-Irish, Congregational, or from low-church Anglican parishes that tended to be controlled by elected laymen.

So there was some "ethnic cleansing" to use the modern term, but rarely by actual killing. As an individual's business was shunned or no one would help bring in the harvest or plow in the spring, families had to choose between enduring in isolation and silence—or packing up and moving to a friendlier area. Before long, everyone in an area agreed with his neighbors on the pressing question of the day. The scene in the movie *The Patriot* accurately depicts a Scotch-Irish town. Soldiers are recruited in the Presbyterian church, and it appears that the whole town supports the rebellion. If anyone doesn't, he holds his tongue.

In modern terms, the Association committees "controlled the debate," generally with the assistance of the county sheriff and militia, who were firmly under their control. The Patriots controlled nearly all the information the citizenry received, and much of it was wrong, exaggerated, or simply anti-British propaganda. The militia was all a committee needed to have power—there was no other body of police. Only the British occupying forces were available to suppress the committees, but to use British troops was the last resort of a governor.

So the Patriots were able to shut down all commerce with England. As the war progressed, outsiders were looked upon with suspicion until their true sentiments could be determined. While the Continental Army may have been a relatively weak force, always poorly supplied and inconsistently led, it nonetheless outlasted the British partly because the home front was always secure. Wives and families supported their menfolk away in the war, and Patriot communities remained dedicated to seeing the rebellion through to victory.

Although the Founding Fathers often get the credit from modern historians for successfully catalyzing public opinion behind the War for Independence, the committees were made up of ordinary citizens who took risks on par with the signers of the Declaration of Independence. Large numbers of ordinary citizens were willing to stand up and risk their lives, property, and their family's survival to win their liberty.

These Association committees and militia units essentially provided the Patriot cause and its armies with the manpower and energy to carry the country through the war. Generally, local leaders themselves did not serve except for short periods, but they saw to it that their county quotas were filled with volunteers, conscripts, or substitutes, usually (except in emergencies) from the less prosperous members of their community. In many areas this manpower was culled from the Scotch-Irish inhabitants—men who possessed an abiding hatred of Redcoats on account of the institutional persecutions the British had regularly carried out against non-Anglicans in Ireland and Scotland. And the militia was *everywhere*, and while the British possessed overwhelming force, the British army was concentrated in large population centers, mostly along the coast. In the countryside, the militia and committee leaders could always be where the British weren't. Even in the South, where there was a substantial Tory population, the British pacified territories only to see them rapidly revert to Patriot control after the British moved out.

Led by the Association, the boycotts of 1774 were extremely successful, in part because wealthy planters in the middle and southern colonies supported them. The Association rendered the planters' substantial debts to British merchants uncollectable, or at least deferred payments until much later. The Navigation Acts had restricted Americans to trading only with the mother country and its dominions, but if independence was won, they could trade anywhere in the world. This element of the economic situation has been seized upon by progressive historians anxious to show that the War of Independence was really fought for monetary gain on the part of the merchant and planter class. In fact, the Patriot merchants and planters were ruined by the Association more frequently than they were enriched.

★ ★ ★
When Salt Loses Its Savor

Some important items for civilian as well as military consumption were in critically short supply from the beginning of the boycott. In December of 1775, a series of salt riots broke out in Virginia. Salt had become unavailable, and the small farmers were faced with a dilemma— either re-open trade for salt by returning to Britain's good graces or win complete independence so trade could be established worldwide—that would only be resolved eight years later, after incredible hardships. Salt was an especially vital commodity, particularly because it was used to preserve foods. Before 1775 it had been imported from Great Britain or Turks Island in the Bahamas, under the control of Bermuda. Turks Island was officially closed to American shipping by the British early in the war, and salt supplies rapidly began to disappear. All along the seacoast, salt works sprang up, boiling seawater in large iron pans—a primitive method perhaps, but the Patriots were desperate to alleviate the salt shortage.

Land Ho!

Unpopular in the port cities, the British government did itself no favors by alienating the western areas of the colonies as well. The Proclamation of 1763 had prohibited settlements west of the Appalachians, but if independence was won, the proclamation would be meaningless. Indian lands would be available for speculation and development by Americans, not British and Canadians, and in particular, not the French Catholics. Even the boycott on the importation of slaves was seen in a positive light. The big landowners were already maintaining or increasing their slave holdings through domestic reproduction, and a moratorium on slave importation would make their slaves more valuable.

In April of 1775, Lord Dunmore, the royal governor of Virginia, seized the Virginia gunpowder supply in Williamsburg and threatened to emancipate the slaves and burn Williamsburg. Reports of Dunmore's actions and threats raced through Virginia and the South, enraging whites of all social classes.

In November of the same year, Dunmore offered freedom to any slave who signed up with the British army, and this act, seen by most colonists as directly endangering their lives and property, turned many ambivalent whites against the British. Londoner Samuel Johnson's *Taxation No Tyranny* pamphlet also received wide distribution, particularly his statement, "Let us give the Indians arms, and teach them discipline, and encourage them now and again to plunder a plantation...." Other British leaders recommended arming slaves and inciting them to revolt against their masters.

Although many British officers in the colonies considered the Revolution to be primarily a religious uprising by Scotch-Irish Presbyterians, others understood that New England Congregationalists and tidewater low-church Anglicans (where parishes were controlled not by clergy but

★ ★ ★

Dunmore's Raid

The royal governor of Virginia, John Murray, the Fourth Earl of Dunmore, had a problem. His father had supported Bonnie Prince Charlie in his failed rebellion of 1745, so there was a cloud over his family. Like many Scots in the colonies, Dunmore was anxious to expunge the failed uprising from British memory and prove his loyalty to the crown.

This "most unfit, the most trifling and most uncalculated person living" (in the words of a contemporary British General, Augustine Prevost) was faced with troublesome subjects and had already removed the flintlocks in Virginia's Williamsburg magazine. He next decided to remove the powder and ordered a detachment of marines and seamen to raid the magazine. On the night of April 20–21, 1775, the Patriots guarding the magazine were seen to retire, and twenty men made their way to the magazine, but not without being spotted and the alarm raised. They each grabbed a half-barrel of powder and raced back to their ship at Burrell's Ferry, making their escape. Dunmore later fled with his family to a British ship, lost the Battle of Great Bridge near Norfolk, bombarded the town, and sailed to New York. He never returned to Virginia, having been instrumental in aiding the revolutionary cause through his stupidity.

★ ★ ★

"A Beggar Never Seen on the Street"

So great was American prosperity before 1775 that arriving Hessian soldiers—German mercenaries in the pay of the British army—considered America a paradise. One German wrote in his diary that "we could perceive the radiance of freedom which the inhabitants of this new world had previously enjoyed.... Every plantation, every farm, seemed a shelter in a fool's paradise; the good harmony between neighbors, where a beggar was never seen on the street and certainly never encountered. All this made us think it to be a blessed land when compared to Germany." Dazzled by the wondrous bounty, the diarist exhibited great sympathy for the Patriots: "Among those inhabitants, love, faith, and freedom of speech were to be found, and now, through war, to have their customs and well-being completely destroyed."

by vestries from the people) were in the fight as well. John Adams estimated that Americans were split into three equal parts, one-third Patriot, one-third Tory, and one-third neutral. A better approximation from the 1780 American population of almost 2.78 million, as worked up by the authors, would probably be five hundred seventy-five thousand slaves, seven hundred thousand Patriots, half a million Tories, and 1.005 million more or less neutral or ambivalent.

Going Short

Under the Association, there were serious shortages, and Americans were forced to do without certain staples or scramble to provide for themselves. Tea, of course, disappeared as the Royal Navy regularly patrolled to stop smuggling, and people began to use almost any plant that could serve as a substitute.

Ironically, the period of deprivation that set in as a result of the boycott took place following a period of extraordinary economic growth that Parliament might have thought would make the colonists extremely happy to be a British dominion. The gross national product of the thirteen colonies had increased by a factor of twenty-five between 1650 and 1770, allowing American colonists to enjoy the highest standard of living in the world. Indeed, according to one account, an American in 1770 had a higher per-capita income than a Russian, Mexican, or Turk...in 1990!

Exports to overseas markets and imports of finished goods had made the colonies increasingly prosperous, and inter-colony trade burgeoned. Unforeseen by Parliament, however, was that such trade between colonies meant not only economic interactions but increased intercommunication that tended to push them into closer association with each other—the prerequisite for becoming a nation.

Parliament's arrogance was also affecting the colonies. British politicians failed to understand that the problem wasn't just the actual financial burden of the taxes, but also the process—*how* the acts were imposed. Parliament's

A Book You're Not Supposed to Read

Propaganda 1776: Secrets, Leaks, and Revolutionary Communications in Early America by Russ Castronovo (New York: Oxford, 2014). The Patriots used propaganda? You betcha! Sam Adams and Tom Paine were experts, but from the opening moments of the Revolution the Patriots figured out that controlling the hearts and minds of the people required a great PR push.

errors were a classical study in governmental stupidity. Even worse, America was enflamed by concerns about potential curtailment of American religious freedom by England (either from the established Anglican Church or by a reassignment of the thirteen colonies to the Catholic Canadian province). All this began to bring the simmer to a boil, particularly since Christian ministers were by and large far more pro-Patriot than has generally been understood. As one Hessian diarist noted upon entering Philadelphia in 1777, "I have seen few churches and those few are mostly in ruins, because their preachers have joined the rebels and led their parishioners into their evil beliefs." Congregational minister William Starnes told his church attendees that "these lands by them first settled they purchased by fair bargain of the natives. The rest was obtained by conquest, in a war entered into them for their own defense, and they defended their acquisitions by themselves alone for a long time with inconceivable expense of blood and treasure…these lands are clearly ours…. What any man acquires by his own labor and toil, he has an exclusive right to."

★ ★ ★

England, Taxes, and Slavery

Modern leftist historians are obsessed with the place of slavery in the American Revolution, meaning African slavery. At the time, Americans, North and South, were concerned about another kind of slavery. They feared English tyranny would enslave all Americans—beginning with the Stamp Act, which they saw as the first of many chains to be fastened upon them.

No one saw the Stamp Act as itself "enslaving," but almost all the commentators, across the board, viewed it as a first step in the enslavement of colonists. Remember, these Americans had

almost all seen indentured servitude in their lives—which didn't look much different from black slavery to them.

John Adams saw the Stamp Act as an "enormous Engine...for battering down all the Rights and Liberties of America"; a Connecticut minister wrote of the Stamp Act's design being to bring "slavish nonresistance and passive disobedience"; and a Virginia planter referred to the Stamp Act as the "first resolution to enslave us." If English law continued to be imposed upon them without their consent? Well, that was no different than what happened to a slave.

Pamphleteers such as Sam Adams further stoked the fires by constantly describing English colonial policies in violent terms: "oppression," "despotism," "slavery," and "tyranny." The Congregational minister Oliver Noble railed against "the oppressive hand of despotic power"; the president of Harvard said that America was "threatened with cruel oppression"; the Presbyterian president of Princeton, John Witherspoon, spoke of the "ambition of mistaken princes, the cunning and cruelty of oppressive and corrupt ministers"; and the Reverend Samuel West said that the people of Massachusetts "find themselves cruelly oppressed by the parent state."

The New Israel

The American Revolution was, far more than modern historians like to admit, a religious event. God was clearly on the side of the Patriots, at least according to American ministers. The Reverend Oliver Noble thundered that the colonists should "commit our cause to God and stand fast.... The cause of America is the cause of God, never did Man struggle in a greater, or more righteous cause." The Presbyterian minister John Carmichael told a company of Pennsylvania militia on June 4, 1775: "[I] congratulate you...on this day, on the certainty we have, for the justice and goodness of our cause...he [God] is on our side...and if God is on our side, we need not fear what man can do unto us." Ministers often prophesied the future greatness of America, a land that would replace the tired lands of Europe suffering under their tyrannical institutions.

America was the new Israel: the Americans were to be "a holy people unto the Lord our God," and an example to the world of the righteousness of liberty. Virtue and patriotism became inseparable. Virtue on the part of the citizenry made a democratic republic work, and patriotism was the obligation the citizen had to defend the republic and its institutions in accordance with God's wishes. Secular happiness depended on Christianity. As John Adams wrote to one minister about preaching against the tyranny of Great Britain, "It is Religion and Morality alone, which can establish the Principles upon which Freedom can securely stand.... You cannot therefore be more pleasantly, or usefully employed than in the Way of your profession, pulling down the Strong Hands of Satan." The modern reader should consider whether America has changed from the vision articulated by these early voices. The boys and girls demonstrating in American universities for benefits might remember that individual liberty was won for them by the Patriots of 1776, who believed in the rights and sovereignty of man over that of kings. It was Protestant Christianity, the common law, free-market capitalism, and a belief in the sovereign right to own property—and the citizens willing to die for those principles and beliefs—that made the Great Revolution.

These interpretations of rights as not only natural but holy appears in almost all of the revolutionary writings. Consider James Otis arguing in the

★ ★ ★

How Diverse Were the Patriots?

It all depends on what the definition of "diverse" is. By modern standards, the white population was ethnically almost homogenous: substantial populations were from the United Kingdom (England, Scotland, and Northern Ireland), France, Holland, Sweden, and Germany. Considering the slaves as a single ethnic group, the United States was made up of immigrants from five Northern European countries and Africa. The inhabitants overwhelmingly spoke English, with German in some local areas the only significant alternative. Protestant Christianity was by far the dominant religion, with denominations including Congregational, Anglican, Presbyterian, Quaker, Baptist, Lutheran, Dutch Reformed, and various pacifist sects. Roman Catholicism was a minor religion, with only twenty priests serving the entire country in 1784. There was little to no persecution for one's beliefs. But diversity? No. What made America strong was the absence of diversity. Only in politics were there sharp divisions, and they were worse than in the twenty-first century.

1760s that no king or Parliament has the right to deprive a man of his life, liberty, or property. Otis made no mistake as to the origin of those rights: "All power is of God." To ensure their liberties and God-given rights, Patriots were willing to suffer massive economic hardships, to risk life and limb and everything they owned.

The American Revolution was not a top-down revolt organized and carried out by the leading figures in the American colonies. The most prominent American at the time the Revolution began was Benjamin Franklin, and he was in England, and not even in favor of independence yet. Washington was just beginning to emerge as a leader; Samuel Adams and his co-conspirators in Boston were almost universally seen in the other twelve colonies as out-of-control radicals. Jefferson was a young man, relatively unknown until he took center stage as the author of the Declaration of Independence in 1776, and important leaders like John Dickerson from Pennsylvania and most of the New York congressional delegation were not in favor of independence from Britain. The grandfather of independence, James Otis, was not even at the Continental Congress. He had passed the baton to his sister, Mercy Otis Warren, but she—by rights the First Lady of the Revolution—was limited in her political influence by her gender. Her definitive biography is still waiting to be written (apparently the story of her life is something that progressive historians, particularly feminists, do not wish to tackle because she is not politically correct).

As the Revolution came to a boil, the problem of governing the colonies had been exacerbated by the long periods of time it took for communications to travel to and from Great Britain. Transit times by the fastest British ships were over a month, and then the king and his ministers often dithered for weeks or months before sending a reply. But the Americans communicated between the colonies within days, and news as interpreted by the Patriots was often circulated months before there could be an effective British response. Worse, the perceived lack of a response told the colonists that Parliament—and the king—wasn't listening.

CHAPTER 3

The Boston Blowup

The American colonies were an armed camp in 1774 and 1775—even a military society, where each able-bodied man was expected to do his duty in the county and state militia. Because local committees of Association that enforced the First Continental Congress's boycott of British goods and the embargo on selling American products to England were acting in concert with the militias, and, even in many cases were made up of the militia officers and personnel, the political, economic, and military forces of the American Revolution were united from the beginning.

So it was in Boston and New England when a common front emerged in response to General Thomas Gage's arrival in Boston in May of 1774 to enforce the Boston Port Bill. By August, Gage had twenty-eight hundred Redcoats quartered in Boston, including an artillery train and detachment of Royal Marines. Surely that would be enough to control the unruly rabble. What the British did not realize was that outside of Boston they had almost no control. Even inside the city, the British could exercise authority only at bayonet point. Whether they were in the colonies or back home in England, British officials simply had no clue as to what was going on—or that they themselves had caused it.

Did you know?

★ Paul Revere never said, "The British are coming!"

★ Londoners raised substantial sums for the relief of the Americans wounded, widowed, and orphaned at Lexington and Concord

★ Revolutionary War cannonballs simply bounced—Sir Henry Shrapnel would not invent the exploding shell until 1787

★ ★ ★
Young Rebels

Half the colonial population was under the age of sixteen, and many of the boys who fought in the Revolution were teenagers.

Gage and his men were like hogs tethered to a mound of fire ants. New England could and did form a militia army of sixteen to twenty thousand men in a few days. Massachusetts alone had a population of about three hundred fifty thousand souls and Connecticut nearly two hundred thousand. The total population of the thirteen colonies was about 2.5 million in 1775, and, with the highest birth rate in the world—thanks to the Scotch-Irish, who often produced over ten children per family—that population was extremely young. Virtually all of these Scotch-Irish were potential anti-British rebels, eager to avenge 150 years of persecution. The aristocrats in England derided the American militia as useless, but there was something they failed to note: whereas militia units would never be able to hold their own in dense lines of battle in open fields, they were often surprisingly effective in fortifications and where they were not exposed to artillery fire and heavy British volleys.

The main advantage General Gage had over the Americans was his superb intelligence service. Dr. Benjamin Church, a prominent Bostonian active in all the Patriot associations, was a particularly valuable asset to the British. Church kept Gage fully informed of Patriot plans and activities; the British general might as well have been present in the meetings of the Sons of Liberty. A second spy, John Hall of Concord, produced the report that resulted in the expedition to Lexington and Concord in April 1775. Hall gave details of Patriot military stores in the Concord area, including the hiding place for the four cannon stolen from the British in Boston. Another leading Tory in Concord, Daniel Bliss, provided sufficient information to plan the expedition route and identify all the local features. Yet another spy told Gage that the Continental Congress was planning to raise an army of one hundred eighty thousand men. Gage decided to act. He couldn't wait any longer.

By April 1, all the Patriot leaders had left Boston except for the redoubtable Dr. Joseph Warren, who was staying in the city to keep an eye on Gage. On April 15, he obtained a copy of Gage's General Orders issued that morning: "The Grenadiers and Light Infantry in order to learn Grenadier exercises and further new evolutions as to be off all duties till further orders."

But Warren could read between the lines: the grenadiers and light infantry would be doing something important in the next few days. He summoned Paul Revere and told him to ride to Lexington and Concord and tell the minutemen there to hide everything since the British soldiers would be coming their way in a few days. Spring had come early to Massachusetts after one of the mildest winters on record.

Revere rode to Lexington on Easter Sunday, met with Samuel Adams and John Hancock, and gave them the news. He then rode on to Concord, warned Colonel James Barrett that the Redcoats were coming, and returned to Charlestown, across the Charles River from Boston. Two days later, Revere was summoned by Dr. Warren and told the British forces were mounting their expedition to Concord that evening. Revere had arranged for one or two lanterns to be lit in the bell tower of the Old North Church; one if the British were marching over the Boston neck, and two if they were crossing the Charles River by boat to Charlestown. After the two lanterns were lit, Revere and another rider,

★ ★ ★
Who Were the Minutemen?

The minutemen were special companies of militia authorized by towns and counties in Massachusetts in the fall of 1774. The Provincial Congress set a quota on all towns of one-fourth of the able-bodied men between sixteen and sixty for these companies. They were to elect their own officers, furnish their own muskets, and outfit themselves to be ready in case of an alarm. Everyone knew what that alarm would be—British troops bent on oppressing the colonists. Concord raised two such companies, filling them out in January 1775 with 104 officers and men. They were to be ready at "a minute's notice" with powder, flints, musket balls, and rifles.

★ ★ ★

"The British Are Coming"?

The common fable is that Paul Revere rode through the night shouting, "The British are coming!" But of course, *he* was British—the Americans still thought of themselves that way—and he wouldn't have said any such thing. He would have yelled "To arms!" or "The Redcoats are coming!" meaning the British regulars. It is worth noting that everyone knew Paul Revere's voice because he belonged to all five of the Boston men's clubs—other than Dawes, no other man belonged to more than two!

A Book You're Not Supposed to Read

Paul Revere's Ride by David Hackett Fischer (New York: Oxford, 1994) is the best in-depth treatment not only of the "Midnight Ride," but of Paul Revere and his context.

William Dawes, left Boston to warn the minutemen; other riders, alerted by the lanterns, would ride out from Charlestown.

The Midnight Ride

Revere and Dawes rode separately to Lexington, Dawes somewhat ahead of Revere, alerting the homes along the way. In Lexington, about 130 militiamen formed up on the Lexington Green at around 1:00 a.m. An hour later, after receiving a report that there was no movement on the road from Boston for seven miles, the commander dismissed the militia. Meanwhile Revere, Dawes, and Dr. Samuel Prescott had decided to press on to Concord, spreading the alarm. About three miles from Concord, they ran into a mounted British patrol led by Major Edward Mitchell, and only Prescott was able to escape. Against all reason—secrecy was vital to the success of the expedition to Lexington and Concord—the British had sent out groups of mounted officers as advance scouts, and their presence gave the game away. Revere and Dawes were being led back toward Lexington when the troops heard a volley of fire. (This seems to have been the militia at Lexington clearing their muskets before dispersing.) Mitchell released his captives (but kept their horses) and returned to the expedition. Revere and Dawes walked into Lexington, their roles in history secure.

Mitchell reported to Colonel Smith that the area was swarming with militia, and that several hundred were waiting for him at Lexington. Smith immediately sent his second in command, Major John Pitcairn, to take a detachment through Lexington to Concord, but prudently sent a courier back to Boston for reinforcements. At 4:30 in the morning, the van of the seven hundred Redcoats in the column began to file onto the Lexington Green, where they were confronted by fewer than eighty militiamen who had not left when dismissed earlier. It was still dark (sunrise was at 4:59), and the militiamen had just filed out of the brightly lit Buckman Tavern. They couldn't see as well as the British troops, as their eyes were not yet accustomed to the dark, but they hastily drew up in a firing line.

A Book You're Not Supposed to Read

The Minutemen and Their World by Robert Gross (New York: Hill and Wang, 1981).

To this day, it is undetermined who fired first in the darkness. Nevertheless, the British definitely unloaded a heavy volley followed by a bayonet attack. Eight militiamen were killed, nine wounded, and only eight militiamen even fired a shot. The single British casualty was one soldier wounded in his thigh as the routed minutemen fled.

From Retreat to Rout

The British infantry formed up and moved to Concord, but suddenly realized the predicament they were in. Pre-dawn shapes played tricks on the soldiers, thick woods seemed full of malevolent moving figures, and then—as they neared the outskirts of Concord with the sun rising behind them—a Patriot band of fifes and drums was waiting for them on the road. It led the column into the center of town. Clearly the Patriots were all around, and wanted the British troops in the town. At 10:00 a.m. an American attack exploded over the North Bridge, sending the British reeling. More attacks followed, and the British retreated back down the Lexington Road, with the grenadiers keeping to the road and the light infantry on the flanks in the fields and woods. Within minutes it became apparent that the Redcoats were surrounded, and lead balls began coming into their ranks from all directions. The four hundred militiamen available for the defense of Concord saw their number swell to over three thousand as Patriots from other towns arrived on the scene. British discipline made the retreat orderly, and the green and poorly officered militiamen failed to turn it into a rout.

The Indian-style fighting by the militia took its toll, but the British flankers often caught individuals and small groups firing on the column from the rear and decimated the Americans with quick bayonet charges before the surprised militiamen could reload. The temperature in the afternoon reached eighty-five, and the heavy wool uniforms and lack of water brought the British troops to the edge of exhaustion. At Lexington, reinforcements under Lord Percy, who had been sent with reserves to rescue the column, greeted Smith's tired and desperate troops. The combined British force numbered nearly fifteen hundred men, but there were many wounded. Percy took command and put the column into motion toward Boston with his Royal Marines providing flank security. On the Patriot side, General William Heath assumed command of the cloud of militia surrounding the British—a force of perhaps ten thousand men—but it was impossible to organize such a disparate force, with active militia companies arriving by the minute. Heath did not even order his men to fire at the artillery horses to immobilize the column's guns.

Other Patriot leaders sent arriving Patriots to the head of the British column, to stay in position as the British passed, then leapfrog back to the front again. But such measures often failed in the broken terrain and heat of battle. Unit cohesion was lost in the orchards and woods, and company commanders failed to exercise the necessary control. Usually a militia company simply closed in on the tail of the British column and, after following the British

★ ★ ★

Lexington and Concord Report Card

The British

Colonel Francis Smith: F

Smith was extremely slow in getting the British expedition under way and failed to take effective action against American resistance at any time. After being wounded, he effectively transferred command to Major Pitcairn.

Major John Pitcairn: B

The real combat leader until Percy arrived, he held the British troops together with some difficulty until reinforced.

General Hugh Percy: A

After taking command of the retreat at Lexington, Lord Percy showed great bravery and led the British troops out of danger.

The British troops: A

The Redcoats remained under tight discipline and fought as well as could be expected under very trying circumstances.

The Americans

General William Heath: F

During the British retreat back to Boston, Heath was unable to establish an effective blocking force to capture Percy's command even though the Americans possessed overwhelming numbers.

The Patriot troops: D

Without effective or even discernable leadership, militia fighters turned back the British at the North Bridge in Concord. Thereafter, they showed a marked lack of marksmanship, and failed to deal with the British flankers, close with the retreating column, and annihilate it.

rear for a short while, retired from the battle. Several good opportunities to cut the Redcoats off from Boston entirely were squandered, and the majority of the British column reached the city safely.

In retrospect, it is almost incredible that the British were able to avoid complete annihilation. Although the militiamen possessed artillery, none was brought to bear on the British column. The vast majority of Patriot arms were evidently muskets, and the kill-per-shot ratio defies belief. Some seventy-five thousand rounds were fired at the British by the colonial militiamen, yet they only managed to kill or wound 247 British troops. The vaunted sure-shot rifleman who would feature in American accounts of the war, and this battle in particular, was nowhere to be seen.

A Battle Lost, Yet Won

The successful retreat to Boston was nothing short of a miracle—a testimony to British discipline and American ineffectiveness in the absence of good commanders. On the British side, one man in five had been killed, wounded, or captured, and the entire British column was in mortal danger for hours. There is no denying the fact that Percy saved his command and brought it back to safety over a single, wretched road while surrounded by thousands of enemy soldiers firing continuously into his column. He had averted a disaster—and learned firsthand that the American Patriot militia were not an "irregular mob."

On the Patriot side, the casualties are traditionally listed as much smaller. But whereas British record-keeping was thorough and probably accurate, American totals were often speculative. In this case, men went into battle almost willy-nilly, sometimes singly, sometimes in small groups, and in many cases without an officer directing their movements or actions. American officers on the scene commanded only those around them, regardless of what militia unit the men belonged to. Most assessments put the number of Americans casualties at forty-nine killed, thirty-nine wounded, and five missing, but this is an example of the war-long *underestimation* of Patriot losses. A better approximation would be 150 total casualties.

On the other hand, the British hadn't expected the colonial militia to attack the column at all. Militia units were thought to be social clubs, organized more for drinking than for doing any actual fighting. To an extent the British were right to see them that way, but the militias had begun to change as they began to enforce the Articles of Association—something the Redcoats were now discovering, to their surprise. Most shocking, it was apparent that the militia had no compunction about shooting down the king's soldiers. Few of them had ever read John Locke—they were fighting for self-government as they saw it.

Among the many myths surrounding the expedition to Lexington and Concord is that it triggered an uprising of the *people*. Supposedly farmers grabbed their guns and went to punish the British for killing and mistreating Patriots and their families. In fact, true civilians were not involved. All of the fighters were members of organized militia companies, and they arrived at the battle in formation.

The American failure to annihilate the British at Lexington and Concord may have been an advantage to the Patriots in the long run. The British continued to treat them with contempt, whereas the total destruction of the force might have sobered up the British high command.

This very first battle between the Patriots and British regulars established a rule that the British failed to learn even to the end of the war: an expedition had to be fully self-contained and of sufficient size to confront and defeat any likely American force in order to be successful. Seven hundred men with limited supplies and ammunition going into a hotbed of resistance was bound to fail. Later in the war similar expeditions and forays at Bennington, Moore's Creek Bridge, King's Mountain, Cowpens, and the Mohawk Valley proved the point. British forces were generally successful only when backed up by the Royal Navy. Even large armies like Burgoyne's at Saratoga and Cornwallis's at Yorktown succumbed when cut off from the sea.

Mightier Than the Sword

Lexington and Concord gave master propagandist Samuel Adams a golden opportunity. Adams produced a fictitious and highly inflammatory account of British behavior on the expedition. He described women pulled from their beds and driven naked through the streets while their menfolk were butchered without mercy—and made such brutal acts of vengeance on the poor people of the colonies out to be the essence of British government. His account made its way to London by a fast ship.

Unaware of the Adams report, Gage produced an account admitting that casualties were heavy on both sides. When Gage's report did not counter Adams's incendiary allegations, the people of Britain were incensed. Substantial sums were raised in England, particularly in London, to aid American wounded, widows, and orphans. It was only the opening campaign, but King George had already lost the propaganda war.

The "hot war" wasn't going so well either. The town of Boston was soon under siege as a cloud of militia sealed it off from the surrounding area. In 1774, Boston's population had numbered about sixteen thousand, but it had fallen rapidly after Gage arrived. With too many mouths to feed, Gage now decided to allow people to leave the city without hindrance, as long as they left their firearms at Faneuil Hall with the Boston Selectmen. By April 27, the very first day of the new policy, several thousand applications had been made to leave Boston, and almost eighteen hundred firearms were received at Faneuil Hall. The Patriots in Boston had been armed to the hilt, Gage was appalled to discover. Meanwhile, hundreds of Tory families waited in Charlestown for entry into Boston.

In the midst of this population exchange, prominent Boston Tories approached General Gage with the idea that Patriot families would better serve the crown as hostages for the good behavior of their menfolk. Boston could hardly be bombarded if Patriot women and children were at risk. Gage changed his mind and halted the exodus, breaking up families and causing great hardship.

Meanwhile, a Patriot army was being organized—actually, four armies, each representing the colony that had furnished the troops: 11,500 from Massachusetts, 2,300 from Connecticut, 1,200 from New Hampshire, and

1,000 from Rhode Island. There were command problems and daunting logistics, and these numbers—particularly the one for Massachusetts troops—were hardly steady, as militia members tended to leave for home at their leisure. Sickness, due to very poor sanitation, was rampant in all the camps except that of the Rhode Islanders. On any given day, the army would be fortunate to muster twelve thousand effectives.

General Artemas Ward was in command of the Massachusetts troops, and in an effort to consolidate command the other colonies instructed their officers—John Stark, Israel Putnam, and Nathanael Greene—to take orders from Ward, but there was never a firmly established chain of command until George Washington arrived to take over in July. The Patriot army began harassing the British in Boston, and Gage's forces there swelled to nearly ten thousand men with the arrival of reinforcements under Sir Richard Howe, John Burgoyne, and Henry Clinton. With these troops, it was decided to attack the town of Dorchester, get behind the Massachusetts troops at Roxbury under John Thomas, and capture his entire force.

It was a good plan, but it was betrayed to the Americans. Ward and the local Committee of Safety decided that Putnam should seize and fortify Bunker Hill north of Charlestown, dissuading Gage from attacking Dorchester. The idea would have shocked any professional military planner: the entire Charlestown peninsula could be cut off by the Royal Navy at the Charlestown Neck, a narrow causeway that connected Charlestown with the mainland but was usually under water at high tide. Landing a British force on the Neck could easily force the capitulation of all Patriot forces on the peninsula. Nonetheless, that was Ward's plan.

The troops selected were three Massachusetts regiments totaling about eight hundred men under Colonel William Prescott, a veteran of the French and Indian War, about two hundred Connecticut troops under Captain Thomas Knowlton, another veteran officer, and two brass cannon under Major Scarborough Gridley. As the detachment approached Bunker Hill in the evening of June 16, it was met by General Israel Putnam, who placed the troops not on Bunker Hill (which would nevertheless give its name to the battle they were about to fight) but on Breed's Hill, a more exposed location, but closer to Charlestown and more of a challenge to the British in Boston. So Putnam countermanded Ward's orders, and the troops moved on to Breed's Hill, putting their heads more firmly in a noose.

Arms and the Man

The firearms carried by the Patriots at the Battle of Bunker Hill were of all type and description, but significantly the American troops had no bayonets. A popular firearm was the New England Club Musket, a gun with a very heavy buttstock that had been found to be an excellent counter to Indian tomahawks. Almost none of the Patriots carried rifles. There was little reserve ammunition, and the wide array of different caliber weapons meant that the men frequently cast their own musket balls and prepared their own cartridge boxes. Before John Stark's New Hampshire men were dispatched to Breed's Hill early in the morning, Stark gave each man a cup of powder, fifteen balls, and a flint. Since many of the balls didn't fit the caliber of the weapons the men were carrying, they hurriedly re-cast them for their own muskets. Then the men had to make up cartridges, which—because they didn't have cartridge boxes—they stuffed into their pockets. To say that the Patriots were poorly armed would be an understatement. British soldiers, on the other hand, bore the traditional "Brown Bess" musket, which at fifty-eight inches had a .69 ball and used the flintlock popular in the American colonies. It also sported a seventeen-inch bayonet. Reliable, easy to produce, and effective, the Brown Bess remained a staple of the British Army for over half a century.

The cannon of the day were named by the weight of the ball they fired—a "three pounder" fired a three-pound ball. Cannonballs did not explode—Henry Shrapnel would not invent the exploding ball until 1787—but rather bounced at the infantry like a bowling ball.

The American troops bent to the task of constructing an earthen fortification beginning about midnight, but the chosen date was one of the longest days of the year, and daybreak was about 4:35 a.m. The men worked feverishly, and Prescott was pleased to see that the parapet reached over six feet high before he allowed them to rest. Although many historians have

★ ★ ★

Fun Fact

The American militiaman who fought at Lexington or Breed's Hill was, on average, between one and two inches taller than his British adversary, or closer to 5'8". Historians credit the good diet and an overall healthier lifestyle in the colonies for this height difference.

recorded that the existence of the fortification came as a shock to the British at daybreak, the activity had been reported to Gage almost as soon as it started, and he had decided to wait until daylight to decide on a course of action.

In fact, it was Colonel Prescott who was shocked when he took a good look at the defenses on Breed's Hill in daylight. The redoubt his men had built was impossible for a thousand men to hold. The position could be easily outflanked on both sides in complete safety, encircled, and reduced at the attacker's pleasure. The danger was underscored a few minutes after daybreak when the HMS *Lively*, the twenty-gun post ship that had brought Gage to Boston, opened fire on the redoubt. Work on the fortification came to a halt during the cannonade, and Prescott called for reinforcements.

Gage called a conference of his officers to discuss the proper course of action. General Henry Clinton was the most outspoken. He pointed out that the rebel fort was incomplete "with no flanks, neither picketed, palisaded or ditched"—nothing more than a small, isolated outpost begging to be gobbled up. Clinton recommended that Admiral Graves position floating batteries to rake the Charlestown Neck continuously to prevent anyone crossing in either direction, then while one detachment landed near Bunker

Hill (west of Breed's Hill and closer to the Neck) from the Mystic River and attacked the fort from the rear, another could attack from Morton's Point in the front. The affair would be over in a matter of minutes, and the Americans hustled away as prisoners.

Gage, supported by his other generals, overruled Clinton. After all, they would only be fighting colonial militia. No complicated maneuvering was necessary. The slope of the hill was gentle, and a whiff of grapeshot followed by a determined assault with the bayonet would capture the fort and its defenders easily. It would be a demonstration to rebels everywhere of the power of the British army. The Americans were cowards, and the only problem would be to catch them as they ran away. This was the same attitude that had been on display from Major Pitcairn and Colonel Smith on the expedition to Lexington and Concord—and that would cripple British generals throughout the war.

The time for the attack was set as soon as possible after high tide at three in the afternoon so the landing at Morton's Point could go smoothly, but that meant that the British had granted Prescott precious time to strengthen his fortification. Nonetheless, Prescott's left flank was still "in the air," and troops marching from Morton's Point could easily encircle him. Stark barely arrived in time with his reinforcements to the northern end of the line.

As the British began landing at Morton's Point, Prescott's artillery deserted. The artillery officers hauled the four field pieces out of the redoubt and headed for Bunker Hall, saying they were out of ammunition. They weren't. Putnam intercepted them and tried to rally the battery, but the artillerymen dashed back across the Neck to safety, leaving the Patriots with no artillery support save two guns northwest of the redoubt.

Other officers, however, were doing everything possible to prepare for the British assault. Thomas Knowlton constructed the three "V"-shaped forts behind the swamp at the end of Prescott's redoubt extension, and also a double fence of rock and rails from the road to Bunker Hill north to the Mystic River. The space between the fences was filled with hay and grass, which afforded no protection from enemy fire, but did screen the defenders. Behind the fence was a ditch in which the men stood.

The British were unimpressed. Howe's plan was simple. His right wing would overwhelm the recent arrivals by attacking in column along the Mystic River beach with light infantry, breach the stone wall, then turn south to gobble up the men behind the double rail fence while the grenadiers attacked the front of the fence. With luck, the farmers would run away, and the remaining fortifications could be easily surrounded and forced to capitulate. One strong blow should do it. General Robert Pigot, commanding the left wing under Howe, would attack the redoubt from the east and south, wrapping around it on the south side to complete the envelopment. The battle should be over before teatime.

The Whites of Their Eyes

Howe's attack was a disaster, with the entire assault along the Mystic beach stopped cold by accurate and rapid fire from Stark's New Hampshire men. Orders ranged from "Don't shoot till you see the whites of their eyes," to withhold fire until the Redcoats were at fifty yards, to "Aim at the handsome coats." The front ranks of the light infantry fell like stalks of corn and were filled from behind, and the following ranks were shot down until just fugitives were left. A stunned General Howe couldn't believe what he saw, but still expected the grenadiers to make short work of the rail fence. But then sheets of flame from the massed muskets in that position blew great holes in Howe's ranks, and only seventy feet from the American line literally all the officers around Howe were dead or dying on the ground, including his entire staff. Howe himself was clearly visible to the American troops, standing alone amidst the carnage, but he enjoyed a charmed life. The grenadiers gave way and ran back to Morton's Point, some even getting into the boats. General Howe walked slowly back, shaking his head at the turn of events. Pigot's attack did not fare any better; his troops were mowed down by accurate fire from the redoubt. As in Howe's wing, the officers seemed to be particularly prone to becoming casualties, and retaining order in the assault became impossible.

Within a quarter of an hour, however, Howe reformed his shattered regiments for a second attack. This time he would forego an assault on the stone fence and instead concentrate on the rail fence. Pigot would attack the redoubt without waiting for Howe. But the British were tiring in the heat and suffering under the weight of their heavy uniforms and packs, which weighed about 125 pounds. Nonetheless they stepped off to meet undiminished fire from Stark and Knowlton, piling up grenadiers and light infantry in front of the rail fence. The uneven ground in front of the American positions, with holes and fences hidden in the long grass, would have made the attacks difficult even without hostile fire. Pigot, on the left, was dismayed at the casualties and retreated.

By the end of the second assault, Prescott was down to perhaps 150 men in the redoubt, another 200 behind the breastwork extension; Knowlton and Stark had perhaps another 400 to 500 men. There was an equal number on Bunker Hill, but they were not moving forward in units to take part in the battle. Those potential reinforcements themselves were less important than the ammunition they carried. Prescott's men were almost out of ammunition, and there was no way he could survive a third assault.

And it came. Howe could not admit defeat; he felt that one last push would drive the Americans away—though the leading companies of grenadiers and light infantry that had assaulted the stone and rail fences had already lost nearly 70 percent of their manpower.

Bolstered by reinforcements, the third assault staggered at first, but the red lines gathered strength and came on again. Patriot fire finally slackened as the troops ran out of ammunition, and a steady stream of men issued forth from the redoubt and from behind the breastworks seeking safety. Only the rail fence held firm, as Knowlton's and Stark's men covered the retreat of the men from the earthen works.

But the killing wasn't over. The Americans still had to negotiate the Charlestown Neck, which was being raked by British cannon fire. It was a gruesome business; the British were out for blood. Until the last American was across the Neck the British fired incessantly, substantially increasing the casualty toll. Still, the American casualties paled beside those of the British: 52 percent of those engaged and almost every officer in the lead companies. As Henry Clinton wrote on the evening of the battle, "A dear bought victory, another such would have ruined us."

American casualties in the Battle of Bunker Hill (really fought on Breed's Hill) were reported by Washington as 138 killed and more than 300 wounded and missing, for a total of 450. Many of these had occurred while the Americans were crossing the Charlestown Neck. British casualties were 226 killed and 828 wounded, for a total of 1,054. An exceptionally high percentage of British losses were officers. In both cases, many of those wounded died in the next few days.

What the battle proved was that militia could fight well under good leadership and when their legs were protected from enemy fire. Marksmanship was greatly improved over the retreat from Concord, mainly because this time the troops were fighting in tight formations commanded by competent officers. But a large number of men in various militia organizations had backed away from the fight, or chosen not to engage. And many of the Patriot officers were still untrained or incompetent. Stark, Knowlton, and Prescott, however, had been given impossible tasks but all acquitted themselves with great gallantry and professionalism. That the Patriots came within an ace of winning the battle was due to those three officers: that the Americans ultimately lost it was due to supply problems, lack of ammunition, and block-headedness at higher levels. It would take the Americans some time to sort out the good officers from the bad.

For the time being, the Continental Army, mostly made up of militia, surrounded the British army at Boston under Howe, who had replaced the disgraced Gage. Meanwhile, Fort Ticonderoga in New York had fallen to Benedict Arnold and Ethan Allen, and Boston was the only place in the thirteen colonies where there was a significant presence of British authority. The Americans had done well so far, inflicting over twice as many casualties on the British as they had suffered. Now the British realized they were in for a long and expensive war. That is, all the British except the king and his

★ ★ ★
Bunker Hill Report Card

The British

General Thomas Gage: F

Gage ignored the perilous position of the Patriots when he could have isolated them by cutting them off at the Charlestown Neck and capturing the whole Patriot army. Instead he decided to show the Patriots the power of Great Britain with a needless frontal assault. Fixated on landing at Morton's Point, he also delayed the attack until mid-afternoon, needlessly and at great cost to his men.

Sir William Howe: F

In command of the British attack, Howe failed to reconnoiter the ground in front of Breed's Hill and the rail fence and did not take the colonists seriously.

He failed to use the Royal Navy—except to bombard the Charlestown Neck—and his artillery effectively. But personally, he exhibited great bravery.

The British troops: A

They did everything expected of them in the face of murderous fire, sustaining 52 percent casualties in killed and wounded.

The Americans

General Artemas Ward: F

In overall command of the Patriots, Ward remained in Cambridge and allowed the battle to run its course without taking any effective action. Fearing British activity elsewhere, he refused to send reinforcements and desperately needed ammunition to Prescott during the battle.

ministers, who were hell-bent on reconquering the colonies and bringing the rebels to account, whatever the cost. Already King George was considering hiring German mercenaries for what he believed would be the final campaign in the coming year.

Lack of Preparation Makes for Desperation

In truth, the Continental Army was hardly prepared for a real war, regardless of the enthusiasm in the ranks. They had no money, little discipline, less sanitation, and almost no military supplies. Each battle used a prodigious

General Israel Putnam: D

He put the whole Patriot army at risk by ignoring his orders to occupy Bunker Hill and moving the army forward to Breed's Hill. He fed troops into the line regardless of unit affiliation and exercised little control over the battle.

Dr. Joseph Warren: F

Although Warren had just been appointed a general, he fought in the redoubt as a private soldier and was killed. The Patriots needed his leadership, not his musket. Egalitarianism takes you only so far.

Colonel John Stark: A

Beyond any reasonable expectation, Stark held the improvised hay-filled fence and rock wall on the left flank with his Scotch-Irish New Hampshire men, was never forced from his position, and covered the Patriot retreat.

Major Thomas Knowlton: A

He handled his Connecticut troops at the fence he had built connecting Stark's position with the redoubt competently and professionally. With Stark, he covered the Patriot retreat.

Colonel William Prescott: B

He commanded the troops in the redoubt well but failed to take any action to replenish his ammunition before the third British attack.

The Patriot troops: A

They held the line until out of ammunition, then still fought hand to hand. American officers learned that militia members would remain in place and fight if their legs were protected and they were well led by their officers. So long as they did not risk leg wounds (so they were confident they could still run if necessary), the militia fought well.

amount of powder and ball, and the colonies were nowhere near self-suffi-cient in gunpowder and lead. Wool was in critically short supply for uni-forms, and there was no American textile industry. Because of the lack of even primitive sanitation in the American camps, disease was rampant. Often less than half of a regiment was fit for duty at any particular time. Although there was a cadre of experienced military officers from the French and Indian War, when the colonists had furnished Great Britain with a hundred thousand troops, few of those veterans had faced solid lines of troops fighting in the current European style. Some, like Artemas Ward and Israel Putnam, were getting old and facing health issues, and could no longer live up to their reputations. The war was being run by committee, and with regimental and company officers being elected by their men, command and discipline issues were an ever-present problem.

"No Harum-Scarum Ranting Swearing Fellow"

Congress, meanwhile, had appointed George Washington of Virginia to command the Continental Army. Washington was known for his personal bravery, and in the French and Indian War he had performed well in the retreat after Braddock's Defeat, but his experience as an independent com-mander was checkered. Still, he was perceived as the only man for the job. Delegates spoke of him as "Sober, steady, and Calm," "dignified," "sensible," and "virtuous, modest, and brave." In one delegate's colorful phrase, Wash-ington was no "harum-scarum ranting swearing fellow." When he traveled to Boston to take charge of the army, few had any idea they had appointed the one man who would almost singlehandedly save the Revolution. As we have already seen, he was, in his biographer James Thomas Flexner's words, "the indispensable man." Now the world would see whether this indispens-able man could mold an army that could survive a head-on confrontation with British Redcoats.

CHAPTER 4

Militia Into Regulars

In May of 1775, even before the Battle of Bunker Hill, the Second Continental Congress convened its meeting in Philadelphia. Once again, only Georgia was absent. The general opinion of the delegates was for making an accommodation with the crown. Many believed that the Tory Party had misled Parliament and that the king could be made to see the colonists' side. Hoping to avoid the war that was already upon them, they failed to understand that the king was the greatest hawk in England, and he controlled Parliament through bribery, rewards to favorites, and intimidation.

A letter from the Massachusetts Provincial Congress woke Congress up. It asked that the Continental Congress take control of the army outside of Boston, as it was providing for the defense of the rights of all the colonies. The New England colonies could not withstand the power of Great Britain by themselves, and John Hancock, Samuel Adams, and John Adams all argued that if New England was defeated, the other colonies would be subjected one by one.

In a contentious debate, the delegates reluctantly agreed that unity was necessary. On June 15 Congress finally voted unanimously to assume control of the army surrounding Boston, named it the Continental Army, and

Did you know?

★ After just a half-dozen rounds, musket barrels became too hot to handle

★ Two of Washington's best officers started out with only book knowledge of the military

★ In 1775 rifles were novelty weapons of astonishing accuracy

★ The Siege of Boston was won by a monumental achievement of military fortification

★ ★ ★

Elected by the Troops

In the American military tradition, dating back to the early colonial wars with the Indians, militias were self-contained units that usually elected their own officers. While many of these men (never women) were wealthy, some were not. Position and rank were not necessarily decided by money, as they tended to be in England. Quite the contrary, the American way of war promoted men from below as long as they could fight and lead. As Larry Schweikart's *America's Victories: Why the U.S. Wins Wars and Will Win the War on Terror* shows, the tradition of electing militia officers would greatly contribute to the American tradition of merit and of a classless society. Americans would place great responsibility on meritorious individuals of all classes—which in turn produced tremendous levels of autonomy and innovation.

appointed George Washington to lead it. Washington was the logical choice: Virginia was the most powerful of the thirteen colonies, and Washington was its foremost military figure. He was reputed to have saved Braddock's army from annihilation in the French and Indian War, and he reminded everyone of his military prowess every day by appearing in Congress in his blue and buff uniform as a colonel in the Virginia militia. Washington wanted the job. He was unanimously elected, along with four major generals and nine brigadier generals.

Many of the selections were badly flawed. Age, along with his inability to make reasonable decisions, should have disqualified the fifty-seven-year-old Israel Putnam. Artemas Ward was a dithering politician with limited military abilities. Charles Lee, a highly experienced former British officer who had immigrated to Virginia in 1773, would prove to be constantly insubordinate and inept in command on the battlefield. And Philip Schuyler, a forty-one-year-old Dutch New Yorker, failed to inspire trust and respect in his soldiers and tended to lead from behind—far behind. The selection of these four generals created a major problem of incompetence and dead wood at the highest rank that became difficult to overcome as the war progressed.

Horatio Gates was one of the brigadier generals, but was actually the adjutant general. Another former British officer, Gates, like Lee, felt he was superior in ability to Washington. He aspired to replace Washington as

★ ★ ★

Going Muzzle to Muzzle with the British

Watching General Gates being annihilated by the British at Camden, the hero of the popular movie *The Patriot* says, "That Gates is a damn fool. Spent too much time in the British Army. Going muzzle to muzzle with Redcoats in an open field is madness, madness." It was hard to believe that American troops, militia or Continentals, would be able to stand toe to toe with British regulars and fight it out. But Indian tactics and sharpshooting riflemen only went so far. Guerrilla tactics couldn't reach the British in their enclaves, and Patriot families were at risk while those of the British weren't. So George Washington attempted to build a respectable army along European lines, but he never succeeded in approaching British numbers of regular troops. What won the war was the militia: floating like butterflies and stinging like bees. The British eventually lost the will to win, partly because they also had to protect their holdings in the Caribbean—which they considered more valuable than the thirteen colonies—from the French.

The linear tactics used by the British and subsequently by the Americans were necessitated by the limitations of the weapons and ammunition. British troops usually formed up in three lines with sergeants and "file-closers" behind to fill in the gaps as casualties occurred. Sometimes the first rank would fire and then kneel to reload while the second rank fired over the heads of the first rank. After just a few volleys, the lines would charge, two ranks with only their bayonets and the third still capable of firing at individual soldiers as necessary. Since the musket barrels became too hot to touch after a half-dozen rounds, the soldiers had to charge with the bayonet while the soldiers could still handle their muskets properly. Contrary to what one sees on television or in movies, the troops were packed in shoulder to shoulder, each man touching the men on either side of him. A bayonet charge against untrained militia never failed to drive the militia from the field—not least because the militia had no bayonets and could only use their muskets as clubs.

commander-in-chief, scheming against him endlessly, but all talk of that ended when he was embarrassingly defeated by Cornwallis at Camden and fled for his life, leaving his troops on the field.

Of all the brigadier generals, Nathanael Greene was probably the best choice. He was chosen by a Rhode Island committee to command the

Rhode Island troops, ostensibly as a compromise on religion—Greene was a Quaker candidate, while the others were Episcopalian and Congregationalist. All of Greene's military knowledge came from books, but he rose to be practically Washington's second-in-command, even if he literally never won a battle.

Washington took over an army of about fifteen thousand troops, poorly armed, wretchedly clad, and nearly without food, powder, and ammunition. The term "army" barely applied. They were undisciplined, without shelter or tents, and the lack of sanitation in the camps had produced nearly three thousand sick, with scores dying every day. None had regularly used bayonets in combat. The only well-organized, well-disciplined regiment was Nathanael Greene's Rhode Islanders. Washington foresaw that the Continental Army would have to learn how to fight the British in the European mode of warfare, standing exposed in rows in open fields.

Musket Balls Were YUGE!

A typical American musket fired a .69 caliber soft lead ball while the British Brown Bess was larger at .74 but could also fire a .69 inch ball, which was undersized, causing the musket to become fouled or inaccurate. These balls were larger in caliber than ammunition used by any infantry rifles or machine guns today. The wounds they made were ghastly, killing or mortally wounding their victims or requiring the amputation of a limb. These are larger caliber "bullets" than the ones fired from the .50 caliber guns on the "technicals" that are commonly seen in the Middle East today!

Pistols were useless except in close combat of fifteen feet or less. Dueling pistols might have some accuracy out to twenty paces, but even then, most duels required second or third shots before anyone was hit. Artillery also figured prominently in linear warfare, as well as during sieges. On the battlefield three, four, and six pounders (from the weight of the ammunition) were used, firing solid round or grape. As we have seen, cannonballs bounced rather than exploded until Sir Henry Shrapnel invented the exploding shell in 1787. At short range, grapeshot—consisting of a bag of iron balls clustered around a rod of iron in the center, like a bunch of grapes on a vine—could be used. It acted like a shotgun against infantry.

To offset the lack of bayonets, the Continental Army attempted to require each soldier to furnish at his own expense a large knife, sword, hatchet, or tomahawk as a cutting weapon for close combat. This was especially important for riflemen, as it took longer to reload a rifle than a musket, and rifles were not outfitted with bayonet lugs. In general, the tomahawk became the preferred sidearm for a rifleman, completing his image as an Indian fighter. And the tomahawk was deadly, but to use it the American soldier had to get inside the reach of the Redcoat's bayonet. The advantage to the British regulars was decisive in most cases. Washington's men were also chronically short of gunpowder. Over 90 percent of the Patriots' gunpowder had to be imported by ship, and the threat of the Royal Navy cutting off the supply was very real. At Boston, the Continentals only possessed enough for nine rounds per man. But improving the supply situation was beyond Washington's grasp at the time, and he turned to another pressing problem, the lack of discipline. Despite the shortage of gunpowder, he ordered that all men fire at least two live rounds in a practice firing.

Washington understood that discipline began with the officers, and he wanted them to be an effective and elite corps in the army, treated with deference. Troops began to be disciplined with severity, including punishment by the lash as in the British army. With better discipline came better sanitation, and the sick list grew smaller. Meanwhile, Washington began a purge of incompetent officers.

As he worked to improve the top end of the military, Washington also sought to bolster the morale of the men by initiating a series of harassment raids on the British to keep them occupied. One particularly successful

A Book You're Not Supposed to Read

The Continental Army by Robert K. Wright Jr. (Fort McNair, DC: U.S. Army Center of Military History, 1983).

sortie was commanded by Colonel John Greaton, who earned renown throughout the war for his daring and successes. Greaton's men rowed across Boston harbor in a group of whaleboats and attacked Long Island at dawn. His troops burned every house on the island and destroyed all British supplies. When the Royal Navy attempted to cut off his escape, he fought his way out, losing only a single man.

Virginia and western Pennsylvania rifle companies, which arrived in August, were a great curiosity. Washington called for them to display their marksmanship with their Pennsylvania rifles. Targets only seven inches in diameter were set at a distance of three hundred yards, and the riflemen charged the targets, firing on the run. Everyone was amazed when most of the shots hit the targets. Washington would learn later that riflemen had to be supported by companies with muskets because of the time required for the riflemen to reload—otherwise they were easily chased away by British bayonets. Nevertheless, the accuracy of their shots gave rise to the myth of the American marksman who was "naturally" better than foreign counterparts (which would reach its apotheosis in heroes like Daniel Boone and Davy Crockett). Washington immediately put the riflemen to work sniping at the British. Soon red-coated sentries were no longer in the open, preferring cover over death.

Meanwhile Washington was informed that seventeen thousand pounds of gunpowder had been taken from the HMS *Betsy* off the harbor of St. Augustine in Florida. It would take weeks for the haul to be brought to Boston, but at least it was on the way. Perhaps the Americans could take supplies they desperately needed from the British on the high seas.

America's first navy was established late in August when Colonel John Glover's schooner the *Hannah* and its crew of thirty-six men were commissioned into the Continental Navy. Soon six other ships were commissioned—although by that time the *Hannah* had been lost to the British. Two months after the establishment of the navy, the British ordnance ship *Nancy* was taken in an outstanding coup. The *Nancy* was carrying a hundred thousand flints, thirty-one tons of musket balls, seven thousand cannonballs, hundreds of barrels of gunpowder, two thousand Brown Bess muskets, and many other items sorely needed by Washington's army. In a single stroke, the Continental Army had gained the supplies it needed. Washington now had the military stores to fight Gage anywhere, anytime.

Forming an Army

In September Benedict Arnold had set out with troops on an expedition to Quebec, which hopefully would meet up with General Schuyler's force traveling from Ticonderoga to Montreal. Schuyler found one reason after another to delay and, after reaching Canada, turned over command of his expedition to General Richard Montgomery and returned to Albany.

Having sent the Canadian expedition off, and now fully supplied with powder, Washington needed to address the pending loss of thousands of troops whose expiring enlistments were threatening the army with dissolution. Washington tried everything possible to keep the troops from heading home, but it was an uphill battle. Then a call went out to the colonies for another levy from the militia. Almost miraculously during December, as Massachusetts and Connecticut troops streamed away for home, thousands of militiamen from New Hampshire, Massachusetts, and Pennsylvania more than made up for the departing troops. The army was disbanding and reassembling right in front of the enemy. Thousands of new arrivals—inexperienced and untrained militia—manned the entrenchments, and Washington had to start all over again with their training. As he had done throughout the fall, he kept up daily harassments of the British to keep them off-balance. It worked—British observers could not detect a difference. By mid-February the Continental Army consisted of fourteen thousand regulars and six thousand militiamen.

But Washington still had a severe shortage of cannon, which he needed to drive the Redcoats out of Boston. In November, ex-bookstore owner Henry Knox, the twenty-five-year-old colonel commanding the colonial artillery—his military knowledge, like Greene's, was all from reading—requested that he be allowed to arrange for the guns at the captured British fort of Ticonderoga to be moved to Boston. It took ten weeks, but during the first part of February 1776 the guns began arriving at Cambridge. In a feat inaccurately heralded by many historians as one of the most outstanding of the Revolutionary War, Knox brought sixty tons of guns and supplies—forty-three cannon, three howitzers, fourteen mortars of various sizes, twenty-three kegs of cannon and musket balls, and other items—almost three hundred miles on sledges through deep snow and very poor roads to the besieging army. Knox's men experienced only a small fraction of the hardships endured by Arnold's troops on their trek to Quebec, but Knox became an American hero and Arnold—his achievements not sufficiently appreciated—drifted into resentment.

Washington now had what he needed to come up with a feasible plan to drive the British from Boston. He would fortify Dorchester Heights, a hill that overlooked Boston and provided a besieging army with an excellent artillery position from which to bombard the city. There were risks: first Dorchester Heights had to be occupied and fortified sufficiently to repel a British assault, and its seizure would certainly bring on a general engagement. General Howe could be expected to isolate the Heights—a bare hillside with frozen ground—and attack before the Continentals could become established in a good defensive position. To solve this dilemma, Washington resolved to seize and fortify the Heights in a single dark night.

To divert British attention from his plan, Washington began nightly bombardments on Boston two days before the designated night, and the British returned fire, their attention drawn away from Dorchester Heights. Then on March 4, some eight hundred riflemen ascended Dorchester Heights, positioning themselves on Nook's Hill where the Heights were the closest to Boston, and to the east to overlook the British-occupied Castle William. Another twelve hundred men followed with materials to build fortifications. The frozen ground didn't cooperate, so the men used thousands of pre-built gabions—wicker cages to hold rock and dirt—and thousands of fascines—long bundles of sticks and saplings. Hundreds of heavy wooden frames called chandeliers were built to hold the fascines. The road to the top was masked with twisted hay, which also helped muffle the noise of the carts. All these fortification materials, along with many of the heavy cannon from Ticonderoga, were carried to the Heights while the cannonade went on throughout the night. When construction was finished, the fortification looked like a long dog bone: one redoubt on Nooks Hill and one to the east, connected by a parapet ten feet high—a formidable structure indeed.

General Howe was astonished; he believed the work must have taken twelve or fourteen thousand men. Nonetheless, he quickly made plans to assault the Heights that very night—with unloaded muskets, depending on the bayonet to do the work. He moved thirty-five hundred troops to Castle William, and sent his main body to assault the Heights. But before they could attack nature took a hand: a furious winter storm blew up, wrecking the barges at Castle William and preventing any further crossings. By the time the storm finally abated, Howe thought the American position to be impregnable. He had no choice but to evacuate Boston.

On March 9, British troops began loading the ships. Howe sent a note to Washington that if his evacuation was not contested, Boston would not be

★ ★ ★

Siege of Boston Report Card

The British

Major General William Howe: B

He had no wish to assault American troops in their entrenchments, and Boston made a poor base of operations against the colonies. His evacuation was hardly a defeat, and a much more promising theater beckoned where British troops could be decisively employed—New York.

The British troops: A

Once again, a wonderful instrument of war.

The Americans

General George Washington: A

It was his presence and prestige that held the Patriots together as a cohesive force, and his plan that caused Howe to evacuate Boston.

The American Troops: A

All flaws were masked, cannon and powder were obtained, and the men were learning the art of war as fast as possible.

burned and destroyed. Eight days later, the Patriots took the city. Over a thousand Tories left with Howe and his men.

The victory was extraordinary. Howe had left behind more than a thousand cannon and tremendous military stores. Washington's army had overcome many problems, including lack of supply and insufficient training. It had also gotten considerable help from nature. But ultimately the lesson both the Patriots and the British took from Boston was that these Americans were capable of amazing achievements.

CHAPTER 5

Declaration

While their force was holed up in Boston waiting for more troops, for more supplies, and for the Americans to come to their senses, the British had not been idle in the rest of the colonies. In North Carolina, Britain made an attempt to marshal Tory forces and turn the Revolution into a civil war. And acting on the British belief that the Southern colonies were intrinsically loyal, they mounted an expedition to seize Charleston.

Even before the Declaration of Independence was written, General William Howe and his brother Admiral Richard Howe were designing a strategy featuring a series of wedges that would dismember the continent into manageable chunks and destroy the fragile unity the Continental Congresses had built.

Dismembering the Rebellion

First the Howes would take New York and gain control of the Hudson River valley as far north as Albany, making use of their greatest asset, the Royal Navy. General Sir Guy Carleton, in Quebec, would complete the sealing off of rebellious New England by coming down Lake Champlain and seizing Forts Ticonderoga and Edward.

Did you know?

★ Thomas Jefferson initially declined to write the Declaration of Independence, but John Adams told him, "You can write ten times better than I can"

★ Adams didn't want to be the author because he was (in his own words) "obnoxious, suspected, and unpopular"

★ Jefferson said the editing of the Declaration was the worst thing he ever went through

A Book You're Not Supposed to Read

The Howe Brothers and the American Revolution by Ira D. Gruber (New York: W. W. Norton, 1975) reveals the Howes, for better and worse.

In the South, as a preliminary move, Admiral Sir Peter Parker and General Henry Clinton planned to occupy Charleston before the colonials could raise an army—and snip off Georgia into the bargain. Josiah Martin, the royal governor of North Carolina, would re-establish the hegemony that former governor Tryon had enjoyed when he had easily eliminated the regulators with militia regiments from the eastern part of the state. From there, southern Virginia could be raided and the hotheads in the House of Burgesses made to see reason. And finally, the Royal Navy would sail up the Chesapeake after the New York operation was over and attack the largest city in America, Philadelphia. It was all eminently logical and reasonable, but the Patriots were yet to weigh in.

The Howe brothers were more than military commanders. They had been designated as peace commissioners, empowered to negotiate with the colonial leaders in order to end the fighting. One thing, however, was missing from their instructions—they could not grant the colonies independence. Quite the contrary, King George expected the rebellion to be stamped out, and the American colonists to return to being good, loyal British subjects.

That wasn't in the cards. But neither side in this conflict understood the resolve of the other. The Americans were out of touch with the situation in Great Britain and could not easily evaluate British intentions. Some delegates to Congress thought that while Parliament was being unreasonable, King George would be more amenable to seeing the American colonies as great and viable trading partners, helping to make England prosperous. Others believed exactly the opposite: since there was a liberal Whig faction in Parliament, it was thought an approach should be made to those individuals rather than the king. Actually, both approaches were doomed to failure. Over the years King George had packed Parliament with men personally loyal to him, and whatever he said, Parliament would do. The Whig minority was emasculated, and any delegation approaching them would be risking the hangman's rope.

But as much as Americans misread the British government, the British ministers, the king, and the leadership of the British army and Royal Navy were even more badly informed about the feelings and intentions of the Americans. Secure in their aristocratic egotism, they believed that no one born an Englishman would want to be anything else—even though they were unwilling to give the colonists their full rights as Englishmen. Accordingly, they assumed the Revolution was only supported by a few malcontents, convicts, and Scotch-Irish who hated England anyway.

North Carolina's Recruitment Dry Run

The first test of this belief came in early 1776, when Josiah Martin, the royal governor of North Carolina, decided to form Tory militia units from his colony. Martin expected to recruit extensively from Catholic Scottish Highlanders in North Carolina. There were also former Regulators who had taken the loyalty oath and decided that working with the colonial administration was more lucrative than being against it. Recruits would be well-compensated for their efforts: they were to receive two hundred acres of land, be exempt from paying taxes for twenty years, and be reimbursed for personal expenses and supplies. In essence, they were mercenaries.

Scottish recruiters were already active in North Carolina signing up men for the Royal Highland Emigrants, the Eighty-Fourth Regiment of Foot. The regiment was supposed to raise five battalions, but in the event only two battalions were filled out, and even those only through enlistments in Quebec and New York as well as North Carolina.

A Book You're Not Supposed to Read

North Carolina in the American Revolution by Hugh F. Rankin (Raleigh, NC: North Carolina Division of Archives and History, 1996) explores the war in a critical colony.

One Colony, Two Governments

Meanwhile, the Patriots in North Carolina had been busy forming an alternate government to that of Governor Martin's. In December of 1773 Richard Caswell and eight others had been appointed to serve as a standing committee to support cooperation throughout the colonies to resist the Intolerable Acts. Caswell, one of the many forgotten Founding Fathers, would become a noted Patriot while serving in all five of North Carolina's provincial congresses and the two Continental Congresses.

He put together a plan to seize the governor and his council and transfer government to the provincial congress. Patriots attempted to capture Martin at the governor's mansion at New Bern, but he eluded them and fled to Fort Johnston on the west bank of the Cape Fear River in June of 1775. There the furious governor initiated an unrealistic plot to arm the slaves. When word of this leaked out, John Ashe of Wilmington led a company of militia in an attack against Fort Johnston. Martin took refuge on board the HMS *Cruiser* at anchor in the Cape Fear River.

When the provincial congress met in August of 1775, Caswell seized the provincial treasury and placed it at the disposal of the provincial congress, which raised three thousand Patriot troops—dwarfing the recruitment efforts of the Tories. Governor Martin, meanwhile, learning that General Henry Clinton's expedition was expected to arrive in the middle of February 1776, ordered the British recruiters to concentrate their men on the Cape Fear River at Cross Creek (modern Fayetteville). From there the Tory army could move on Wilmington, a hotbed of Patriot resistance. He expected at least six thousand Tory troops. Instead, he got about thirty-five hundred, under General Donald MacDonald, and even that had dwindled to barely half its strength by the time they reached the lower Cape Fear River.

Word of the British concentrations at Cross Creek arrived at the North Carolina provincial congress from spies almost as soon as it took place. The call went out for the Patriot forces to mobilize and prevent the Tories at Cross Creek from reaching the coast and joining the British.

Out-Marching and Out-Fighting the Tories

On February 15, Colonel James Moore and 650 Patriots camped on the southern shore of Rockfish Creek, blocking the easiest and most direct route for the Tories to the coast. Caswell set out from New Bern with 850 men to join Moore. MacDonald, blocked from the best route to the coast by Moore, headed toward Corbett's Ferry on the Black River. Caswell swiftly responded, reached the ferry after a lightning march, and set up defensive positions. At the same time Moore sent forces to build entrenchments on the east bank of Moore's Creek to protect the Moore's Creek Bridge, which was on the next best route to the coast.

Finding Corbett's Ferry blocked, MacDonald sent his main force to cross Moore's Creek at Moore's Creek Bridge ten miles away, but again Caswell was quicker. As soon as MacDonald departed for the bridge, Caswell raced ahead and crossed the bridge to confront him.

MacDonald, whose army had dwindled to fewer than twelve hundred men, decided to collect his stragglers and attack Caswell in the morning. Then, feeling ill under the strain of marching, MacDonald turned over command of the army to Captain Donald MacLeod, a veteran of Bunker Hill, to conduct the attack.

Meanwhile, Caswell saw the weakness of his position covering the approaches to the bridge, crossed back to the east side of the creek, and disabled the bridge by removing its planking. He strengthened the east side's entrenchments—the Patriot militia would be fighting behind cover for their legs—and awaited MacDonald's attack.

★ ★ ★
Battle of Moore's Creek Report Card

The British

General Donald MacDonald: F

Every decision the Tory commander made was wrong.

The Americans

Colonel James Moore: A

He planned for every contingency.

Richard Caswell: A

By quick marches and inspired leadership, Caswell won North Carolina for the Revolution.

MacLeod assembled his force, and in the morning led a disastrous attack. Within minutes over thirty Tories, including MacLeod himself, lay dead on the field, and about sixty were wounded. Everyone who had crossed the creek and was still moving surrendered. On the Patriot side, only one man was killed and twenty were wounded.

This mini-campaign between Tories and Patriots was a harbinger of things to come. MacDonald's march had involved various atrocities and the burning of Patriot farms. Troops that had committed such acts were not allowed to surrender honorably but rather were treated as criminals and summarily executed. Nonetheless, in all about 850 Tories were captured and processed for release or prison. General MacDonald himself was captured and imprisoned in Halifax. With their leadership eliminated, the Scots in North Carolina were never again a major factor as active Tory partisans.

Not a Slaughter Pen

The British side of the North Carolina operation began while Generals Howe and Clinton were still besieged in Boston. In addition to planning the seizure of New York City and the Hudson Valley, they had organized an expedition to the Southern colonies, where they were assured by local governors that even a modest presence of the British army would bring the two Carolinas back under the king's control. Clinton and Parker set out from Boston to Cape Fear, North Carolina, where they planned to join with the mostly Scottish Tories recruited in North Carolina and a British force of twenty-five hundred men coming from Ireland.

Arriving at Cape Fear on March 12, Clinton learned that the Tory army had been defeated at Moore's Creek Bridge two weeks earlier, and there would be no help forthcoming from colonial forces. The British force under Lord Charles Cornwallis, scheduled to leave Cork, Ireland, in December 1775, had been delayed and was still in the middle of the Atlantic. Even after Cornwallis arrived, his troops dallied, raiding North Carolina for provisions, and the British command concluded that Cape Fear was unsuitable for a base in the South. Hearing that Charleston had almost no defensive works, Royal Navy Admiral Parker convinced the army commanders to set out for South Carolina.

Meanwhile, Congress had appointed General Charles Lee to command the Continental Army troops in the Southern colonies. At Wilmington Lee was told the British fleet had sailed from Cape Fear, but he didn't know if it was headed for Virginia or South Carolina. Lee opted to go to Charleston and arrived a day after the British fleet anchored outside the mouth of the Charles River. He immediately took command of the city's defenses, but found the South Carolina militia in no mood to recognize his authority.

The main defensive fort was located on Sullivan's Island, a sandy spit of land at the entrance to Charleston Harbor, extending north about four miles and only a few hundred yards wide. A ship sailing into Charleston had to negotiate the southern end of Sullivan's Island as it entered the channel to the inner harbor. A second fort on the tip of James Island to the southeast of the city protected the city itself. In December of 1775, a company of South Carolinians secured Sullivan's Island and began construction of what would become Fort Sullivan. When Patriot Colonel William Moultrie arrived and assumed command in March of 1776, he put a great number of soldiers and slaves to work using thousands of Palmetto logs and tons of sand to build a fort sufficient to contain a thousand men, but it was only half completed when the British arrived. Moultrie also assigned Colonel William Thomson to build a breastwork at the north end of the island to guard against British infantry attempting to attack the fort from that direction.

Lee took one look at the fort and ordered it to be abandoned, calling it "a slaughter pen" that British cannons would easily knock to pieces. But Colonel Moultrie refused to budge, and the work continued. Lee appealed to President John Rutledge of the South Carolina General Assembly to remove Moultrie and dismantle the fort, but Rutledge backed Moultrie, ordering the colonel to "obey [Lee] in everything, except in leaving Fort Sullivan." Lee's primary concern seemed to be that Moultrie should build a bridge to allow the fort's garrison to retreat in an orderly fashion from the island. In Moultrie's *Memoirs of the American Revolution*, published in 1802, he stated that, "all [Lee's] letters to me shew how anxious he was at not having a bridge for a retreat; for my part, I was never uneasy on not having a retreat because I never imagined that the enemy could force me to that necessity." Lee did not approve of Moultrie's style of command with his militia. Everything Lee did until late in the battle, when he ordered ammunition to be sent to Moultrie, was harmful to the Patriot cause and the defense of Charleston.

While the British remained outside the harbor getting ready to attack, Moultrie continued his work on the fort over Lee's objections. Fort Sullivan was essentially to be a square. The mostly completed seaward wall rose ten feet above the wooden gun platforms—made of planks two inches thick and fastened with wooden spikes into retaining logs—on which the artillery were mounted. A palisade of thick planks helped guard the powder

★ ★ ★
Unfit for Command

The commander of the Southern Department, Major General Charles Lee, was favored by many in Congress to be the commander-in-chief—until he was captured by the British in December of 1776. But Lee was distinguished for:

- His outspoken insubordination and opposition to General Washington at Boston
- His refusal to prepare a defense for New York City
- His ordering that Fort Sullivan be abandoned, which would have left Charleston defenseless
- His refusal to obey Washington's orders during the New York Campaign (see chapter seven)
- His cooperation with the British after his capture—amounting to treason (see chapter eight)
- His ordering of a retreat at the first opportunity at Monmouth (see chapter eleven)
- His court martial, which ended his career (thank God—some people really do finally get their just deserts!)

magazine and served as the fort's wall on the northern side. Only thirty-one cannon were emplaced. That was all the Patriots had.

Finish the Bridge

The British fleet arrived outside Charleston on June 1 and began to scout the port's defenses. The expedition was composed of nine man-of-war ships including two fifty-gun ships, several frigates, and a number of smaller vessels, totaling nearly three hundred cannon and mortars, most heavier that what Moultrie had. Early in June, Clinton landed five hundred troops on Long Island (today called the Isle of Palms), immediately to the north of Sullivan's Island, to secure a position from which his infantry could attack Fort Sullivan. Clinton's initial plan was to wade across the Breach, the channel between Long Island and Sullivan's Island, and attack the fort from its unfinished rear while Admiral Parker's ships bombarded it from the sea. But even at ebb tide the depth was impassable, at seven feet, and Colonel

A Book You're Not Supposed to Read

The Struggle for Sea Power: A Naval History of the American Revolution by Sam Willis (New York: W. W. Norton, 2016). Although most historians focus on the ground war, the war at sea, as Willis shows, was equally important.

Moultrie had already stationed an advance guard of three hundred men under Colonel Thomson to cover the Breach. So the British strategy changed: Clinton sent notice to Parker that he would use longboats to land his troops.

Lee seemed to give up on Moultrie and began reinforcing his positions on the mainland in case the British launch an attack directly on Charleston. His idea of building a bridge of boats to Sullivan's Island was proven to be impracticable by one of his own engineers, and so he redoubled his demands that Moultrie build a bridge. Then on June 21, Lee demanded that Moultrie build a traverse inside the fort to minimize casualties. Four days later, Lee simply ordered Moultrie, "Finish the bridge." Instead, Moultrie continued to strengthen the fort.

News was circulating through the British fleet that no quarter would be given the Americans, and that five thousand pounds had been offered for General Lee. When British ships opened fire upon the half-completed fort and its Patriot defenders, Lee attempted to cross from the mainland to the island, but rough water forced his small boat back. From across the cove behind Sullivan's Island, Lee could only watch as the British ships bombarded the fort.

The Patriots slowly returned fire with their guns, outnumbered ten to one. But what the fort's firepower lacked in quantity it made up in effectiveness. Moultrie ordered his men to concentrate their fire on the two double-decker warships, *Bristol* and *Experiment*, which took hit after hit from the fort's guns. Chain shot fired at the *Bristol* eventually destroyed much of her rigging and one round hit her quarterdeck, wounding Parker in the knee and thigh, and carrying away the seat of his britches. The two British ships shuddered from the impact of the iron balls tearing through them and sending splinters flying in all directions. The decks ran red with blood, and the *Bristol* unintentionally drifted out of the broadside line and presented her stern to the fort. A lucky cannonball from the fort had cut her anchor cable, and, for the moment, the *Bristol* was helpless. Moultrie doubled his fire, and the *Bristol* became a charnel house. Her main mast was shot through and crashed over the side, followed by her mizzen. Broken and all but sinking, the British flagship drifted away with heavy casualties. Even worse was what happened to the frigate *Actaeon*. She lost her bowsprit, her rudder jammed, and she grounded herself hard and fast on the shoal that later became the site of Fort Sumter.

By 3:00 in the afternoon, however, the fort was out of gunpowder, and all cannon fire was suspended for an hour and a half. President Rutledge sent over five hundred pounds of powder, and Charles Lee, in his only positive act during the fight, approved Moultrie's request to obtain additional ammunition and gunpowder from Haddrell's Point. Lee visited the fort during this lull in firing, but left before the fire resumed.

"The Most Important Hour Britain Ever Knew"

While the British cannonade was in process, General Sir Henry Clinton's twenty-two hundred troops attempted to cross the Breach using their long boats. The British troops, all carrying their normal packs weighing seventy-five pounds, got out of their boats in the surf and tried to push, wade, and swim them across the channel. Many disappeared in water over their heads as the sandbars gave way to deeper water. The Patriots under Colonel Thomson didn't make the passage any easier: American rifle fire and grape shot from two small cannons raked the British soldiers with devastating accuracy, and they retreated as best they could back to Long Island.

There was nothing Clinton could do. Parker's warships were fully engaged, and even if there had been ships to spare, there was no way for them to achieve a position from which they could effectively drive Thomson

★ ★ ★

The 1776 Siege of Charleston Report Card

The British

Admiral Sir Peter Parker: F

Ever disdainful of the Patriots and their ability to fight, Parker chose to reduce Fort Sullivan instead of making an attack inside the harbor towards Charleston itself.

General Clinton: D

He made little use of the three weeks preparation time to gather intelligence on the Breach and to devise a plan to overcome the problems it posed.

The Americans

Colonel William Moultrie: A

He was aided immeasurably by British block-headedness, but it was his decisions and effective leadership that won the day.

General Charles Lee: D-

More of a hindrance than a help, ex-British officer Lee respected British competence to a fault, and nearly single-handedly prevented an American victory. But since it was he who reported the victory to Congress, he was given the lion's share of the credit.

from his position. For the remainder of the day, the British and American forces harassed each other, but both knew a crossing of the Breach was now out of the question. Clinton reluctantly abandoned the attempt.

Before the British sailed away, they set fire to the grounded *Actaeon* to prevent her from falling into American hands. It was a fitting end to a Patriot victory. For the next two years, Charleston would escape the ravages of war. The campaign that Clinton called "the most important hour Britain ever knew" was a resounding defeat.

American Scripture

While musket balls flew and bayonets flashed across the colonies, an even more important battle was under way in Philadelphia, as delegates from the thirteen colonies gathered at the Second Continental Congress, which had convened in June 1776. Many of America's greatest legends and heroes were there, including Benjamin Franklin, John Adams, and Thomas Jefferson. Adams noted that merely attending—having the "courage to ride in this Whirlwind"—constituted an act of moral determination. Adams had pressed for a document declaring independence from England, thinking it was not only necessary but critical to unite the colonies. But he saw that his personal unpopularity made it impossible for him to successfully introduce such a resolution—and moreover that the motion needed to come from Virginia as the most populous state (and as a state not named "Massachusetts"!). So it fell to Richard Henry Lee on June 7 to propose a first draft, whose words were similar to the final: "Resolved, That these United Colonies are, and of right ought to be, free and independent States, that they are absolved from all allegiance to the British Crown, and that all political connection between them and the State of Great Britain is, and ought to be, totally dissolved."

On June 11 Congress appointed a committee of five to create the first draft, including Roger Sherman, Benjamin Franklin, Thomas Jefferson, John Adams, and Robert Livingston. Quickly the actual writing fell to Jefferson—who tried to shove it off on Adams again! Jefferson had initially refused to draft the document, but Adams insisted that, "a Virginian ought to appear at the head of this business." Adams added, "I am obnoxious, suspected, and unpopular," and "You can write ten times better than I can."

"Very well," said the Sage of Monticello.

At least that's how Adams reported their conversation; Jefferson said it never happened.

At any rate, the committee reworked Jefferson's original draft, and then it underwent

A Book You're Not Supposed to Read

Our Lives, Our Fortunes and Our Sacred Honor by Richard R. Beeman (New York: Basic Books, 2013) contains Jefferson's original draft and the additions and changes by the committee and Congress.

extensive editorial revision by Congress, sitting as a committee of the whole. Jefferson said that enduring the editing of his work was the worst experience he ever underwent. His mention of the Scots and other foreign mercenaries being sent against the Patriots was stricken, as was his blaming King George for the slave trade.

The final document, while blunt and pulling no punches, had none of the vitriol that some of the Patriots had hoped to see. When John Hancock spoke of the "Strain of Rapine and Violence" that had infested all of England, Jefferson wisely left those sentiments out.

In the end, the Declaration of Independence was so brilliant and so perfect that historian Pauline Maier called it "American Scripture." It made an unanswerable case that the colonies had been abused, and it appealed repeatedly to the very "rights of Englishmen" that their opponents claimed as their birthright.

Believe it or not, there is a great deal of historical controversy about when the Declaration was actually signed. Jefferson, Franklin, and Adams all claimed (later) that it was signed on July 4. A signed copy with the July 4 date indeed exists, and journals of Congress accept that date. But the "Secret Journals of Congress," first published in 1821, said that the final document was not signed until August. (This was a state department folio book of under fifty pages consisting of diplomacy papers, not transferred from the state department to the Library of Congress until 1821.) In fact, some of the fifty-six signers were not in Philadelphia on July 4. Most, however, were there and did sign, and others added their names later.

Every one of the men who pledged "our Lives, our Fortunes and our sacred Honor," was committing high treason by signing the

An Article You're Not Supposed to Read

"The Authentication of the Engrossed Declaration of Independence on July 4, 1776," by Wilfred J. Ritz, *Law and History Review* 4:1 (April 1986), 179–204.

Declaration of Independence. And they understood the risks. As he signed, John Hancock
quipped that his handwriting was so large that
King George would not need his spectacles to
read it. And almost all of them suffered dire
hardships. The signers lost property and some
even ended up in debtors' prison. They endured
the deaths of close family members at the
hands of the British, and various signers themselves were driven to an early grave. And yet
the Declaration of Independence was no more
treasonable than the hundreds of Association
Resolves that had been passed in cities, towns,
and counties throughout the colonies and
signed by ordinary citizens. Americans in all
the colonies—from the immortal men at Philadelphia to ordinary people
in Massachusetts towns and the North Carolina countryside—were staking
everything they had on freedom.

A Speech You're Not Supposed to Hear

Rush H. Limbaugh, Jr., the father of the famous radio talk show host, delivered a speech called "The Americans Who Risked Everything" many times in many places, recounting the biographies and wartime hardships of all of the signers—every one. The text of the speech is available at http://www.rushlimbaugh.com/pages/static/my_father_s_speech.

CHAPTER 6

The Fourteenth Colony

Back when the Patriot forces were still besieging Boston, an invasion of Canada was mounted. The idea had permeated Patriot thinking since the earliest days of the war. Many assumed that Canada would become the fourteenth colony. Even before Lexington and Concord, Canada had been invited to send delegates to the First Continental Congress, but the Patriots were as deluded about the Canadians as Parliament was about them.

The Maple Leaf State?

Early contacts by Americans suggested that there was considerable support for independence in Canada, especially in the area around Montreal. After all, Quebec had only been taken from the French by the British in 1759, and most Canadians were French farmers who might still be antagonistic towards their recent conquerors. All it would take for Canada to throw off her putative chains would be a slight push from her southern neighbors. Or so the Americans believed.

Did you know?

★ In harrowing hardships, suffering, and endurance by the soldiers, the American expedition to Canada is comparable only to Napoleon's retreat from Moscow

★ Arnold set out for Quebec with more than 1,000 men and reached it with only 510

★ General Guy Carleton might have won the war for Britain if he had been in charge in the middle states instead of the Howe brothers

Two Books You're Not Supposed to Read

The Invasion of Canada by the Americans, 1775–1776: As Told through Jean-Baptiste Badeaux's Three Rivers Journal and New York Captain William Goforth's Letters edited by Mark Anderson and translated by Teresa L. Meadows (Albany, NY: State University of New York Press, 2016) and *Benedict Arnold's Army: The 1775 American Invasion of Canada During the Revolutionary War* by Arthur F. Lefkowitz (El Dorado Hills, CA: Savas Beatie, 2008) comprise a first person and a historian's account of the ill-fated expedition to Canada.

The initial plan for the Canadian invasion, as developed in Congress, was to attack north through Lake Champlain to St. John's and Montreal. General Washington then authored or supported a plan to eradicate the British presence in Canada by adding a second expedition, under the command of Colonel Benedict Arnold. Arnold's force would travel up the Kennebec River in Maine, through the northern wilderness to the Chaudière River, and downstream to the Saint Lawrence and Quebec. Washington personally selected Arnold and gave the plan a high chance of success. In many respects it was a sound one, incorporating the elements of surprise and superior force against an unprepared and dispersed enemy. The Lake Champlain route was well known and traveled, and the British were likely to concentrate their efforts at Montreal to ward off an invasion by that route. General Richard Montgomery, an experienced Scotch-Irish veteran of the British army, was selected to command the force moving northward through Lake Champlain. (Philip Schuyler would have headed the expedition, but, as we have already seen, he bowed out once he reached Canada—Schuyler had what was described as a "Barbarous Complication of Disorders," and was generally a nervous wreck.) While General Guy Carleton, the British governor, was distracted by Montgomery, Arnold would fall on Carleton's rear, capture a lightly held Quebec, and cut the British off from support from England. Success depended on Arnold's reaching Quebec without the British being forewarned of his approach.

Where Are We Going Here?

Unfortunately, there were three problems with the Canadian plan that were unrecognized at the time. The first was that Arnold's route through the Maine wilderness was highly speculative; it had been traveled only by a few bands of Indians and trappers. Essentially nothing was known about its difficulty.

The second problem was that the First Continental Congress, in its October 1774 broadside written by John Jay and addressed to the people of Great Britain, had inveighed against French jurisprudence and Roman Catholicism in no uncertain terms. This attack on their religion and their legal system had alienated most of the French-Canadian Roman Catholic clergy, who proceeded to lecture their flocks from the pulpit against the heresies of the thirteen Protestant colonies. Canadians feared American Protestantism as much as Americans feared Canadian Catholicism.

But third, even assuming that the British could be expelled from Canada by an American expedition, there would be no possibility of defending Quebec and Montreal against British sea power. The Royal Navy was the greatest sea power in the world at the time and essentially invincible when attacking a port city. The St. Lawrence estuary provided the deep-water access needed by the British, and a resolute English commander could easily retake and hold Canada against subsequent invasions. So at best the invasion had little hope of achieving any permanent gain, and at worst it might result in the loss of desperately needed American forces.

Altogether about 1,050 men were assigned to Arnold's expedition. Many of the Pennsylvania rifleman companies (and approximately 250 of the entire force) were recent Scotch-Irish immigrants, brave and hardy to a fault. These men were willing enough to undergo hardship and privation, but they had little experience fighting Indians and knew nothing about handling boats. Moreover, none were equipped with bayonets.

★ ★ ★

Row, Row, Row Your Bateaux

The bateaux (usually spelled "battoes" by the Americans) that Colburn constructed were similar in shape to the modern "John boat" favored by many American fishermen. Flat-bottomed boats with flaring sides, long, overhanging ends, the front higher than the stern, and without a keel or rudder, they were difficult to manage in swift water. They could hold six to seven men with their arms and supplies of one hundred pounds per man. Colburn furnished each boat with four oars, two paddles, and two long "setting" poles. The ribs were made of white oak, but the bottoms and sides were green pine, thin, weak, and difficult to caulk. The boats turned out to be leaky, and easily cracked or broke on rocks.

Seeking "Active Woodsmen"

The entire expedition was made up of very young men: the American high command wanted "active woodsmen," but what they got were inexperienced soldiers, and even the officers were no exception. Arnold was only thirty-four, Henry Dearborn twenty-four, and Aaron Burr nineteen. Most of the enlisted men were in their late teens or early twenties.

A contract was sent early in September to Reuben Colburn, a resident of the Kennebec Valley, to construct two hundred bateaux for the expedition. Somehow Colburn was able to finish the bateaux just in time to greet the expedition when it arrived two weeks later. This was a remarkable achievement, but there had been no opportunity to dry or season the wood. So the bateaux proved to be heavy, up to a thousand pounds each with their loaded provisions, and almost unmanageable.

The Americans who undertook the invasion of Quebec would experience hardship and privation almost beyond human endurance—something to be repeated only in Napoleon's retreat from Moscow. But, as we have seen, it was eclipsed in the public imagination by Henry's Knox's much less taxing achievement—the transportation of the captured British guns three hundred miles from Ticonderoga to Boston. And by the twenty-first century, Arnold's saga would disappear completely from the story of the Revolution as it was taught in American schools.

Arnold's army sailed from Newburyport, Massachusetts, on September 19, 1775, and disembarked at Gardiner on the Kennebec River. Here Arnold received the bateaux that had been constructed by Colburn's carpenters for the Kennebec passage, and the expedition moved up the river to Fort Western, learning how to handle the unmanageable boats. Another problem became immediately apparent: even in this richest part of what would one day be the state of Maine, there were no supplies to be gathered from the surrounding area.

The first division of riflemen departed Fort Western under the command of Daniel Morgan. They had orders to blaze the trail for the following divisions and cut a road across the "Great Carrying Place," as the distance between the Kennebec and the Dead River was called. The seven-man boats were loaded above the falls at Fort Western, then polled and paddled upstream by three or four men while the rest marched on the road to Fort Halifax. The boatmen were forced to wade in the cold river up to their waists through over six miles of rapids, pushing the bateaux upstream while onrushing water forced its way through warping seams on the boats to soak the cargo and increase the dead weight they were handling.

Upon reaching Fort Halifax they found it little more than a ruin, unusable by the expedition. Half a mile above Fort Halifax the Kennebec descended over a series of rock ledges now called the Ticonic Falls, so the bateaux were manhandled out of the river, off-loaded, and carried by four-man teams on poles passed underneath the boats. But that was nothing compared to the passage of Skowhegan Falls, twenty-one miles from Fort Halifax. Wading, slipping, falling into the water, the men suffered horribly, their misery worsened by weather so cold that it froze their clothes solid. Their footwear was totally inadequate. By the time the expedition reached the last outpost of civilization at Norridgewock, the sick list was beginning to mushroom. They had only managed fifty miles in ten days, not a good omen with 295 miles yet before them.

At Norridgewock the cargos were inspected and found to be heavily damaged by water, particularly the salted beef, dried fish, bread, and biscuits.

The spoiled provisions were discarded, making the bateaux lighter but also reducing the food supply to a dangerously low level. Some attempts were made to shoot game, but little sustenance was obtained other than a few moose. The noise of the army kept game animals far away, and the men had little time to spare for side trips to hunt.

It took the riflemen six days to traverse the Great Carrying Place, and they arrived at the Dead River on October 13. At that pace—the total length of the Great Carrying Place was about thirteen and a half miles—they would not reach Quebec before the end of 1775. Fortunately, reports came in of an easier passage ahead, and morale soared as the troops assumed the worst was over. They were wrong. Rains started and became progressively heavier over the next several days. Then a furious gale buffeted the men, filling the Dead River with uprooted trees and causing it to rise by several feet. Food supplies were lost, critical equipment was swept away, and game disappeared. The very survival of the expedition was threatened. Progress was excruciatingly slow against the swift river, but the riflemen had little choice but to press on. They labeled one of their camps "Camp Disaster."

Arnold called a council of war with his commanders, who decided to send back the invalids, while an advance party of fifty men under Arnold himself would hurry forward to secure provisions from the Chaudière valley. Colonels Roger Enos and Christopher Greene, with their divisions, would press on to catch up, leading as many men as could be provided with fifteen days' rations, while sending the remainder back to Fort Western. It was a plan born of desperation, but it seemed the only one that might offer any hope of survival—much less of success—for the expedition.

Greene's division trudged onward, but Colonel Enos and his men in the rear democratically voted to return downstream. The remainder of the troops, undeterred by this mass desertion, forged ahead. The riflemen in the lead crossed into Canada on October 20, weak and freezing, but the troops behind were in even worse shape. The rest of the men would have to reach the French settlements within days, or die in the wilderness from starvation or exposure. But the soldiers found themselves in the depths of a horrible and icy swamp.

Most of them were now without food, having consumed their meager supply of fire cakes several days before. Their clothes were little more than filthy rags, and their shoes had long since given out. They tied rags around their feet for warmth and used bark strips for soles, but the snow and wet ground defeated all attempts to keep the men's feet warm and dry. They were wet to the skin, and they had no shelter, no food, and almost no hope. The expedition was rapidly disintegrating into helpless individual fugitives desperately trying to survive. Finally, the company commanders announced that it was every man for himself.

Salvation arrived on November 3 when a relief party of locals sent back by the advance party met the van of the army. They brought cattle, oxen, flour, and other provisions, saving the starving troops by the narrowest of margins. Only 510 stalwart souls remained to conquer Quebec. This was not an army—it was a rabble of nearly naked, sick, and starving men. They needed six months in a rest camp to recuperate. Yet here they were, almost at Quebec.

The Battle for Quebec

By November 13 the men had mustered on the south side of the St. Lawrence River—barefoot and in rags. During the next two nights, the little army crossed the St. Lawrence to the Quebec side in canoes and dugouts supplied by French Canadians. After ascending the bluff by the same route taken by General Wolfe and his British army sixteen years earlier, Arnold placed his force in position on the Plains of Abraham to begin the siege.

The British may have been laughing too hard to take Arnold's army seriously, especially after he paraded it under the walls of Quebec to induce the city fathers to surrender. Quebec was defended by a Scottish regiment, a battalion of seamen who handled the artillery, and various militia units, totaling 1,248 men. This was more than twice the strength of Arnold's force, and they enjoyed abundant food and other supplies, large quantities of artillery, and professional military leadership.

Arnold faced a critical situation. Something had to be done about the condition of the army. Most of the men were walking on hunks of freshly cut hide tied onto their feet with strips of leather or fabric, and the ammunition was down to four cartridges per rifleman. The 510 men in Arnold's army needed to be entirely re-outfitted and re-equipped. Nevertheless, the riflemen took up positions near the walls of Quebec and began sniping at the defenders whenever a Redcoat exposed himself.

In spite of the dangers and defying all odds, Arnold did his best to remain in place in front of Quebec. But when it was learned that the British were preparing a sally with seven field pieces, Arnold withdrew the army twenty miles westwards to await the arrival of Montgomery with reinforcements. (The attack through Lake Champlain had gone according to plan, Montgomery now held Montreal, and Governor Carleton had fled to Quebec.) The weather was bitterly cold, and marching in the snow and ice was exceedingly depressing. Montgomery finally arrived with a few captured British uniforms and some food, as well as three hundred men and artillery. The meager reinforcements were disappointing, but reflected the democratic processes prevalent in some units. A number of the Vermonters in Montgomery's force had served under Ethan Allen, who had been captured by the British at Montreal, and many of his men had gone home.

With fewer than a thousand men and greatly outnumbered by British forces, Arnold and Montgomery returned to the task of capturing Quebec. By nightfall on December 3, they were back in position in front of the city, where the British were holed up. Carleton had built up the city's defenses quickly and had over eighteen hundred men under arms. He had accumulated provisions for eight months and emplaced 150 pieces of artillery. Once again, as before Montgomery arrived, the Americans were outnumbered two to one.

Montgomery and Arnold thought that the British would surrender the Upper Town of Quebec if Lower Town was taken, and assaulting Lower Town at the river level was felt to be a much less perilous undertaking than facing Carleton's artillery, which covered the approach to Upper Town. The cover of bad weather was considered to be a prerequisite condition for a successful attack, and the Americans had plenty of bad weather—it was so terrible that they bogged down for almost two weeks in deep snow, ice, and a smallpox outbreak. Several New England companies threatened to leave, as their enlistments expired on December 31. If Arnold did not attack by then, they were going home. Arnold, beside himself with rage and frustration, had no other choice than to attack before his army vanished. As luck would have it, the weather turned even worse on December 30. A desperate last-ditch attempt to capture Quebec followed, as American riflemen put white paper bands with the words "Liberty or Death" around their caps and prepared for the assault.

The plan was foolhardy in many respects. The Americans would attack at both ends of Lower Town: Arnold on the north with the five hundred men in his detachment storming the barrier at Sault-au-Matelot; Montgomery's three hundred would come from the beach of the St. Lawrence on the south. The two would presumably meet at Mountain Street. It was a plan that looked good on paper but could not possibly work with the pitiful state of communication and control in 1775.

The storm reached its height at about 3:00 in the morning, and the assault companies moved off in the dark and snow. Visibility was negligible as the large, heavy, and wet snowflakes fell thickly and covered everything, even the marching soldiers, with a blanket of white. The snow quickly soaked the attacking troops' uniforms and equipment as thoroughly as if they were in a rainstorm. Arnold and Morgan were in the van of Arnold's contingent.

A Book You're Not Supposed to Read

The Battle for the Fourteenth Colony: America's War of Liberation in Canada, 1774–1776 by Mark Anderson (Lebanon, NH: University Press of New England, 2013).

Snow was already up to the men's knees when the column passed through St. Roque towards the Palace Gate.

Against all odds and the withering British fire that cut down Arnold, the van of the attack under Daniel Morgan stormed over the barricades. Hardly stopping to control the prisoners, the riflemen dashed on down the street to a second barrier and seized it without opposition. Half of the assault had been successful, and Morgan's contingent was in position to link up with Montgomery's. Although the way to the Upper Town lay open, Morgan followed his orders and waited. It was a fatal error. Montgomery never arrived. He lay dead in the arms of Aaron Burr on the other side of town, killed in the single British volley fired. His troops were being led in a precipitate retreat up the northern side of the St. Lawrence River by his second-in-command, Colonel Donald Campbell, who had lost heart when Montgomery was cut down.

The British retook the second barricade and with overwhelming force pushed Morgan and his men into a row of houses. Out of ammunition, Morgan's force surrendered. The invasion of Canada had been a disaster, and the attempt to make Canada the Maple Leaf State was over.

Canadians Were Not Americans

The three main groups inhabiting Canada in 1775 were the Indians, Catholic French Canadians, and recent Scottish Highlander immigrants, who were also Catholic. The Indians would fight for anyone who gave them provisions, the Highlanders were out to prove their loyalty to King George to make up for Bonnie Prince Charlie's rebellion in 1745, and the French had little understanding of liberty in the English sense—the jealously guarded "rights of Englishmen" that the Americans were fighting for. The French king was an absolute monarch, French citizens lived under civil rather than common law, and they could lose their property at the stroke of a pen. Three of the four pillars of American exceptionalism were missing: the common law, Protestant Christianity, and the sanctity of private property. Only free market capitalism was present to any substantial degree. The French sat out the fight, the Highlanders became devout Tories, and the Indians were the king's mercenaries.

The Canadian Invasion of America?

The invasion of Canada failed, and now it suddenly looked as if there would be no way of stopping a British invasion of Lake Champlain and the upper Hudson valley from Montreal.

When General Montgomery had departed Montreal for Quebec City, he left the administration of the city in the hands of Connecticut's Brigadier General David Wooster. While Wooster initially enjoyed good relations with the community, he rapidly alienated the local population. A stalwart anti-Papist, he distrusted French-Canadians and threatened to arrest anyone opposed to American ideals. He disarmed communities he believed might support the British and imprisoned a number of local leaders at Fort Chambly. Even worse, the Americans were paying for supplies in Continental script while the British paid in gold. On March 20, Wooster left to take command of the forces at Quebec, relieving Arnold and sending him back to Montreal on April 19.

On April 29, a delegation consisting of three members of the Continental Congress, including the Catholic priest John Carroll, met with Arnold, now the commandant of Montreal. This delegation had not brought any hard currency with which to purchase supplies, and they were unable to repair the

★ ★ ★
A Pox on Both Your Houses

Smallpox plagued both armies. It was an equal opportunity killer. At Morristown in 1777, Washington's army would face starvation and freezing cold while British troops stayed warm and well-fed in New York and Philadelphia; but the greatest potential enemy for Washington's troops that winter would be disease: smallpox. During the winter of 1775–76, this killer took 17 percent of Washington's troops, but at Morristown, Washington heard of a new vaccine for the disease. He ordered all his men to receive it, and according to medical historian Donald Henderson, deaths fell to only 1 percent.

damage Wooster had done to American–French Canadian relations. Carroll was unable to make any headway with the Catholic clergy, mostly because the Quebec Act by Parliament in 1774 had already given the French Canadians complete religious freedom and restored French civil law to the province. The most constructive thing accomplished by the congressional delegation was the dismissal of General Wooster, who immediately collected his baggage and headed home to Connecticut.

The newly minted Major General John Thomas was sent to take Wooster's place, and he arrived at Montreal on May 1, 1776. He found his whole force in Canada to consist of a thousand men fit for duty. Smallpox was raging out of control, and Wooster had done little about camp sanitation. But worse, Wooster had divided up his forces in small units scattered throughout Canada, few of which could be considered mutually supportive. No more than three hundred men could be brought together quickly at any given point, and Wooster only had on hand 150 barrels of powder and six days' provisions for the whole force. When Thomas arrived at Quebec on May 5, he immediately decided to raise the siege.

Then intelligence was received that a British fleet was below Quebec, and the next morning five ships entered the Quebec harbor. General Carleton rapidly unloaded the arriving troops and attacked the unprepared Patriot camp. The Americans were in critical danger of losing their whole army. Thomas ordered his troops to retreat up the river, and the retreat immediately became chaotic. Many of the sick and wounded, and all of the army's military stores, fell into British hands, along with the troops south of the St. Lawrence. It could have been even worse for the Americans, but Carleton was a Whig who hoped to win over the American rebels by being lenient in victory. Thomas's army continued to retreat to the Lake Champlain Valley east of Montreal. In the retreat, Thomas also lost two tons of powder that had just been received from General Schuyler, and five hundred stands of small arms.

"Not a Mouthful of Food"

Samuel Chase, a member of the delegation from the Continental Congress, wrote on May 17, "We have now 4,000 Troops in Canada and not a Mouthful of food.... Our affairs here are almost desperate...." With the arrival of new troops under Brigadier General John Sullivan at St. Johns, the total American commitment to Canada reached ten thousand men, and ultimately there would be nothing to show for it. Meanwhile Thomas, who himself was stricken with smallpox on May 21, finally agreed to a mass inoculation of the troops. He died on June 2, while retreating up the Richelieu River near Chambly, and Sullivan assumed command.

Carleton, still hoping for reconciliation, had stopped after capturing Trois-Rivières, allowing Sullivan time to consolidate and re-organize. But Carleton now had General John Burgoyne's army of six thousand troops on hand in addition to another seven thousand of his own, and his halt was sure to be only temporary. After another ill-advised American attack, Sullivan resumed his retreat.

With Carleton dogging his heels, Sullivan abandoned his army and sailed from St. Johns to Crown Point on Lake Champlain. All remaining units headed for Ticonderoga. Arnold stayed with a rearguard, finally pushing off his own boat at the very end—the last American soldier to leave Canada.

★ ★ ★

Invasion of Canada Report Card

The British

Sir Guy Carleton: A

After a harrowing escape from Montgomery's forces at Montreal, General Carleton thoroughly fortified and garrisoned Quebec, dooming American efforts to take the city. He managed the defense of the city superbly. General Carleton's only error during 1776 was to refrain from pursuing the American forces from Quebec when he could have annihilated them. He chose reasonableness rather than ruthlessness, and left the Americans to fight again. In his instructions to his wife upon his death, he ordered her to destroy all his correspondence during the time he was in the Americas. It was speculated that he was more of a friend to the Americans than he wanted known. But had Carleton, instead of the Howe brothers, been in command in the middle states, the British might well have emerged from the Revolutionary War victorious.

The Americans

Lieutenant Colonel Roger Enos: F

A faint-hearted leader, he deserted the expedition when it most needed him and denied it critical supplies.

Captain Daniel Morgan: B

The toughest fighter in the American army was an effective commander after Arnold was wounded. But the fact that Morgan obeyed orders rather than taking advantage of the open gate in Lower Town doomed the Americans to defeat.

The campaign for Canada had been fought and lost. It had been a complete debacle. Canadians just weren't Americans. Canada would not gain dominion status until 1867, it would not become fully independent from Great Britain until the 1960s, and it still acknowledges the sovereignty of the British monarch to this day.

Another Miracle

Before he sailed south on Lake Champlain, Arnold had destroyed every boat that the Americans did not need for their own escape in order to hinder any

General Richard Montgomery: B
He captured Montreal and chased Carleton to Quebec. His unfortunate death doomed the American attack on Quebec to defeat.

Colonel Donald Campbell: F
When he saw that General Montgomery was dead, Campbell fell apart and ordered an unwarranted retreat.

Brigadier General David Wooster: F
Incompetent as a military leader, he also irretrievably alienated the Canadian population.

Major General John Thomas: F
Under his command the retreat from Quebec was a shambles. All his command decisions were wrong or taken too late.

Brigadier General John Sullivan: F
He clearly could not handle independent command, and abandoned his army to its fate.

Benedict Arnold: A
Arnold did all he could as a commander. The approach march was ghastly, but once the expedition was under way Arnold could not have done better on the excruciating trek to Canada. At Quebec, he had no choice but to attack before his troops' enlistments ran out. His only possible error there was to use a signal cannon to coordinate the attacks—all that did was alert the defenders. He managed the retreat from Canada effectively. Probably no other American general at the time could have accomplished so much with so little. His leadership was outstanding.

British advance. General Carleton, like the Howe brothers, expected that New York City and the Hudson Valley would fall to the British late in the summer or fall, by which time Carleton would take control of Lake Champlain and quickly move to meet Howe's troops in Albany. But Carleton possessed no ships on which to sail down Lake Champlain, so he was forced to take three months to build an inland navy. Horatio Gates, the new American commander of the Northern Army at Fort Ticonderoga, soon heard that Carleton was massing boats and troops at St. Johns for an attack on his position. He resolved to meet the invasion on Lake Champlain and commissioned Benedict Arnold—chafing after having been run out of Canada—to build a fleet to counter Carleton. It was a daunting assignment for someone who possessed very limited knowledge of fighting at sea, and even of sailing itself. But, characteristically, Arnold eagerly took on the assignment.

For once, Arnold received help; shipbuilders and carpenters came to Crown Point and other construction points from all over New England to build his ships. But there was still a significant problem: lacking volunteers to man his ships, Arnold was forced to draft nearly three hundred men, primarily from two New Hampshire regiments. None of Arnold's men were seamen or experienced in naval affairs, and few had ever sighted or even loaded a cannon. By October 1776, the American fleet had fifteen armed vessels: two schooners, one sloop, one cutter, three galleys, and eight gondolas, firing a total weight of 460 pounds.

In contrast, Carleton's vessels had been built for him by the Royal Navy and were manned by naval personnel. His fleet consisted of twenty-nine armed vessels: one ship, two schooners, one gondola, one bateaux, twenty gunboats, and four long boats, firing a total weight of nearly thirteen hundred pounds. Arnold's fleet was woefully outgunned, and the British guns were heavier and operated by experienced gunners.

Arnold took up a position behind Valcour Island—located about ten miles south of Plattsburg near the western shore of Lake Champlain—facing south, more or less in a position to ambush the British as they sailed south past the island. Theoretically, it was a dangerous position, as the British fleet could cut off Arnold from his base at Crown Point. But Arnold had no intention of ever going back to his base—he would fight it out here to the extinction of one fleet or the other.

Early in the morning of October 11, the British fleet came into view, rounding the eastern edge of the island. Arnold ordered the *Royal Savage* and his three galleys to advance and engage the enemy, but the ship ran aground almost immediately and could not be freed. Arnold ordered the ship to be set afire and the men transferred to other boats. The British formed a battle line, moved forward to the attack and anchored within musket range. As night closed in, the American fleet was in shambles with sixty killed and wounded, while the British had taken much less damage. Nonetheless, Arnold and his men had done well: the schooner *Carleton* was wrecked and temporarily out of action, and three gunboats had been sunk. But now the wind trapped the Americans against the British line, and the little fleet was facing annihilation.

Then, in another near miracle, the British withdrew some distance to avoid rifle fire, and Arnold saw his chance. The night was extremely dark, and a heavy fog further reduced visibility. In the dark Arnold sent his ships past the British line in single file, heading south toward Crown Point, each ship guided only by a hooded lantern at the stern of the vessel ahead of it in the line. The sailors muffled their oars and moved silently past the British ships. It was tense, but all the American boats made their escape. Ultimately the American ships were beached or captured, but Arnold and the bulk of his troops escaped once again, despite terrible losses.

Carleton was astounded at the fierce resistance of the little band of Patriots. This fight took time he didn't have. When he finally arrived at Crown Point on October 20, snow was already falling and winter setting in, leaving him no option but to sail back to Canada and make plans to attack again the following year. The Americans had lost battle after battle, only to gain strategically. And what success the Americans had was all due to Arnold, who by now could claim to be the savior of the Revolution. He would bolster that claim the following year, and in the process make a great many enemies.

CHAPTER 7

Disaster in New York

Britain's strategy for winning the war was schizophrenic from the beginning. On the one hand, this was a rebellion that had to be put down—and England had no reputation for mercy or subtlety in such matters. On the other hand, the king knew he had a problem if he turned the American colonies into a permanent enemy. The Howe brothers, one commanding the British fleet (Sir Richard Howe) and the other the British army (General William Howe), were charged with ending the rebellion, but as we have seen they were also peace commissioners. General Howe had already unsuccessfully attempted to crush the rebellion through a demonstration of raw British power: the assault at Bunker Hill. That gambit had failed, not only leaving the British with heavy casualties, but also strengthening American resolve and inspiring the Patriots to believe England could be whipped. Yet in a policy that presaged Lyndon Johnson's in Vietnam, the British continued to vacillate between the carrot and the stick, unsure whether they wanted to win the war or befriend the colonists. General Howe would roundly defeat Washington at New York, but subsequently turn dovish and exhibit a curious reluctance to engage in the ruthless pursuit necessary to finish the Patriot forces once and for all. Then General Charles

Did you know?

★ George III was the first Hanoverian king of England whose native tongue was English rather than German

★ The Hessians' rate of desertion was so high that they were no longer used as pickets after 1781

★ Fake atrocity stories made it dangerous for Patriots to be captured carrying tomahawks

Cornwallis's Southern campaign would see terror administered by Lieutenant Colonel Banastre Tarleton and his Tory allies to subdue the population.

In the summer of 1776 there probably wasn't a person in the colonies who didn't expect the Howes to sail from Halifax to New York City as soon as the British army was resupplied. New York City was by far the most logical point to attack. It featured a deep harbor that could shelter the entire Royal Navy, and the British army could be supplied almost completely from Long Island, if necessary. New York was already a hotbed of Tory sentiment, and best of all, it was the key to detaching the rebellious New England colonies from their lukewarm cousins farther south. The British would simply take possession of the Hudson River Valley and Lake Champlain all the way to Montreal.

New York, New York

In fact, though neither the British nor the Patriots saw this clearly at first, New York City and its environs would be impossible for the Patriots to defend against General Howe's army supported by the Royal Navy. Staten Island could not be held against a seaborne attack, and Long Island was a trap that threatened to ensnare any Patriot army that attempted to defend it. New York City itself was open to attack on three sides, and any attempt to hold the city—then clustered at the south end of Manhattan Island—would probably mean the loss of the defending army.

On the other hand, if only for reasons of propaganda and morale, Washington could not readily abandon New York City.

Bunker Hill had shown that militia could repel hardened professional troops (though only, it would turn out, under certain conditions that were as yet unrecognized), and the British had been defeated at Charleston and forced to evacuate Boston. Even the failed Quebec expedition had shown that Americans could fight well when led by competent commanders.

★ ★ ★
Who Were the Hessians?

George III had deep ties to Germany. He was the first of the Hanoverian kings of England even to speak English as his first language. And when the war with America arrived, he was forced to hire mercenaries to fight it, on account of the lack of enthusiasm for the war among the English population. English armies were always relatively small compared to their continental adversaries, but recruitment suffered more than usual in the American Revolution. The population of London was against the war, as was East Anglia and the southern and eastern parts of England. There was some support from the Midlands, but by far the greatest fervor for fighting came from the Catholic Highland Scots. But their numbers were insufficient, so George turned to his kinsmen in the petty princedoms of Germany. The Germans came mostly from north-central Germany, Brunswick, Waldeck, Ansbach, Kassel, and the Duchy of Hesse, all Lutheran states. Collectively they became known to the Patriots as Hessians. The officer corps was made up of aristocrats, but the enlisted men generally came from the lower strata of German society—the poor, the unemployed. Not a few German boys enlisted for the chance to go to America, and many deserted when the opportunity arose. After 1781, Hessians were no longer used as pickets as the desertions rates were too high. As with the British regulars, discipline in Hessian ranks was draconian. Many, if not most, of the Hessians who surrendered at Trenton stayed after the war to become American citizens.

Washington's army was attracting volunteers, fluctuating between sixteen and twenty thousand men. Even the British expected him to fight hard to retain New York City, and thus when General William Howe arrived off Sandy Hook at the entrance to New York Harbor in July 1776 he had thirty-two thousand troops—the largest British expeditionary force in history up to that time. Little did he dream it would not be sufficient for the task.

Howe scouted the harbor and as early as July 2 began landing troops on Staten Island. His brother Richard arrived from Great Britain by way of Halifax ten days later and brought more troops to Staten Island, including mercenaries from the German principality of Hesse-Cassel. The Germans immediately won the hatred of Americans, Tory and Patriot alike, by treating all the local inhabitants as rebel scum—pillaging, raping, and killing civilians indiscriminately. General Howe found himself using terror tactics against the population inadvertently—simply by having the Hessians in his army.

The Patriot defenses of New York were under the command of General Charles Lee from January until March 1776, when he was sent to Charleston to command that city's defenses. Upon Lee's departure, Washington put General Israel Putnam in charge of New York until he himself could assume command in April. Neither Lee nor Putnam made any headway in devising a plan for New York City's defense or even constructing defensive works.

But first the Howe brothers announced themselves as "peace commissioners," implying that they had the power to negotiate on behalf of Parliament and the king. In June 1776 Admiral Howe sent a letter to all of the royal governors who had been expelled from their colonies, imploring them to use all their powers and contacts to promote negotiations for peace. He stated that the king had authorized two commissioners to grant general or specific pardons to all those who had departed from the obedience due to the crown but now desired to return to their duty, and participate in the benefits of royal clemency. The commissioners were empowered to proclaim any province or city to be in the king's peace, thus sheltering them from the penal laws for a revolt against the king. Lastly, Lord Howe promised large recompense to all those who would contribute to help reestablish royal authority. Many cities, such as Albany, New York, published this document in the hopes of somehow settling the conflict as peaceably as possible.

George Washington, Esq.

Howe even sent a personal letter to Washington, but addressed it simply to "George Washington, Esq." Washington refused the letter because it had not been addressed to him in his capacity as commander-in-chief of the American army, arguing that as a private individual he could not hold any communications with emissaries from the king or commanders of his forces. Howe tried again, addressing the letter to "George Washington, &c. &c." Washington answered that "et ceteras" implied everything and nothing, and stood on his prerogative to demand he be addressed by his title. Congress, however, in September sent a delegation to meet with the Howes in what became known as the Staten Island Peace Conference. The delegates—John Adams, Benjamin Franklin, and Edward Rutledge—learned that the Howes had no real power to negotiate; everything still had to be referred back to Parliament and the king. Even worse, the only result acceptable to the British side was a full return to the king's allegiance, but without the rights that Englishmen in Great Britain enjoyed. It was clear that Americans could secure their "rights as Englishmen" only through war with England.

On August 22, British troops began to land on the west end of Long Island. For whatever reason, Washington failed to perceive that the Royal Navy could isolate Long Island by patrolling the East River, and he sent additional troops to Putnam for the defense of Brooklyn. Clearly a battle was in the offing, and Putnam caused the Patriot line to be moved forward of the entrenchment on Brooklyn Heights to the heights of Guan, a chain of hills running east-west and dividing the island into two parts. But sending half of his command to fight on the heights while holding the remainder behind entrenchments in Brooklyn was a recipe for disaster. Four thousand Patriots with little artillery and no bayonets would be facing over twenty thousand hardened professional British and Hessians.

Worse, there were five passes through or around these hills. One, called Gowan's Road, actually skirted the hills along the shore of the Narrows from New Utrecht to Brooklyn. The Jamaica Pass was another; it went from Jamaica to Bedford. Patriot General William Alexander (Lord Stirling) commanded Putnam's right wing along the shore of the Narrows, and Major General John Sullivan, the same man who had deserted his army in Canada, was assigned to cover the roads on the left, including two from Flatbush and two from Flatland. The leftmost road came through Jamaica Pass. He sent only five men to guard the pass—to Howard's Tavern, three miles east of Bedford. Sullivan apparently thought Washington had sent a regiment of 500 Pennsylvania riflemen to protect Jamaica Pass, but in fact those men ended up elsewhere. Sullivan missed the other road from Flatland altogether. Unfortunately, Washington apparently believed that Sullivan would do his job and that, if not, Sullivan's superior Putnam would fill the gap. But at this stage of the war Washington really needed to be everywhere—a feat even the "indispensable man" could not pull off.

Putnam had a total of about ten thousand troops at the beginning of the battle, including those remaining behind the fortifications at Brooklyn Heights, and Washington sent him nearly three thousand reinforcements from New York City after the battle opened. About seventeen hundred defended Putnam's right wing, while Sullivan had twenty-two hundred on the left. Against all logic, Washington had declined to employ a cavalry regiment from Connecticut on Long Island, supposedly because he didn't want the burden of providing forage for their mounts. Unfortunately, the lack of mounted scouts limited his ability to gather intelligence about British positions and movements.

Americans on the Run

On the British side, General James Grant led more than five thousand English troops into battle along Gowan's Road against Stirling. The Hessian commander General Leopold Philip von Heister employed approximately five thousand German troops in the center against Sullivan's men guarding the Flatbush passes, and General Clinton marched around the Patriot position with ten thousand men through Jamaica Pass. At every point of contact, the Americans were woefully outnumbered.

Although the Patriots initially acquitted themselves very well against Grant's left wing and the Hessians in the center, Clinton coming into their rear decided the battle. The Americans were surrounded, and many fought grimly to the end. The Hessians and Scottish Highlanders bayonetted many of the trapped Americans who were trying to surrender. They even formed up in circles to comb the woods, driving the wounded or defenseless Americans into a smaller and smaller area, then dispatching the trapped Patriots with bayonets. As if the Hessians needed any more excuse for brutality, the British had lied to them, telling the Germans that the Americans would take no prisoners, but rather hack to death and mutilate them with tomahawks. As a result, any Patriot carrying a tomahawk—and that was true for almost all riflemen—was summarily bayoneted after he surrendered.

American casualty reports are fragmentary, but the British took 1,006 prisoners, including three general officers: Sullivan, Stirling, and Woodhull. A reasonable guess on killed and wounded would probably be another thousand. Sullivan's force was wrecked. The British loss was less than four hundred.

Yet Howe declined to follow up with an attack against the Patriot position at Brooklyn Heights. His officers, particularly Clinton, argued for an immediate offensive, but the Americans had a fortified position (better than at Bunker Hill) and Howe demurred, envisioning the enormous casualties he would incur with a frontal assault. More to the point, the British army could not depend on an endless supply of reinforcements, as the Americans could. Howe had to make every man count and minimize casualties. Ironically, his position was very similar to the one the United States would find itself in during the Vietnam War.

In any case, Howe had Washington cooped up in a jail of his own making. The British army was in front of Brooklyn Heights, and the Royal Navy behind it. Washington would surely surrender in a few days, without further

★ ★ ★

Divine Intervention?

During the night that Washington withdrew his troops across the East River, a thick fog, completely out of season, arose to blanket Long Island. Even more remarkable was the fact that it did not cover New York City—only Washington's withdrawal.

loss of life. Indeed, Washington was in a precarious position. He was trapped in the fortifications of Brooklyn Heights with nine thousand men, surrounded by almost three times as many British troops and the Royal Navy.

Then came what many have seen as interference by providence. For two days and nights it rained, rendering military operations infeasible, and Lord Howe declined to take his ships into the East River because of a strong north wind. Washington gave the order to retreat across the East River.

Colonel John Glover and his Marblehead, Massachusetts, sailors handled the boats, and as they started, the wind shifted to the northeast. All night long the ferries went back and forth, with Washington being the last to step on board a boat. The miracle escape had taken place. The two regiments on Governor's Island were also evacuated, and the army was united in central Manhattan.

"Give an American Army a Wall to Fight Behind and They Will Fight Forever"

Somehow Washington had still not realized that the island of Manhattan could be cut off by the British landing high up the East River, but he did query Congress on the advisability of evacuating New York. Finally a council of war decided that the army should relinquish New York City to the British, and the forty-five hundred troops under Putnam in the city (south of Wall Street) were told to evacuate to Harlem, where sixty-five hundred American troops were already stationed. Washington himself was in Harlem when the British landed a division at Kips Bay on the East River, and he raced to confront the British van while his troops were still marching northward from the city. Militia sent to oppose the landing fled north up the island, and nothing Washington could do made the slightest difference. Legend has it that Washington threw down his hat and yelled, "Are these the men with whom I am to defend America?" Fortunately, Clinton, in command of the British advance, delayed his movement inland, and Putnam's troops slipped by to the north, taking up a new position behind entrenchments at Harlem Heights (now Morningside Heights). The incompetent Putnam nearly marched his men into the waiting arms of the British at Murray Hill because he was ignorant of the roads, but Captain Aaron Burr led the column to safety on a road to the west of the British position.

On September 16, Washington ordered Colonel Thomas Knowlton and his rangers to reconnoiter the British lines, and Knowlton provoked the advancing British light infantry into attacking him. Knowlton soon perceived that the British—in particular the renowned Black Watch, the Royal Highland Regiment—were becoming over-extended. So Washington set a trap for the hotly pursuing Scots in an area of open ground called "The Hollow Way," ambushing them with over a thousand men. Knowlton's Rangers had nearly surrounded the British troops when Knowlton, a hero of Bunker Hill and one of the first American "follow me" combat leaders, was killed. In spite of Knowlton's death, the Patriots pushed the British back, inflicting heavy casualties.

Harlem Heights was Washington's first victory against the British, and it greatly improved morale in his army. Casualties are controversial, but the Patriots apparently suffered about thirty killed and one hundred wounded, while the British lost about seventy-five killed and nearly three hundred wounded.

The lines on Harlem Heights were very strong and defended by about 14,750 men. Once again it had been demonstrated that Americans—especially fresh recruits and militia members—felt far more secure behind a wall that protected their legs, under the assumption they could always run away and fight another day. General Putnam once said, "Give an American army a wall to fight behind and they will fight forever." Walls could be outflanked, however, and Howe went east through Long Island Sound, around Washington's flank. This tactic of maneuvering and outflanking the enemy using the Royal Navy would become a staple of British imperial military engagements for almost 150 years.

Leaving a division under Lord Percy (Lieutenant General Hugh Percy, Duke of Northumberland) to protect New York City, Howe moved across to Throg's Neck where he effected a landing. When he marched up the neck to the ford and bridge connecting Throg's Point to the mainland, he found the Patriots had destroyed the bridge and were there in substantial force. Howe remained several days awaiting supplies on what was essentially an island. During the lull, Washington extended his left flank to Pelham and sent Colonel John Glover to watch Pell's Point about four miles south of New Rochelle. Glover hurried to a position above the point, and was stunned: the British had managed to land at least four thousand men overnight.

Outnumbered at least five to one, Glover did what any aggressive officer would do—he pushed his men forward to oppose the British advance. Glover placed his four small regiments behind the stone walls that were so common in the area and established a relay system wherein one regiment would fire a few volleys from close range, then retreat behind another regiment and take up a position behind a new stone wall. Most of the advancing Redcoats were Hessians, and they stoically forged ahead on the road and on both sides of it in solid lines, which were shredded, often at ranges of only thirty to forty yards. Glover finally ran out of stone walls and retreated.

Once again the Patriots had fought superbly, protected by the stone walls. Glover lost only eight killed and thirteen wounded, but the Hessians lost about two hundred killed and six hundred wounded. Significantly, the British advance had been delayed by a day, and Washington was able to arrive at White Plains, about eight miles north of New Rochelle, in advance of the British. There the American army dug entrenchments, including some on the dominating landmass known as Chatterton's Hill. When Howe arrived at White Plains, Washington had arrayed about thirteen thousand men against the British advance, leaving only two thousand at Fort Washington, and forty-five hundred at or near Fort Lee in New Jersey. Howe once again outnumbered Washington, but this time by a smaller margin.

Washington had stationed about a thousand men at Chatterton's Hill, and Howe attacked with about four thousand, including three regiments of Hessians. The first attack failed, but when Hessian Lieutenant Colonel Johann Rall and his regiment worked their way around to attack the hill from the right flank and rear of the defenders, the Americans had to retreat. The British and Hessian loss was over 230 in killed and wounded; the Americans lost fewer than two hundred.

Two days later, Howe received reinforcements, including another Hessian division under Lieutenant General Baron Wilhelm von Knyphausen. This brought Howe's strength up to twenty thousand men, and he determined to attack the following day. But once again, protected by a raging storm, Washington evacuated his positions and withdrew five miles to a very strong position on the Heights of North Castle. Howe, perhaps realizing the danger of being drawn deep into the New York backwoods, did not follow.

"I Am Bereft of Every Peaceful Moment"

Washington had been driven out of New York City. His main body of troops at North Castle now numbered fewer than twelve thousand, with another five thousand split between Fort Washington and Fort Lee.

Fort Washington stood on the highest elevation on Manhattan Island, where 182nd Street is today, overlooking the Hudson River. It, along with a like installation named Fort Lee on the Jersey side of the Hudson, was intended to prevent the passage of the Royal Navy up the river. A large chain and other obstructions had been placed between the forts, but two frigates sailed past the forts without difficulty, showing them to be ineffective in achieving their purposes.

Washington sank into a depression ("I am bereft of every peaceful moment") and began to think that a last stand was all that remained. Though not easily depressed by nature, Washington saw himself as running out of options. Congress had no money or supplies. His men could fight well under controlled circumstances—behind walls, well positioned, under reasonably solid leadership. But battles far too often required officers to think on the run, and the men to adapt and overcome. Most of all, even in the 1700s, armies had to move and maneuver, and these untrained volunteers could not begin to pull off critical maneuvers under fire.

Howe, having retreated to New York City, sent von Knyphausen from New Rochelle to seize Fort Independence guarding the Harlem River, then followed with the remainder of his army, putting himself squarely between the main body of Washington's army and Fort Washington.

These movements by Howe left Washington confused, leading him to continue to divide his forces. He sent two thousand more troops to Fort Lee in Jersey, dispatched four thousand under General Heath to Peekskill to watch the Hudson River, and left Charles Lee, newly returned from Charleston, at North Castle Heights with seven thousand men. Washington himself traveled to Fort Lee, believing that Howe had designs on New Jersey. Washington gave Lee orders to join him "with all dispatch" if Howe moved across the Hudson, and to be prepared for an attack if the movement towards Jersey was a feint. Those were orders that Lee would not obey.

In fact Howe was taking steps to gobble up Fort Washington in preparation for a move into New Jersey. As Howe's strategy became apparent, Washington conferred with Nathanael Greene, who had slowly raised the garrison at the fort from twelve to twenty-eight thousand men and appointed Colonel Robert Magaw commander. The prevailing belief among Washington's subordinates, in particular Generals Israel Putnam, Henry Knox, and Nathanael Greene, was that if the fort were properly garrisoned, it would be essentially impregnable to a direct assault. Greene should have known better; he himself had determined that eight thousand men were needed to properly defend the approaches to the fort—the three fortified lines and King's Bridge. Washington left it to Greene's discretion whether to defend the fort or evacuate, and Greene opted for a defense. When Magaw received a British demand to surrender on November 15, Greene advised him to reject the demand. And after conferring with Magaw, Greene returned to Fort Lee, confident that Fort Washington would be well defended.

The next day Hessian and British troops attacked all remaining Patriot forces on Manhattan Island. The British and Hessians rapidly forced the Americans in the outer defensive lines into the fort and gave Magaw only thirty minutes to surrender. He delivered up his sword to Baron von Knyphausen, and twenty-eight hundred Americans marched out between two ranks of Hessians. Fort Washington had fallen, in the worst defeat so far suffered by the Patriots. While the numbers of killed and wounded on both sides were relatively small, nearly three thousand officers and men were captured, and most of them would not survive British captivity.

There was only one more American strongpoint anywhere close to New York City: Fort Lee on the Hudson, opposite the captured Fort Washington. Howe quickly sent Cornwallis against Fort Lee, and the Americans fled their posts in panic, leaving meals unfinished and fires still burning. The Continentals had now suffered a string of humiliating and costly defeats.

★ ★ ★

New York Campaign Report Card

The British

General Sir William Howe: C

Although his tactics in the Battle for Long Island nearly destroyed the American army, Howe failed to capture Washington. He also established a corrupt system for handling prisoners, allowing over 60 percent of American prisoners to die in British custody, mostly by starvation.

Admiral Sir Richard Howe: F

He failed to seal off the East River and allowed Washington to escape from Long Island.

The British troops: A

The British army continued to be well-served by its personnel in the ranks.

The Hessians: C

Although the Hessians fought extremely well, they committed excessive depredations against civilians—Patriots and Tories alike—that aroused the colonists.

The Americans

General George Washington: F

Washington failed miserably to command his troops, issuing suggestions rather than orders, and allowing subordinates to overrule him. From August to December his army went from nearly twenty thousand to thirty-four hundred men, with six thousand being taken prisoner. Other than the small engagement at Harlem Heights and Glover's delaying fight at Pelham, every battle was a defeat.

General Israel Putnam: F

Putnam proved incompetent on Long Island, in the retreat from New York City, and once again in agreeing with Greene's decision to defend Fort Washington.

General John Sullivan: F

In command at Brooklyn, Sullivan left two British attack routes unguarded. When Howe came through the easternmost pass, Sullivan had no effective response.

Washington found himself retreating down New Jersey until only a tiny remnant of the once imposing Patriot army crossed the icy Delaware River into Pennsylvania.

After capturing Fort Lee, General Howe turned dovish again, exhibiting a reluctance to finish Washington once and for all through ruthless pursuit. The reasons are unclear. Already the Patriots had shown that they could

General William Stirling: B

Stirling did well against General Grant on the right flank, but failed to note Sullivan's disaster on his left and effect a timely retreat.

General Nathanael Greene: F

After the battle of White Plains, Greene still thought Fort Washington on Manhattan could be held. Washington didn't think so, but he left the decision to evacuate or not up to Greene. Greene reinforced the fort, and the British captured it in a matter of hours.

General Charles Lee: F

A constant thorn in Washington's side, Lee refused to help Washington after White Plains, assuming that Washington's poor generalship would cause his dismissal and he himself would become commander-in-chief. Lee intrigued to set up an army outside of Washington's command, and moved to New Jersey to watch New York instead of combining his troops with Washington's, as the commander-in-chief had ordered.

Colonel John Glover: A

He and his Marblehead mariners pulled off the rescue of Washington's army from Long Island literally under the nose of the Royal Navy in a single night. He also won the delaying fight at Pelham, inflicting a large number of casualties on the Hessians.

The American troops: C

The performance by American troops, both continentals and militia, was decidedly mixed. Certain continental units fought extremely well, but some did not. In line of battle, exposed militia could not yet stand against British regulars.

The Weather: A+ for the Americans

Time and again, Mother Nature or the Lord God Almighty had intervened to provide concealment and cover to retreating American forces that surely would have been destroyed without it.

retreat fast without completely disintegrating, while the British repeatedly showed slothful, European-style movement. But it's also possible that the Howe brothers' Whiggish views were stronger than publically acknowledged. After the Howes were gone, everything would change. General Clinton would make maximum use of Tory partisan raiding parties around New York, New Jersey, Connecticut, and Rhode Island. General Burgoyne would unleash his Indian allies against Americans in upper New York and the Mohawk Valley. And General Cornwallis would use terror tactics against the population in the South.

For now, Howe established a large stores depot at New Brunswick, New Jersey, and a series of outposts in New Jersey to keep Washington at bay. He wasn't worried. In the debacles of Fort Washington and Fort Lee, Washington had lost some 146 cannon, 12,000 musket balls and shells, 2,800 muskets, 400,000 cartridges, and thousands of other tools and items of equipment that he needed to wage war. It was a disaster of epic proportions for the Patriots. General Howe could rightfully expect to easily extinguish the rebellion in the 1777 campaign season.

CHAPTER 8

Christmas Miracle

The Patriots could not have faced a bleaker moment than the dawn of December 1776. Their situation was dire, and little did they dream that within a month, the entire course of the war would change in their favor. Washington had bivouacked at New Brunswick, New Jersey, with about five thousand men, two thousand of whom had enlistments that were up on December 1, and another thousand on December 31. In other words, Washington was about to lose 60 percent of his army by the first of the year. He paraded the men whose enlistments were expiring and personally exhorted them to stay, but his efforts failed, and over two thousand troops left camp for home. (Washington was not particularly known for stirring, emotional speeches until the end of the war, with his Newburgh Address heading off the officers' revolt and his farewell address at Fraunces Tavern.) Howe, meanwhile, had nearly thirty thousand regular troops, including Hessian mercenaries, at his disposal. He sent Cornwallis to invest New Brunswick. Washington pulled up stakes and led his small force toward Pennsylvania.

As had become a (bad) habit with the British, Cornwallis pursued somewhat slowly. Perhaps he expected to be attacked by Lee, whose army was

Did you know?

★ Emanuel Leutze's famous painting of *Washington Crossing the Delaware* shows an African-American rowing the boat because Leutze was an abolitionist

★ Colonel Rall's absolute faith in his Hessians led him to neglect appropriate defensive measures

★ Cornwallis hesitated and lost his chance to finish Washington at Assunpink Creek

***
A Cautionary Tale

Perhaps because British land forces were always relatively small compared to those of the continental powers—even up through World War II—England's generals have been notoriously cautious. Field Marshal Bernard Montgomery infuriated General George Patton with his plodding movements in the Second World War. The Duke of Wellington's caution, on the other hand, saved his army at Waterloo against Napoleon in 1815. And in the American Revolution, the slow-moving British field commanders missed numerous opportunities to eliminate American armies.

still at his rear. In fact, neither the British nor Washington knew Lee's whereabouts, and somewhat comically, both sides kept expecting him to show up at any time.

On December 2, the little Continental Army filed into Princeton. Washington left a blocking force there in case Cornwallis showed up, then took the rest of his men to Trenton. Meanwhile, in a truly brilliant move, Washington had ordered his troops to seize all the boats on the Delaware River and bring them to Trenton. Now the Americans could cross the river at will, while Cornwallis could not.

Howe controlled New York City, Long Island, and the Hudson River Valley as far north as Peekskill. For whatever reason, though, he neglected to send the Royal Navy up the Hudson. The way was open, and he easily could have driven away or captured the American forces at Peekskill. When the British did move, as usual, they were successful, capturing American-held forts Montgomery and Clinton on opposite sides of the Hudson with minimal effort. Then, typically, Howe thought defensively and supported his army at Newport, Rhode Island, to secure Long Island from attack and to prepare for an overland invasion of New England in the spring. Thinking Washington was neutralized, Howe spread Cornwallis's twelve thousand men out through a series of outposts in New Jersey, from New Brunswick through Princeton to Trenton, Bordentown, and Burlington on the Delaware River. It was a foolish move, especially for a commander as well-trained as Howe.

Cornwallis arrived in Princeton on December 7. His British and Hessians plundered and looted without restraint, as New Jersey paid the price for being "rebel-land," as compared to "loyal" New York.

Meanwhile, Washington crossed the Delaware and moved all the boats and ferries to the Pennsylvania side. The exasperated British arrived at Trenton the next day to see Washington on the other side of the river. Oddly enough, Howe was completely satisfied with his own position: he had accomplished all his objectives for the year with very few losses; his chain of posts secured New Jersey from Washington and raiding militia. The Hessians were given the posts of honor of the most exposed points: Trenton and Bordentown, with fifteen hundred Hessians stationed at Bordentown under Colonel Carl von Donop, and fourteen hundred at Trenton under Colonel Johann Rall. Howe returned to New York to enjoy his mistress, Mrs. Elizabeth Loring, the wife of Joshua Loring, Howe's commissary general of military prisoners. (Loring and Provost Marshal William Cunningham were responsible for the mass ill-treatment and starvation of American prisoners; today they would be tried for war crimes.)

Two Books You're Not Supposed to Read

Read together, *Hell on the East River: British Prison Ships in the American Revolution* by Larry Lowenthal (Fleischmann's, NY: Purple Mountain Press, 2009) and *Forgotten Patriots: The Untold Story of American Prisoners During the Revolutionary War* by Edwin G. Burrows (New York: Basic Books, 2008). These books will destroy all sympathy for the British that a reader may possess.

Adding by Subtracting

Lower New York and all of New Jersey were cleared of American troops in December of 1776. The last Patriot troops to depart New Jersey were those of Charles Lee, who had finally crossed the Hudson at King's Ferry on December 2 with only twenty-seven hundred men—out of an army of seventy-five hundred just a month earlier. Sickness, desertion, and expiring enlistments had taken their toll. Lee avoided Cornwallis, but seemed to march as slowly as possible, making only five miles a day. On December 13 at White's Tavern in Basking Ridge, New Jersey, three miles away from his army, Lee was captured by a cavalry detachment including Banastre Tarleton. What a break for the Patriots! Not only was an incompetent commander taken out of the picture, but Lee's remaining forces eventually joined Washington in Pennsylvania, an event that probably would not have occurred had Lee remained in command.

In captivity, Lee became a traitor to the Patriot cause—making himself extremely useful to the British, advising Howe on the strengths and positions of the American units and their tactics. On his own initiative, Lee even produced a plan for the British spring campaign and promoted it to Howe. But Lee's treason would remain secret until the 1850s, when his plan was found in General Howe's papers.

Lose One, Gain Two

Unfortunately for the Patriots, Charles Lee was not the only less than stellar general they had—though he may have been the very worst. Horatio Gates and John Sullivan—the latter newly exchanged with Lord Stirling for two high-ranking prisoners held by Washington—were soon informed of Lee's capture, and both men headed west to cross the Delaware as soon as possible. Sullivan's competence was highly questionable, but at least he was loyal to Washington. And his role as the only Catholic general on the American side was important to keep the war at least partially ecumenical. On December 20, Sullivan's troops—formerly Lee's—began arriving in Washington's camp, soon joined by Gates and his men, bringing Washington's total force to over four thousand. His army had survived

A Book You're Not Supposed to Read

Washington's Crossing by David Hackett Fischer (New York: Oxford University Press, 2006).

and was being reinforced—but what could it do against Howe's enormous number of troops?

Washington quickly resolved to attack the British outpost at Trenton. The dramatic attack Washington had planned began with a body of militia attacking Bordentown. That assault succeeded in drawing von Donop's units away to Mount Holly, where they remained for several days, gathering provisions and keeping an eye on their opponents. The British didn't see what Washington had done—enticed a large body of enemy troops eighteen miles away from his real objective, the Trenton garrison.

Contrary to popular myth, the Hessians under Colonel Rall at Trenton were neither totally unprepared nor lax in their defensive measures. Rall had established six outposts around Trenton to give him early warning of an attack. Nor were these small outposts: the contingent at the Fox Chase Tavern at the edge of Trenton comprised seventy-three men, while the Crosswicks Creek drawbridge detachment was made up of a hundred men. But Rall had not fortified his main position in Trenton, believing that his men, when warned by the pickets, could turn out rapidly and defeat any Patriot force sent against them.

Washington prepared an overly complex plan with three simultaneous attacks: the main attack, composed of two columns under Nathanael Greene and John Sullivan of about 2,400 troops and eighteen cannon, would cross the Delaware nine miles north of Trenton. A second assault would be made across the river at the Trenton Ferry by 700 Pennsylvania militiamen under James Ewing, to seize the bridge over Assunpink Creek on the south side of Trenton. And a third party led by General John

★ ★ ★
Their Last Hurrah

It was John Glover's Marblehead militia, the "amphibious regiment" composed almost entirely of fishermen, that ferried Washington's troops across the Delaware. These were the same men who had evacuated Washington's army after the defeat at the Battle of Long Island in August 1776. But after their successful crossing of the Delaware on Christmas night, the regiment disbanded at year's end.

★ ★ ★

The Painting

Washington Crossing the Delaware, painted by Emanuel Leutze in 1851, depicts a daytime crossing and a Washington much older than he really was. The American flag in the painting did not exist until a year later. And the river looks more like the Rhine than the Delaware. But if Leutze was in error in some details, he got the symbolism exactly right. Each of the twelve soldiers pictured (including Washington) is wearing distinctive clothing—symbolic of the different ranks of society and regions of America represented in the Patriot army. There is a black man rowing, as Leutze was an abolitionist, and it appears that the man holding the flag is supposed to represent James Monroe. Some have even suggested that there is a woman in the boat. Despite the artistic license, Leutze's *Crossing* remains one of the most inspiring and heroic paintings of the Revolution.

Cadwalader would cross at Bristol to threaten von Donop and pin him down.

The famous crossing by the main assault, captured in the memorable painting by Emanuel Leutze, went slowly because of ice in the river; Washington's artillery did not reach the east bank until at least 3:00 a.m. It was pitch black and snowing throughout the night—which was a blessing. The storm ensured that the Hessians remained indoors and the storm covered the noise of the crossing and approaching march. Realizing the critical nature of the attack, Washington made the password for the night "Victory or Death."

Rall had received warnings that Washington might attack Trenton. But after a party of American militia skirmished with a Hessian picket post on the Pennington Road earlier in the evening of the twenty-fifth and Rall sent a patrol that found nothing, he concluded there was no real threat.

The Hessians spent the remainder of their Christmas evening drinking and playing cards. Legend has it that while Colonel Rall was playing cards, he received a note from a Tory spy that Washington was closing in on Trenton. Rall stuffed it into his breast pocket without reading it—it was finally found and read by Rall when his tunic was being removed after he was mortally wounded.

Meanwhile, Washington learned that Ewing, in charge of the second assault party, had been prevented from crossing at Trenton Ferry by the weather. So he instructed Sullivan to take the River Road all the way to

Assunpink Creek to prevent the Hessians from escaping southwards. Sullivan reached the creek crossing late, and when he finally reached his target, he sent a note to Washington that his troops' powder was too wet to fire. Washington's terse answer: "Tell Sullivan to use the bayonet."

It wasn't until almost 8:00 in the morning that the Americans finally attacked—and yet even at that late hour, the Hessians were taken by surprise. After initial volleys, artillery was sent into action, sweeping the streets clean of the confused Hessians. Still, over four hundred Hessians escaped across the creek before Sullivan was able to close off their avenue of retreat.

The disorganized and half-awake Hessians attempted to make a stand but were overwhelmed and surrounded by Washington's troops. Rall was shot down, fatally wounded, and his leaderless regiments surrendered. Amazingly, the Patriots suffered only four casualties, all wounded, including future president James Monroe. (Two soldiers had frozen to death during the approach march.) The Hessians suffered twenty-two killed and 948 captured.

Only after the battle did Washington learn that some of his units never got into the fight. Cadwalader, in charge of the third assault party, had crossed only six hundred troops at Bristol—and then withdrawn them when the rest of his force was unable to follow. General Putnam, who had been supposed to arrive with reinforcements from Philadelphia, never appeared at all. Washington, with only a fraction of the force he had intended to have at Trenton—and with prisoners who required a substantial guard force—deemed it prudent to withdraw back across the Delaware.

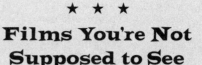

★ ★ ★
Films You're Not Supposed to See

While we don't include many films here, there are a few that are worth mentioning. The Revolution is very poorly represented in American cinema, apparently because it is not politically correct. Aside from *The Patriot* (2000), *Revolution* (1985), and *1776* (1972), there are very few movies about America's birth. One that stands out is *The Crossing* (2000), a made-for-television movie directed by Robert Harmon and starring Jeff Daniels as George Washington. Harmon gets most of the details correct, and Daniels is at his best.

Once back in Pennsylvania, Washington found that General Cadwalader had re-crossed the Delaware with his entire command on December 27. Appreciating his subordinate's bold action, Washington decided to re-cross the river himself, but again he was bedeviled with expiring terms of enlistment. The enlistments of nearly his entire force would expire on December 31. Washington offered a bounty of ten dollars to everyone who would remain another six weeks, and the problem was temporarily alleviated. He ordered a contingent under General William Heath to Morristown for winter quarters, re-crossed the Delaware with fifteen hundred men on December 29, and set up a defensive position on the south side of Assunpink Creek.

Meanwhile, a furious Howe, assessing the Hessians' heavy losses, ordered Cornwallis to reestablish the British positions on the Delaware. Cornwallis arrived in Trenton on January 2 and began feeling out Washington's position. To any trained military observer, Washington's deployments must have seemed the height of folly. His only avenue of retreat lay over the Delaware River again, and attempting to effect a crossing under hot pursuit by a superior force would probably be disastrous. His position behind Assunpink Creek was hardly strong; it could be easily flanked to the east. Facing him were fifty-five hundred veteran British troops with twenty-five hundred more within supporting distance. Washington at that time had barely five thousand men.

We'll Bag the Old Fox in the Morning

Cornwallis began a cannonade of Washington's defenses, and the Hessians attempted to storm the Patriot position at the bridge—three times. They were repulsed with heavy casualties, by one account 150 dead Germans on the field. Cornwallis pulled back in the evening. Assunpink Creek was not fordable at Trenton, the bridge was well-guarded, and it was nearly dark: he told a subordinate, "We've got the old fox safe now. We'll go over and bag him in the morning." Cornwallis did not realize the creek was fordable only a mile east of the bridge.

The "old fox" was not there in the morning. During the night Washington had had a picked force of five hundred men keep the campfires burning and work on the entrenchments while he marched his army around Cornwallis using little-used roads. By daylight the army had covered eleven miles, and was approaching Princeton, in Cornwallis's rear.

The Patriots smashed into the British regiments moving through Princeton, but it took time for all of Washington's army to arrive. The Redcoats put up a stout defense, and American general Hugh Mercer was killed. When the American attack seemed to slow, Washington took control. Riding between British and American lines that were only seventy yards apart, he shouted, "Parade with us, my brave fellows. There is but a handful of the enemy, and we shall have them directly." That was all it took for Mercer's leaderless men to re-form. The Americans advanced on the British, with Washington on horseback leading the charge. Washington shouted, "Halt!" and "Make Ready!" But before he could give the order to fire, the British unleashed a volley. The Patriots responded—with the general still between the two lines of the armies. Washington and his horse disappeared in the smoke, unscathed.

When the British retreated toward Trenton, the Pennsylvania Light Horse followed them, and the retreat became a total rout. The remainder of the British force held out for a while on the grounds of Princeton College, but after their escape toward New Brunswick was cut off they readily surrendered. British casualties were about one hundred killed, and three hundred captured, of whom eighty were wounded. The American losses were about

★ ★ ★
Another Miracle

At the Battle of Princeton, George Washington charged to the front of the Patriot lines—*between them and the British*—to rally his troops. Both armies unleashed volleys, yet Washington was not scratched nor was his horse shot. It was yet another miracle in a string of providential events that saved the American Revolution.

Battles of Trenton and Princeton Report Card

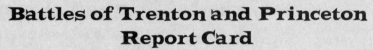

The British

Richard Howe: C

His underestimation of Washington created the opportunity for Trenton.

Colonel Johann Rall: D

A brave man, but with too much faith in his Hessians as the best soldiers in the world.

Charles Cornwallis: F

Given the opportunity to defeat Washington once and for all, he waited for the morning.

The Americans

George Washington: B

His plan of attack on Trenton was overly complex and could not be executed as expected by his sub-par commanders. And his subsequent return to New Jersey was a huge unnecessary gamble: staking his command on a night march around the British flank was reckless. But the personal bravery he showed at Princeton was a huge boost to Patriot morale, and all his gambles paid off.

John Sullivan: D

Another lackluster performance from an incompetent officer.

Israel Putnam: F

He never showed up with the reinforcements Washington was expecting.

James Ewing: F

Ewing let the weather stop him from even getting across the Delaware.

John Cadwalader: B

His bold action in re-crossing the Delaware gave Washington an opportunity to follow up the Battle of Trenton with another impressive Patriot victory.

eighty killed and wounded. Young America had had its second noteworthy victory in a matter of days.

Having achieved a remarkable pair of victories, Washington turned north from Princeton and headed for Morristown, reluctantly abandoning a huge prize: the British depot at New Brunswick. It would have been a town too far. Besides, both he and Cornwallis now knew there would be another spring for "the old fox." The war had entered a new phase.

Washington, gambling everything on British complacency, made his winter camp in Morristown, a defensible camp to be sure, but within easy striking distance of the British at New York. A British assault might end the Revolution, but the ever-cautious Howe had no stomach for a winter campaign. By staying in Morristown, Washington was laying claim to most of New Jersey and kicking sand at the bear. As Benjamin Franklin had predicted, there were not enough Englishmen willing to die for their country to subdue the growing American nation. At least not in 1776.

CHAPTER 9

Washington under Siege

Even as the feisty Continental Army delivered a pair of shocking defeats to the Redcoats over Christmas at Trenton and Princeton, the scales of war still weighed heavily in favor of the British. It was easy to see how the Revolution could be defeated in 1777. In the spring General Johnny Burgoyne would move south from Montreal down Lake Champlain to Ticonderoga and Albany, isolating New England from the other colonies and establishing British control throughout the Hudson Valley and New York. Once the Royal Navy began patrolling the Hudson, Howe could expect American communications and troop movements to be severed, the rebellious regions separated and open to be crushed individually.

Everything looked peachy for the Redcoats on parchment. But as Secretary of Defense Donald Rumsfeld said during the Iraq War, "The enemy always gets a vote." And Americans definitely voted—with their muskets and rifles.

Howe's troop strength was a problem. As in any human endeavor, the prospects for victory changed based on confidence. Americans seemed to be able to grow armies out of thin air—especially when news of Trenton got out—while British casualties were difficult to replace. At best it took a

Did you know?

★ "Tarleton's Quarter" became Revolutionary War slang for *no mercy* after British general Banastre Tarleton murdered 113 surrendering Patriot soldiers

★ Attempts to stop war profiteering with wage and price controls were a dismal failure

★ The Battle of the Brandywine demonstrated Washington's tactical shortcomings—and strategic genius

month to simply move new troops from England to North America. And that was assuming Britain had the troops to send. Recruitment in England had suffered from the beginning, with the king forced to recruit large numbers of Catholic Irish and Scottish Highlanders and to employ mercenaries from German principalities. These troops, stationed in America, seemed as alien to the Tories as to the Patriots.

How Bad Were the British?

The British did not help themselves with their treatment of civilians. British and Hessian troops alienated the American population, even Americans with pro-British politics. By today's standards, the behavior of British and Hessian troops was off the chart. Women, whether Tory or Patriot, were regularly subjected to indignities; incidents of rape, including gang rape, were common. Civilians were well advised to stay indoors at night, as those caught outside were often molested, beaten, and robbed. Complaining to British authorities was futile, as complaints were seen as slurs on the British troops or even outright treason. Merchants providing supplies were never paid promptly, and personal debts incurred by officers were sometimes paid by murdering the merchant. Long Island, under British occupation for seven years, became a wasteland of ruined farms and burned-down houses. Worse of all were the Hessians. They seemed to take advantage of the language barrier to misunderstand everything, and had a penchant for murder, rape, robbery, plundering, and personal cruelty. Discipline within their own ranks was draconian, and they turned around and visited the same violence on American civilians. As with the British, there was no appeal to their commanders.

In the film *The Patriot*, the evil Colonel Tavington, modeled on Banastre Tarleton, forces an entire town of civilians he suspects of Patriot sympathies into a church and sets it on fire, burning them all to death. The real Tarleton never burned down a church of civilians, yet the story told in *The Patriot* would ring true to the original Patriots. There were many instances of British horrors to support such legends.

For example, after George Washington withdrew from New York, a fire broke out and soon consumed the city. Patriots thought to be arsonists were hurled into burning buildings—including women. Others were hung by their heels and bayoneted, or hanged in the old-fashioned way. And Tarleton did commit atrocities, though not the one in the movie. He murdered 113 Patriot soldiers from Colonel Abraham Buford's detachment who had surrendered. This incident gave rise to the phrase "Tarleton's Quarter," meaning the indiscriminate slaughter of anyone surrendering.

On the other hand, Patriot forces also exacted a toll on Tories. The Articles of Association as enforced by the various committees were keeping many local Tories from trading with the British forces. Often, Tories were caught between British thuggism and retaliation from the Patriots. Theirs was not an enviable position.

Civilian Life in Time of War

What was it like to be a non-combatant in 1775 –1783? Occupation of major American cities by the British produced an uneasy truce between the majority Tory populations who supported them and the minority Patriots who opposed their presence; the latter were in a dangerous situation. Civilians were often turned out of their homes to make room for officers, although this was a practice frowned upon by the Howes and other top commanders. While the British army brought income to inn keepers, stables, and suppliers of all types, they were not always sure to pay; and the provider had no recourse except to appeal to…British magistrates. The army was a major buyer of hay, oats, and livestock. But the need for supplies was always a double-edged sword—the soldiers might decide to simply confiscate the

★ ★ ★

Price and Wage Controls

War profiteering, mostly by Tories and neutrals, was an immense problem during the Revolutionary War. At the time of the Association in 1775, Congress had produced schedules that restrained the prices of items that were then currently being imported. The schedules were widely ignored, and near the end of 1776 the four New England colonies held a convention in Providence, Rhode Island, to set controls on wages and prices. A regulation was produced on December 31 setting a scale for farm labor and maximum wages for a wide variety of occupations. This effort at government regulation of wages and prices failed miserably, and it was discontinued in the fall of 1777.

In November of 1777, Congress tried its hand. The best it could do was call for regional conventions to set wages and prices. Only one was held—in New Haven, Connecticut, setting new schedules for wages and prices for New England and some Middle States. These controls didn't work either. Association committees at the local level attempted with some success to hold profiteering down by intimidation and the outright use of force, but still profiteering was widespread. It became an American institution in all later wars—often involving members of government themselves.

Substantial efforts were made by Congress, state, and local governments to curb war profiteering through wage and price controls, but all except the most local initiatives failed miserably. Young America learned that the market controlled wages and prices. But then, the United States has been doomed to relearn this principle over and over again, to the present day.

goods. The British did have one thing the Continental Army did not: gold. British gold pieces remained in circulation and in high demand.

The cities definitely lost population: Philadelphia went from thirty-two thousand in 1775 to about twenty-four thousand in 1778; New York from twenty-one thousand in 1770 to only five thousand in 1776; and Charleston had lost about one-third of its population by 1782. Naturally most cities' populations—and especially their Patriot populations—were more female than male, with so many men gone to the fight. And women took over a number of jobs formerly done by males. British officers tended to prefer the luxuries of the cities, and retreated back to them whenever possible. But that meant that while the British were safe in their urban comfort, they were surrendering the countryside to the Patriot forces.

Divide and Conquer?

After Trenton and Princeton, the winter of 1776–77 was mostly uneventful. In January 1777 a small battle occurred at Fort Independence, which guarded the northern approaches to Manhattan. Washington ordered General William Heath, who was still in the Hudson Valley Highlands, to attack the fort, held by two thousand Hessians, with his six thousand men. Like Rall's command at Trenton, the Hessians were beyond supporting distance from other British units. But Heath, like so many other early Patriot commanders, proved incompetent, and after the weather turned sour, he retreated. Washington never gave him another combat command.

The British plan for the summer campaign in 1777 was to divide the colonies. Burgoyne had an army of ten thousand men, two thousand of whom would travel down Lake Ontario and attack east through the Mohawk Valley toward Albany. Originally Howe and Burgoyne had planned to join forces at Albany, but Howe inexplicably decided not to proceed with his northward march, *and not to bother to inform Burgoyne of that fact*! Without informing his generals, Howe decided on an expedition of his own to the largest American city—now its new capital—Philadelphia. This way, Howe thought he could destroy Washington's army while Burgoyne defeated whatever militia might be raised from New England. If both Howe and Burgoyne were successful, it stood to reason that Howe could then turn to the south and send troops into Virginia or the Carolinas while Burgoyne and Clinton mopped up resistance in New England. Britain would win the war. And Howe would win the PR campaign: he, rather than Burgoyne, would emerge from the campaign with the victory and the headlines.

When Howe put his army on transports, Washington needed to know where they were going. Washington assumed Howe's designs were against the Highlands and shifted most of his army toward West Point. But on July 24, Washington learned that Howe had put out to sea rather than sail up the Hudson. Uncertainty reigned, but Washington moved his army to the Delaware River north of Trenton, prepared to return to the Hudson or continue on to Philadelphia. For the moment, however, Washington was most concerned with Burgoyne. He sent Putnam and his troops to bolster the Northern Department, and began detaching some of his own units to go north.

At this point a row between generals Horatio Gates, commanding the Northern Army, and Philip Schuyler, commander of the Northern Department overseeing it, threatened to rip the Patriot forces apart. Schuyler refused to leave his comfortable quarters in Albany, and Gates appealed to his friends in Congress to set matters right. His friends proved to be all he needed: Schuyler was removed, and Gates put in command. Unfortunately, one incompetent general had been removed only to make room for another incompetent general.

Meanwhile, on August 22, Howe's intentions became obvious: he was moving against Philadelphia from the upper reaches of the Chesapeake Bay, apparently to avoid the defenses the Americans had constructed along the Delaware River. Other than his extreme caution and lack of aggressiveness, this was perhaps Howe's only strategic mistake during his time in command in America. Landing at New Castle on the Delaware would have saved him twenty-five overland miles to Philadelphia, and he probably would have arrived at the city a month earlier. His forces finally landed at Head of Elk in Maryland with thirteen thousand men. Lurking close by, however, was Washington's army, comprised of fifteen thousand men and organized into five divisions commanded by Major Generals Nathanael Greene, John Sullivan, Adam Stephen, John Alexander (Lord Stirling), and Brigadier General William Maxwell. Two of the five, Sullivan and Stephen, would fail miserably.

The British advanced slowly (yet again) after having been cooped up at sea for six weeks. Meanwhile Washington, in a morale building demonstration, paraded his army through Philadelphia on August 24. Washington naturally assumed that Howe would take the shortest route to Philadelphia, namely through Wilmington, Delaware. So he positioned his troops in front of Wilmington on White Clay Creek and threw up entrenchments in front of the city. Apparently Washington and his staff performed little scouting and did not inform themselves about the available road net or about where fords were on Brandywine Creek. The Continental Army's scouting and intelligence-gathering continued to be dismal, as in New York.

Howe's rare incompetence ironically proved beneficial to him. Washington expected Howe to march northeast towards Philadelphia, but instead, Howe put his army into motion on September 8, heading north through the town of Newark, five miles to the west of Newport. The British army crossed White Clay Creek and marched through stunningly good defensive terrain without being molested. One defile took a half hour to traverse; according to a Hessian named Jaeger, a hundred riflemen could have held up the column there for days. Howe then headed northwest toward Lancaster, actually leaving Washington and Wilmington in his rear!

Late on the night of September 8, the American army finally began to move, abandoning their entrenchments at Wilmington and heading for the assumed crossing point of Brandywine Creek—at Chad's Ford. Washington took up positions on the northeast bank of the Brandywine, with Greene's forces in the center, Sullivan commanding his division and those of Stirling and Stephen on the right, two miles to the northwest, and the Pennsylvania militia on the left guarding the downstream crossings from Chad's Ford.

On September 10, Howe made camp about eight miles south of Chad's Ford. He scouted the road net, checked the creek for fords, and conferred with local Tories concerning his options, learning that Trimble's Ford on

★ ★ ★

Another Miracle for America

So far, miracles had saved Washington's army at Boston from a British attack on American positions when a storm blew up; the army again at Long Island by a mysterious fog bank that saved Washington's army as it crossed the East River under the guns of the Royal Navy; and Washington himself when he had ridden unscathed *between* two armies that simultaneously fired at short range. Now a fourth miracle took place: at Brandywine Washington was riding with only one escort, away from his adjutants, when he ran slap into the British army. As British Major Patrick Ferguson saw the incident, a rebel cavalryman in a Hussar uniform appeared less than a hundred yards away from him, followed by another rebel officer in green or blue, with a "remarkable large high cocked hat." The man in the cocked hat was riding a very good bay horse, and Ferguson gave the order for three of his green-coated riflemen to creep forward and pick the two officers off. Then the idea disgusted him, and he recalled his men. Ferguson himself rode forward with a breech-loading rifle (his own invention) to take the rebels prisoner and shouted for them to stop. The officer on the bay horse stopped for a moment, looked at him, but then continued to ride slowly away. Ferguson couldn't bring himself to shoot an "unoffending" individual in the back, and so let him go. Later he determined the man had been General Washington, and the Hussar most likely Casimir Pulaski, the Polish hero who had volunteered to fight for the Patriots and is sometimes called "Father of the American cavalry." In yet another miracle, Washington was neither killed nor captured.

the West Branch of the Brandywine was left unguarded. The next day, Howe initiated a repeat of Long Island.

Howe sent von Knyphausen's columns against the middle of Washington's line at Chad's Ford at 5:00 a.m. A little before noon Washington received information that a heavy column of British troops were on the Valley Road heading northwest beyond his right flank. This was very much like what had happened to the Patriot forces on Long Island, but since it was only a single report and unconfirmed, Washington assumed the column was a feint to draw him off. He decided to attack the troops before him at Chad's Ford and ordered all wings of his forces forward.

At about 2:00 p.m., Patriot General John Sullivan received a report that the British were some two miles away and behind him. He and Stirling immediately moved their troops at a right angle to meet this existential threat, taking routes across open ground because of the lack of roads in their sector. Sullivan complained, "I neither knew where the Enemy were or what route the other two divisions were to take, and of course could not determine where I should form a junction with them." That was an interesting complaint, as Sullivan was in command of the right wing, and Stirling and Stephen were his subordinates.

Then, almost predictably, the British stopped. But even an hour's respite didn't help the Americans. Sullivan, Stirling, and Stephen were unable to sort out where they should go, and Washington remained at Chad's Ford. When Howe finally resumed his advance, he was still able to nearly cut off parts of the American right wing. The end appeared near: Cornwallis began his descent from Osborne's Hill toward the Patriot forces, matching eight thousand hardened veterans against four thousand Continentals who were disorganized and unsure of where they should be.

A hole appeared between the lines of Sullivan and Stirling, which the British quickly exploited. Sullivan's division was the first to give way, and as it scattered, Stirling's troops were hard pressed. Washington, meanwhile,

★ ★ ★
Whistle While You Work

American troops reported that the British took heavy casualties everywhere on the battlefield, but the British had modified their tactics to compensate for the accurate American fire. Company commanders carried whistles. Seeing the Americans about ready to fire a volley, they would blow their whistles and their companies would drop to the ground. After the volley was fired, the British would rise up and charge with the bayonet. (Some British regiments also ran out of ammunition during the long battle—their cartridge boxes only held twenty-four rounds—and American troops assumed the decreasing volume of fire indicated heavy casualties.)

left a force to hold Chad's Ford and ordered Nathanael Greene's troops to reinforce Sullivan. They arrived just in time to cover the retreat of the defeated right wing, but now Washington's center was weakened. As soon as von Knyphausen saw Greene's division leave, he formed an attack column of five thousand men to descend on Chad's Ford, pushing the remaining Patriots from their positions. Americans retreated across the field, and only a brigade-sized battle stopped the British pursuit in the darkness. Brandywine, the longest one-day battle of the war—eleven hours—was over, and Washington had lost again.

Pyrrhic Victory

But again a British success had come at a disastrous cost. The British and Hessians probably lost more than seven hundred men, although official totals were somewhat lower. Washington's losses were controversial, but definitely greater than Howe's. General Howe reported that Washington's casualties were three hundred killed, six hundred wounded, and nearly four hundred captured, in addition to considerable losses in officers killed and wounded. Those numbers are generally accepted as valid. Most of the wounded were brought off in the retreat, indicating an orderly withdrawal.

In spite of its defeat, Washington's army retained good morale after the battle. Many combatants had seen the British and Hessians go down in rows for the first time, and most believed the enemy's casualties to be far greater than their own. They were emboldened by their

★ ★ ★

The American Army— Nationality Count

According to the numbers in a letter by Tory guide James Parker to a friend in Scotland, the 315 American prisoners sent to Wilmington from the battlefield were 42.5 percent Scotch-Irish (called "Irish"), 20.6 percent English, 5.1 percent German, 2.9 percent Scottish, 26.0 percent "American," and 2.9 percent (nine individuals) from other countries. There was not a great deal of diversity in the American army.

ability to fight toe-to-toe with Redcoats. Perhaps intuitively, they knew that British casualties could not be sustained. Washington had
once again demonstrated his tactical shortcomings: he had trusted incompetent subordinates
and had been outflanked, just as at Long Island.
On the other hand, he had again kept the army
together, displaying his strategic genius.

Even as victor, Howe knew he had gained
little. Once again, Washington's force was still
intact while his own was losing men and bleeding supplies by the minute.
Tories from Philadelphia were flocking to Howe's army, adding to his
supply problems. Meanwhile, both armies were suffering in a torrential
rainstorm.

Brigadier General Anthony Wayne's troops, the Patriot rearguard under
orders to watch Howe closely, warned Washington that Howe was being
guided by Tories familiar with the region. Washington ignored the warning.
He decided to cross the Schuylkill River and block Howe from crossing,
leaving Wayne on Howe's left flank to harass the British as they maneuvered. But Wayne stuck too close to the enemy.

Howe decided to rid himself of Wayne's presence by a night attack. On the
night of September 20, Major General Charles Grey began silently marching
a contingent of troops toward Wayne's position,
after ordering them to remove their flints and
attack with only their bayonets. Wayne's troops
were surprised by the stealthy British, and the
battle became known as "The Paoli Massacre"
after the nearby Paoli Tavern. The blow to American morale was out of proportion to the actual
casualties. Fewer than three hundred Patriots

A Book You're Not Supposed to Read

Brandywine: A Military History of the Battle that Lost Philadelphia but Saved America, September 11, 1777 by Michael C. Harris (El Dorado Hills, CA: Savas Beatie, 2014).

★ ★ ★
Fun Fact

"Mad" Anthony Wayne was neither crazy nor perpetually angry. His volatile personality and risky military exploits gave him the nickname.

had been killed, wounded, or captured, but a thousand of the Maryland militia had deserted as the bayonets approached. British brutality became the talk of the army. Philadelphia fell to the British not with a bang but a whimper.

Turning Point

Washington immediately and aggressively attacked at the British encampment near Germantown, taking on a large British army. The attack was bungled in part by Ticonderoga's hero Henry Knox, who insisted on leveling the stone "Chew House" with British soldiers in it rather than bypassing it. Still, the American army didn't feel defeated, only disappointed. And this attack shocked the British: up to that point they had been carrying the war to the Americans, not the other way around. Colonial soldiers were learning, and getting better—and while the bane of Washington's command was the constant turnover of enlistments, many Patriot soldiers returned, again and again. When they did, they came back to Washington's army as trained soldiers, not fresh recruits. Washington's volunteer army was slowly becoming professionalized. The French were also impressed. Germantown, along with Burgoyne's surrender at Saratoga two weeks later, would convince them to support the Americans.

Howe made one more attempt to strike Washington before going into winter quarters. Forewarned by a Patriot sympathizer in Philadelphia who sewed intelligence reports into her clothes, Washington knew that Howe intended to attack him at Whitemarsh with a large force. On December 6, Howe maneuvered his troops in front of Washington, in essence offering Washington the option to precipitate a battle as he had done the previous June in upper New Jersey. This time Washington refused the bait, and the British began a return to Philadelphia.

Washington followed with Daniel Morgan's rifle corps. At Edge Hill, Howe suddenly turned and attacked Morgan's men. The Patriot riflemen

★ ★ ★

Philadelphia Campaign Report Card

The British

General Howe: B

He showed the world that he was a master tactician, but was weak in pursuit and incapable of putting Washington away once and for all.

The British troops: A

They accomplished every task required of them.

The Americans

George Washington: C-

He was learning, but he neglected intelligence, failed to organize proper scouting, made overly complicated battle plans, and relied too often on incompetent officers. Most of all, he repeated his mistake at Long Island.

John Sullivan: F

Once again he seemed to take little interest in scouting and learning the land and roads in his area of responsibility. He was unable to form an adequate defensive line on the right flank at Brandywine.

Henry Knox: F

He convinced Washington to reduce the Chew House, and lost the battle of Germantown.

American troops: A

They generally performed well. It was not their fault that their generals misused them.

poured destructive fire on the attacking British light infantry but were then forced to flee, having nothing with which to meet the British bayonets. All Howe got out of the exchange was more casualties he could ill afford, and an interruption of his retreat to Philadelphia.

Washington then withdrew to Valley Forge for the winter while Howe resided in comfortable Philadelphia. Wintering in Valley Forge would be a trial for Washington's men, but a hardened and trained army came out of the encampment. In the summer of 1778, the war would look dramatically different—and yet the victory at Saratoga was a mere continuation of the ominous trends for the British. Unable to land a knockout punch, the Redcoats saw their logistics and their will to win sapped by the moment.

CHAPTER 10

The Saratoga Surrender

The summer and fall campaigns of 1777 were not kind to Washington, but they were a gift to another American general. Like Charles Lee, Horatio Gates had been a career British army officer before coming to America. Gates had experienced little combat in his twenty-four years in the British army before he sold his major's commission in 1769, and he was not known as a leader. But he had made a name for himself as an administrator. Gates would reap the benefits of American military successes in 1777, even though he would do little to earn them. He did do everything he could to game the system to enhance his reputation.

The real hero responsible for the crucial American victory at Saratoga was Benedict Arnold. His contribution began the previous year, with his heroic defense of Lake Champlain, which had delayed the British invasion from Canada. Arnold had won a strategic victory at Valcour Island in October of 1776, and the British invasion force had returned to Canada for the winter. But the following year, they were ready to try again, with a new commander, Major General John ("Gentleman Johnny") Burgoyne, who arrived in Lake Champlain off Crown Point on June 30.

Did you know?

★ Polish engineer Tadeusz Kościuszko warned American general Arthur St. Clair of Fort Ticonderoga's vulnerability to attack, but he ignored the advice and lost the fort

★ Benedict Arnold had no official role in the American army at the time he was responsible for the victory at Saratoga

★ General Gates sat out one battle in the Saratoga campaign arguing politics with a captured British officer in his tent

"Weak in Numbers, Dispirited, Naked"

Burgoyne quickly established Crown Point as a forward base and began moving his army of over seven thousand men, British and Hessians, toward Fort Ticonderoga. The American garrisons at Ticonderoga and Fort Independence, the fort's accompanying work on the Vermont side of the lake, numbered over three thousand men, commanded by General Arthur St. Clair. Ticonderoga did not last long, as Burgoyne's artillery officers noticed that an unoccupied mountain, Mount Defiance, dominated the fort. Tadeusz Kościuszko, a young Polish engineer who was volunteering for the Patriot cause, had actually told St. Clair that Mount Defiance needed to be occupied for that very reason, but he had dismissed the advice out of hand. From Mount Defiance the British would be able to rain shells on Ticonderoga if they could wrestle artillery to the top of the mountain. They achieved this feat under cover of darkness during the night of July 4–5, and St. Clair was forced to evacuate the next night in a panic. Burgoyne took Fort Independence the following day, gladly seizing the fifty cannon that St. Clair had left. St. Clair's army straggled out, in General Schuyler's words, "weak in Numbers, dispirited, naked… destitute of provision…. with little Ammunition, and not a single piece of Cannon."

Other defeats soon followed. A British advance under Brigadier General Simon Fraser caught up with the American rearguard at Hubbardton,

An Officer and a Gentleman

Traditional depictions of British general John Burgoyne portray him as "Gentleman Johnny," a braggadocios womanizer who endangered his column by bringing along his mistress and her four cartloads of belongings. But according to new research into Burgoygne's papers published in Douglas Cubbison's *Burgoyne and the Saratoga Campaign*, the British commander has gotten a raw deal. Cubbison describes Burgoyne as a "consummate, dedicated, progressive officer" held in high admiration by his men, and finds no evidence that Burgoyne brought along his mistress, or that he was ill-prepared. Cubbison only admits that after the British general moved south from Lake Champlain, he failed to establish the necessary bases to support his army.

Vermont and, after a sharp engagement, was able to scatter the rear elements of the main American force. St. Clair lost forty killed, ninety wounded, and three hundred men captured, including most of the wounded. But Fraser was not without his own losses and had to remain at Hubbardton for a day to tend to his wounded. Several other rearguard fights occurred. At Skenesborough, Burgoyne was joined by over five hundred Indians, who soon made their presence felt in the Patriot backcountry.

A Book You're Not Supposed to Read

Valiant Ambition: George Washington, Benedict Arnold, and the Fate of the American Revolution by Nathaniel Philbrick (New York: Viking, 2016).

Burgoyne's Indians wreaked havoc on friend and foe alike. The day Burgoyne left Skenesborough for Fort Edward on the Hudson River, a party of Indians attacked the farm of Tory John Allen in Camden Valley, and killed and scalped his entire family. No one was safe.

Adding Indians to the mix was viewed by most Patriots as a violation of the rules of war, and militia and volunteers flocked to St. Clair's army. First the British had brought over Hessian mercenaries, and now they were enlisting Indians! It was a major mistake on Burgoyne's part, turning many who would not otherwise have supported the Patriot cause against the British. A beautiful young woman named Jane McCrea was murdered by Burgoyne's Indians, and though she was the fiancée of a Tory in Burgoyne's army, the general was unable or unwilling to punish her murderers, causing Tory support of the English to decline overnight.

Burgoyne also made a tactical mistake: he decided to march by the very poor road connecting Skenesborough to Fort Edward, rather than returning to Lake George and transporting his army by boat. General Schuyler, commander of the American Northern Department, put hundreds of woodsmen to work folling trees, thoroughly blocking the road. His men destroyed bridges, dammed creeks, and turned lowlands into swamps. They chased off livestock, set up barriers, and flooded crossings. (Washington described it as "letting the forest fight for him.") Schuyler's Fabian tactics slowed the British advance to a crawl, and they were forced to build an entirely new road for the next twenty-two miles. It took three weeks, delaying Burgoyne's arrival at Fort Edward until July 29. Even worse, Burgoyne found his army running short of supplies. The fifteen miles from Fort Edward back to his secondary base of Fort George were literally wilderness, and the movement of supplies slow and tedious. For the first time in the Revolution, the British began to confront the logistical nightmare of fighting a war three thousand miles from home in an interior inaccessible to all but mules and eagles!

General Baron Friedrich von Riedesel, in command of Burgoyne's Hessians (actually Germans from Brunswick, in this case), had noted that the areas east of Burgoyne's route were rich in horses, draft animals, and forage. He convinced Burgoyne to send out a foraging expedition composed mainly of his troops. The Germans headed east towards Bennington on August 16 but ran into John Stark's force of fifteen hundred New Hampshire militia,

The Murder of Jane McCrea

In July 1777, a Tory woman, Jane McCrea, was traveling to Ticonderoga to join her fiancé. She had stopped at a village by Fort Edward on her journey when the village was attacked by Wyandot Indians led by Wyandot Panther. Several people in the village were killed, and McCrea and another woman named Sara McNeill were captured and separated. Eventually McNeill was taken to a British camp, where she saw McCrea's scalp on an Indian. Later it was claimed that McCrea had been accidentally hit by pursuing Americans, not killed with a tomahawk. But that story didn't explain the scalping, and a 2005 exhumation of McCrea's body found that her skull was in fact missing, forever ending the debate. In any case, the killing of Jane McCrea became a rallying cry in the region. The story played no small part in attracting American militia to the Saratoga Campaign. Reportedly, McCrea's fiancé's hair turned permanently white when he heard the news of her death.

who enveloped the entire detachment, killing or capturing nearly all of them. When more Germans under Colonel Heinrich von Breymann were sent, they also came under attack from Stark's force, with assistance from Seth Warner's Vermont militiamen. Breymann managed to escape, but his regiment suffered heavy casualties. In a day, Burgoyne had lost nearly a thousand veteran troops. His Indians began to desert in large numbers, and he had a tenuous link to his supply base. A disaster was brewing.

Ultimately Burgoyne would have to capitulate. Events seemed to be conspiring against him. We have already seen how General Howe decided to attack Philadelphia, leaving any consolidation with Burgoyne's forces up to his successor, Sir Henry Clinton. Then Colonel Barry St. Leger's expedition through the Mohawk Valley to reinforce Burgoyne at Albany was defeated—partly as a result of George Washington's decision to reinforce Schuyler's command. Washington had dispatched Benedict Arnold to put some verve into the combat leadership, a step that would have a decisive effect.

The starting point of St. Leger's attack through the Mohawk Valley was Oswego, on Lake Ontario. When he left Oswego on July 25, he had about three hundred regulars, supported by four hundred Tory militia and a detachment of about a thousand Indians. St. Leger reached Fort Stanwix and began a siege. General Nicholas Herkimer, in command of the Tryon County militia, raised eight hundred Patriot troops at Fort Dayton, and started to the relief of Stanwix the day after St. Leger arrived.

Hearing of Herkimer's approach, St. Leger sent all his Indians, supported by Tory militia, to ambush the Americans near Oriskany. Herkimer

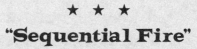

★ ★ ★
"Sequential Fire"

Herkimer noticed that as soon as a rifleman fired, an Indian would rush up to tomahawk him while he was reloading. So Herkimer put his men in two-man teams, firing in rotation. Sequential volley fire was the standard in Western armies. Some armies, including that of Gustavus Adolphus a hundred years earlier, had experimented with single volleys for more mass. But the constant outpouring of fire was psychologically difficult to sustain.

★ ★ ★

The Business of America Is Business?

Many of the better-known figures of the American Revolution were successful businessmen before the war. Benedict Arnold became a pharmacist in 1762 in New Haven, Connecticut and soon expanded his enterprises into shipping with a fleet of three ships. John Hancock, a Massachusetts merchant, had become one of the richest residents of Boston thanks to his import-export business. Obviously, farmers such as George Washington knew the business of agriculture. But no one was more successful in business than Benjamin Franklin, who had worked in publishing since a very young age. By the 1760s, Franklin was quite possibly the wealthiest man in America.

It is not surprising, then, that changes in British regulations on trade—not to mention taxes—turned many against the crown. But Benedict Arnold had a special reputation for his financial ambitions. "Money is this man's God," wrote fellow officer John Brown.

Yet there was little money in fighting, and Arnold was arguably one of America's most pugnacious generals (along with Daniel Morgan and Anthony Wayne). Money can't have been his only motivation. He must have been aiming for another prize: fame. In the end, he got infamy.

was wounded in the leg at almost the first fire, but he organized a solid all-around defense. No quarter was asked for or given, and the proportion of killed to the total engaged was enormous.

Informed that Herkimer had been ambushed, Colonel Willett, second in command of Fort Stanwix, made a sortie with 250 men, captured the Tory and Indian camps, and returned with all the supplies his men could carry—and St. Leger's papers. An hour later, the Indians at Oriskany heard the news and fled the field. Herkimer, mortally wounded, retired to Fort Dayton, leaving over a third of his command dead on the field.

Informed that Herkimer's relief had failed and that St. Leger was still besieging Fort Stanwix, General Schuyler asked for a volunteer to head a new relief force. Benedict Arnold, ever ready for military glory, volunteered.

Schuyler sent him with eight hundred volunteers. The cagey Arnold sent several "deserters" to the British with exaggerated estimates of the size of the relief force, and St. Leger's Indians deserted in a body. St. Leger fled back to Canada, while his Indians ritually murdered their captives before returning to their home territory.

The loss of Ticonderoga without a battle had severely shaken Congress, and on August 19 General Horatio Gates arrived in Albany to take command of the Northern Department from Schuyler. One administrator—excellent at slow-down tactics, no doubt—was replaced with another administrator. But at least Gates would pitch his tent somewhere near the battlefield. Gates also raised American hopes, probably a more significant factor than the change in generalship.

When Gates took over from Schuyler, he found the army scattered between Arnold's command at Fort Stanwix and Stark's command at Bennington, Vermont. Arnold hurried back to Albany, and Gates put him in charge of the army's left wing. Apparently on his own initiative, Arnold took the Polish engineer Tadeusz Kościuszko with him to build defensive works. They selected Bemis Heights, about six miles in front of Gates's camp at Saratoga, as the best position, and Arnold assigned a large detachment to build the necessary works under the Pole's direction. As the news of St. Leger's retreat and the dissolution of the Indian forces spread, the Patriot army's size swelled to nine thousand men. Gates took the right wing along the Hudson River, while Arnold defended the hills on the left.

The Battle of Freeman's Farm

Meanwhile, oblivious to St. Leger's plight and still expecting that supporting troops were coming northward from New York City, Burgoyne struggled down the Hudson. Enduring bad roads, bad weather, and constant harassment, he did not approach the American works on Bemis Heights until September 19.

★ ★ ★
Gates vs. Arnold

There was no love lost between American generals Benedict Arnold and Horatio Gates. The latter was in command of the Continental forces at Saratoga, and Arnold was his putative subordinate. Gates was not happy to have another prima donna in his army, but for a time he retained Arnold because of his combat reputation. In the Battle of Freeman's Farm on September 19, Arnold took charge of the fighting while Gates remained in his tent.

All that time his men were consuming supplies and rations; Burgoyne would have to attack soon, or decide to retreat. Viewing the American position, he resolved to attack it at three points: he would send General Fraser around on the British right to flank the Patriot works on the hills, attack the center with his main force, and demonstrate along the Hudson on his left. His preparations for the attack were easily visible from the American entrenchments on Bemis Heights, but Gates did nothing. After an hour, Arnold finally received permission to send Morgan's riflemen to attack Burgoyne's Canadians and Indians, who were spearheading Fraser's attack on the far left of the American line.

Morgan's men attacked with such fury that the Canadians and Indians were forced back on Fraser's main force, which became disorganized and suffered heavy casualties. Without waiting for further orders, Arnold brought up the remainder of his wing and led the assault on Fraser in person. The fighting continued at close quarters for several hours, and Arnold requested reinforcements to finish off Fraser. Gates refused, fearing he might leave his camp too lightly defended. British and Hessian generals William Phillips and Friedrich Riedesel, in position along the Hudson, saw that Gates did not advance and marched to the support of Fraser. Soon most of the British army was slugging it out with the troops led by Arnold, who held his ground until sunset before retiring in perfect order. Losses on the American side in what became known as the Battle of Freeman's Farm, were 319 in killed, wounded, and missing, while the British lost more than five hundred. The outnumbered Americans had outfought the professional British in a standup battle. It was a bad omen for Burgoyne.

The Battle of Bemis Heights

It was also bad for Arnold in terms of his relationship with Gates, who became intensely jealous of Arnold's battlefield success, something Gates himself had never experienced. Gates purposely omitted Arnold's name from his reports to Congress and to Washington, and Gates's aide, the odious and devious James Wilkinson, actually spread reports that Arnold had not even been on the field. The bad blood between the two generals only became worse as Arnold's staff, consisting of General Schuyler's old officers and aides who had been ill-treated by Gates, expressed contempt for Gates at every opportunity. With his position becoming more difficult by the hour, Arnold applied to leave the army, and Gates promptly approved his request. When Arnold was besieged by officers and troops begging him to stay and asked to retain his command after all, Gates refused this request. So when the Battle of Bemis Heights occurred on October 7, Arnold had no official function in the army. Nevertheless, Arnold would shoot out of his tent without orders and take control of a Patriot brigade, and other men soon followed him. Though wounded in the leg, he would lead the troops to drive the British from their critical position, adding to his reputation.

During all the bickering among the American command, British troops under General Clinton had taken the Hudson River Highlands forts, and there was nothing between them and Gates. But Clinton did not want to be far from New York City, and would not be advancing northward. Burgoyne now knew he was on his own, and his situation was becoming desperate. On October 3, he put his army on half rations.

Four days later, on October 7, Burgoyne attempted a reconnaissance in force with fifteen hundred regulars and six cannon to turn the American left. The movement was detected, and Gates sent Morgan's riflemen to attack the right wing of Burgoyne's attack force. Arnold argued vehemently that more force was needed. Gates peremptorily dismissed him, but nonetheless added new troops to Morgan's assault. Without orders, Arnold jumped into

the fight and led an attack against Breymann's redoubt, which had been constructed since they arrived, carrying the position and killing Breymann. It was the first time that an American force had taken British entrenchments by storm. Arnold had won the day. The Americans had suffered 150 men in killed and wounded, including Arnold, and the British over 800. (Gates had not left his tent; he spent most of the day arguing the merits of the Revolution with a captured aide of Burgoyne's.) Now, not only were the British failing to defeat American forces in standup battles, their casualty lists were growing so rapidly that Burgoyne might not have a force left at all. His supplies were nearly exhausted, and more American militia were arriving every minute.

The "Convention"

Retreating northward was not feasible, and Burgoyne had no choice but to open surrender negotiations. Protracted discussions began but without urgency, as Burgoyne still harbored the belief that since Clinton had taken the two Hudson Valley forts, help might somehow arrive in time to save his army. Finally Gates acceded to nearly all of Burgoyne's demands, and the "Articles of Convention"—not a "surrender"—were signed. A total of 5,763 officers and enlisted men laid down their arms on October 17.

Not surprisingly, Burgoyne had outwitted Gates. By the terms of the "Convention," the troops were not prisoners of war, and not subject to the normal rules. The Articles of Convention stated that Burgoyne's troops were to march out with the honors of war and lay down their arms on the command of their own officers. Then they were to march to Boston and sail to

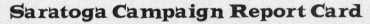

★ ★ ★
Saratoga Campaign Report Card

The British

General Burgoyne: F
He lost his army.

Sir Henry Clinton: F
Apparently unable to function more than a day's march from the Royal Navy, he refused to save Burgoyne.

The Americans

Arthur St. Clair: F
Although held in high esteem by other officers, St. Clair was perhaps the worst commander in the American army, unable to make reasonable decisions—as when he refused to take Kościuszko's advice and occupy Mount Defiance.

Philip Schuyler: F
Ineffective in command, Schuyler lost the confidence of the men he led and that of Congress.

Horatio Gates: F
The only thing worse than his actual performance would have been if he had acted as a real commander in the battles—he might well have lost them.

Benedict Arnold: A
He was the battlefield commander the Americans needed.

Daniel Morgan: A
An outstanding performance.

George Washington: B
While not directly involved in the battles, Washington perceived the danger a multipronged advance posed and saw an opportunity to strike a serious blow against a foe who was far removed from his line of supply. His dispatch of additional troops—and the aggressive Arnold—was decisive.

England on the condition of not serving again in North America unless properly exchanged. Somehow Gates had not grasped that the troops could perform garrison duties elsewhere, immediately freeing up a like number of British or German troops to take their places in America. Washington saw this defect immediately, and the "Convention" became a matter of dispute. The upshot of the deal Burgoyne had engineered was that his troops, called the "Convention Army," were marched to locations including Lancaster, Pennsylvania, and Charlottesville, Virginia, and parceled out to farmers as laborers to help compensate for Patriot losses. By the end of the war most of the officers had been exchanged, and many enlisted men—particularly the Brunswickers—had been allowed to "escape" and settle on farms in western Virginia and Pennsylvania, often marrying into Patriot or Quaker families. British and German desertions in general increased as the war went along.

British incompetence in the Saratoga Campaign had provided opportunities, seized upon by relentless American leaders—including a commander who technically was not even in the army—to give the Patriots their most decisive victory yet. But it had been a near-run thing: Gates had almost given away the fruits of the victory through his incompetence.

CHAPTER 11

The Devil's Anvil: From Valley Forge to Monmouth

Valley Forge. The very name means extreme hardship and persever-
ance. More than any success in battle, the survival of Washington's
army at Valley Forge epitomized the Patriots' will to win the war. But in
addition to the well-known hardships suffered by the troops, three other
developments during Washington's 1777–78 encampment in winter quarters
also shaped the Revolution: the Conway Cabal, the transformation of Quakers from neutrals to Tories, and Baron von Steuben's training of the American troops.

The winter of 1777–78—when Washington's troops were at Valley Forge—
was actually one of the mildest winters in years. But it was still winter in
Pennsylvania! Even at its best, a Pennsylvania winter is difficult, and the
three thousand men who first arrived at Valley Forge were hardly in good
shape. They had no coats or blankets, in many cases no shoes, and many
were practically starving. Typhus was rampant.

As soon as the troops arrived at Valley Forge, they set to work like a "family of Beavers" according to Thomas Paine, erecting "a Curious Collection
of Buildings in the true rustic order." And why not? As historian John
Ferling points out…. they were in a massive forest! There was no want of

Did you know?

★ The Valley Forge
winter of 1777–78
was actually one
of the warmest in
years

★ "Neutral" Quak-
ers traded with the
British but not with
the Patriots

★ Friedrich William
Baron von Steuben
exaggerated both
his military experi-
ence and his noble
rank—but his pro-
fessionalization of
the American army
was genuine

A Book You're Not Supposed to Read

Valley Forge: George Washington and the Crucible of Victory by Newt Gingrich and William R. Forstchen (New York: St. Martin's, 2011). This is a historical novel, but one that offers great insight into the winter at Valley Forge.

lumber or logs for fires, hut construction, and basic wooden implements. The troops assembled 14 x 16–foot huts to accommodate every twelve enlisted men, while officers had less crowded accommodations. Once the leaky, poorly ventilated shelters were built, at least there was some respite from the cold. A steady stream of men followed the first arrivals into Valley Forge, but large numbers of them perished.

Washington, alert to the danger that he could lose the army altogether, actively involved himself in procuring food and other supplies. He dispatched officers to locate specifically needed items, dispatched teams to drive cattle to camp, and sent out foraging parties of up to a thousand men. General Greene thought Washington acted like a "Pharaoh" in stripping the countryside, but admitted it was necessary to save the Continental Army. The Marquis de Lafayette, the young French officer and nobleman who had come to America to fight for the Revolution and who served as one of Washington's generals, said that no European army could have suffered what the Americans endured at Valley Forge and still survived.

The Conway Cabal

But the weather wasn't the only danger Washington faced that winter. In early autumn of 1777 Thomas Conway—a French army officer who had come to the United States to earn fame and fortune—decided that George Washington was not an effective general. Conway began working to make Horatio Gates, the victor of Saratoga, commander-in-chief of the army. Gates readily conspired with men like Conway to further his own career, and others sniped at Washington for their own reasons. Dr. Benjamin Rush, General Thomas Mifflin, and several members of Congress joined in the chorus. No doubt General Charles Lee would have been up to his eyebrows in the cabal, except it was hard for him to conspire from a British prison!

Rush's criticism of Washington in a letter he wrote to Patrick Henry was typical of what was being said: "The northern army has shown us what Americans are capable of doing with a GENERAL at their head. The spirit of the southern army is no ways inferior to the spirit of the northern. A Gates, a Lee, or a Conway would in a few weeks render them an irresistible body of men." Rush quoted General John Sullivan on Conway, who had performed well at Brandywine, his only battle in a Continental uniform: "His regulations in his Brigade are much better than any in the Army, and his knowledge of military matters far exceeds any officer we have." The Rush letter also included critical remarks on Washington's performance from Conway, who had told Gates, "Heaven has determined to save your Country, or a weak General and bad Counselors would have ruined it." Patrick Henry forwarded the letter to Washington, and it ruined Rush's career.

Conway had written to Congress requesting promotion to major general and disparaged Washington with comments such as, "as to his (Washington's) talents for the command of an Army, they were miserable indeed." But when his campaign against Washington was exposed, Conway hastily retreated, blaming everyone around him. He offered his resignation to Congress, and it was sent on to the Board of War, where Conway's friend Thomas Mifflin—another conspirator against Washington—stalled any action. Meanwhile Congress promoted Conway to major general and made him inspector general of the army, in which position he devoted himself to preparing training manual materials on maneuvers and tactics. He served alongside Washington at Valley Forge but reported only to the Board of War—actually functioning as a spy for the board, whose president was…General Gates.

Conway's relationship with Washington continued to deteriorate, and in January 1778 Conway and Gates were called before Congress to clear their names. They failed miserably; Congress supported Washington.

The "Neutral" Quakers (and the Culper Ring)

The second major development during the winter at Valley Forge involved the Quakers. Up until the winter of 1777–78, they were regarded as neutrals. Their pacifism would not allow them to serve in the Patriot army. And yet they had provided guides for Howe and his army. Then, during the winter of Valley Forge, they flouted the Association by actively trading with Howe in Philadelphia. Even worse, they refused to trade with the Continental Army because of the declining value of Continental currency, whereas the British could pay in gold. The Quakers were effectively no longer neutral—their self-interested dealings with the British turned the opinion of the American public in general against them. Philadelphia, the most populous city in the colonies, would remain important for another twenty years on account of its central location, but it was marginalized politically thereafter.

But one Quaker—or "half-Quaker"—would play an important role in support of the Patriot cause. Robert Townsend, alias Samuel Culper Jr., was one of two secret agents (the other was Abraham Woodhull, a.k.a. Samuel Culper Sr.) after whom Washington's "Culper Ring" spy network is named.

Espionage and intelligence gathering were significant factors in the war. At first both the British and the Americans had mostly relied on traditional scouting by cavalry units for their military intelligence. But Washington would begin developing his own spy ring as early as August 1778, when he received a letter from Caleb Brewster, a lieutenant in Connecticut, offering to report on enemy actions. After several accurate reports from Brewster, Washington assigned General Charles Scott to supervise him and recruit other spies. Major Benjamin Talmadge was Scott's subordinate, but he eventually took over most of the work and was made head of the spy ring by Washington. The name Culper was an abbreviation of Culpeper County in Virginia, where Washington had worked as a surveyor in his youth.

A Book You're Not Supposed to Read

Washington's Spies: The Story of America's First Spy Ring by Alexander Rose (New York: Bantam, 2007).

Although vastly romanticized and enhanced on American television, Washington's spies gave him good service. One of the earliest American secret agents, Nathan Hale, was unsuitable and easily compromised, but thereafter, Washington's men gave the British fits. Caleb Brewster in particular provided excellent assessments of the strength and location of British units, even adding his own analysis of new boatbuilding by Tories. Townsend was also especially helpful on account of his position as an innkeeper inside New York City. Even Washington did not know the names of most of the operatives and the team used intricate variations on European code techniques that were extremely difficult to break, even for experienced code breakers.

While the Culper Ring would produce no major coups—nothing equivalent to showing that the Japanese navy was about to invade Midway in 1942, for example—neither did it have any disastrous lapses. The identity of Robert Townsend as Samuel Culper Jr. was secret until 1929, and the general public remained unaware of the Ring's activities until the 1930s—a coup in itself. Whereas the British didn't make much use of such clandestine operations—Howe was still largely wedded to cavalry reconnaissance—Washington so desperately needed intelligence that he resorted to other methods.

A Professional Army

A third major development during the winter at Valley Forge was the molding of the citizen army into a well-trained body of troops able to consistently stand up to European professionals. This came about through the efforts of Frederick William Baron Steuben. (Steuben was something of an imposter, claiming to be a lieutenant general in the army of Frederick the Great of Prussia, while in reality he was a lowly captain without prospects. He also claimed to have a European estate but did not, and he was deeply in debt. Nor was he a true aristocrat—he didn't have a "von" in his name, and he had the title of "baron" from being a chamberlain at the court of the Hohenzollerns.) Nevertheless, he favorably impressed Benjamin Franklin, Congress, and Washington, and soon rose to become one of Washington's most trusted officers. His American career was particularly remarkable since he spoke virtually no English—except to curse efficiently—and had to work through interpreters.

Steuben immediately noted the sad condition of the army, the lack of discipline, and the ignorance—in all ranks—about drill standards, regulations, tactics, and maneuvering in formation on command. It seemed that the only battle commands the Americans understood were "get into a line abreast" and "get into a column of fours." He recommended to Washington that he form an elite unit that would become the model training company for the entire army. Washington immediately approved the idea and issued the following general order on March 17, 1778: "One hundred men are to be annexed to the Guard of the Commander-in-Chief, for the purpose of forming a corps to be instructed in the maneuvers necessary to be introduced in the army and serve as a model for the execution of them. As the General's Guard is composed entirely of Virginians, the one hundred draughts are to be taken from the troops of the other states."

Washington also used Steuben as a de facto inspector general in place of the despised Thomas Conway. Steuben went out into the camp to talk with the officers and men, inspect their huts, and scrutinize their equipment. Everything was wrong, and it was a question of what to tackle first. Steuben decided the first order of business was to have healthy soldiers.

He established standards of sanitation, bringing order and improving the health of the troops. Kitchens and latrines were moved to opposite sides of the camp, with latrines downhill from kitchens and away from sources of water. Some of Steuben's success came merely from the end of the winter. As the severe cold weather abated, foraging parties finally started to find food and game.

Steuben wrote out the drills in French, and as he wrote they were translated into English by a secretary to produce a full training program. A man far ahead of his time, Steuben introduced a formal system of military instruction, beginning with basic training for an individual soldier without arms; then with arms, muskets, and bayonets; then in small units; then companies; and finally in regiments and brigades. Company commanders were made the chief trainers, with instruction and repetition on the parade field the purview of sergeants. This was revolutionary in 1778 America. During the winter of 1778–79, Steuben prepared his *Regulations for the Order and Discipline of the Troops of the United States* using the training plan he had devised at Valley Forge. Now the American army could do things "by the book" like a real professional army.

Steuben began drilling the model company on March 19 with twice-a-day drills. He set an example for all ranks by taking a musket himself to show the men proper weapon handling. He amused the men and onlookers constantly with his colorful curses delivered in a number of languages and soon became well liked for his readiness to relate to the men. He taught them how to march, form in column, deploy into various formations for combat, and execute various maneuvers necessary to meet changing conditions on the battlefield.

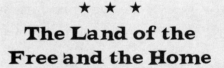

★ ★ ★

The Land of the Free and the Home of the Brave

Steuben found that Americans were a different sort of soldier than Europeans. He wrote to one European officer that in the Prussian army he would tell soldiers to do something and they would do it, but in the American army he needed to tell the soldiers why they needed to do something before they would do it.

A Book You're Not Supposed to Read

The Drillmaster of Valley Forge: The Baron de Steuben and the Making of the American Army by Paul Lockhart (New York: Harper, 2010).

By April Steuben was confident enough to put on an exhibition drill for general officers. By all accounts the exhibition was an astounding success, and the Guard spent the next six weeks demonstrating and teaching the drills and maneuvers throughout the army. Steuben's maneuver techniques, using columns for movement and line formations for fighting, were simple but efficient. Skirmishers covered the columns while marching, and then moved through gaps in the line to re-form behind as reserves. Volley fire was achieved through strict manual-of-arms training, and all units were taught effective techniques for bayonet use.

The first action involving the newly trained Guard took place on May 18 when Washington detailed over a hundred men from his Guard to General Lafayette to safeguard his person while performing a reconnaissance in force towards Philadelphia. Lafayette was to interdict any British foraging parties he might encounter. With the winter thaw, Washington was beginning new probes of British positions. Lafayette moved his detachment of twenty-four hundred men midway between Valley Forge and Philadelphia and took up a position near Barren Hill Church. General Clinton, who had replaced Howe as the British commander-in-chief, immediately sent out a substantial force in three columns to bag Lafayette. The young Frenchman was almost trapped, but after skillful maneuvering for two days he managed to extricate his command and return safely to Valley Forge with minimal losses. Steuben's new maneuvering capabilities had proven themselves almost immediately, for only a well-disciplined army could have turned itself around so many times.

In June, Clinton evacuated Philadelphia and began crossing the Delaware with about ten thousand effectives, slowed by an additional three thousand

Tory civilians—men, women, and children from Philadelphia who dared not remain when the city was re-occupied by the Patriots. A train of fifteen hundred wagons stretching for twelve miles substantially slowed Clinton's progress. Washington saw an opportunity, and he ordered his army to pursue. With Clinton moving slowly to protect the British wagon train, Washington stood a good chance of intercepting Clinton's force—if the Continental Army marched with dispatch.

On June 23, Washington detailed eighty of his Steuben-trained Guard to Daniel Morgan's Rifle Regiment of six hundred men "to take the most effectual means of gaining the enemy's right flank and giving them as much annoyance as possible in that quarter." Morgan immediately set out on a long march across Clinton's front to harass him. Washington had assigned the Guard to Morgan based on recent experience, when Morgan's men had faced British light infantry who charged them with bayonets. Although skilled marksmen, Morgan's men had a slow rate of fire and no bayonets themselves, and they were routed. Washington reasoned that sprinkling regular troops trained with bayonets liberally among the riflemen would stiffen their resolve substantially. This was the same "learning curve" that the Europeans had taken over one hundred years to master, experimenting with pikemen and bowmen, then pikemen and muskets. Washington picked it up in less than two years.

Lafayette's vanguard was camped at Cranbury, fifteen miles northwest of Clinton's camp at Allentown, New Jersey, and squarely athwart Clinton's route. Clinton abandoned all thought of heading toward New York over a land route and turned to the northeast toward Monmouth Courthouse, taking his main army away from Washington. The Patriots had to make a forced night march back to Monmouth Courthouse. Soon, the van of Washington's force was within five miles of the British camp and was threatening Clinton's army strung out along its route of march. If Washington could gather together a solid striking force, Clinton's army could be attacked and defeated.

After severe thunderstorms on the night of June 26–27, 1778, both main armies rested. Even with the rain, an oppressive heat set in (105 degrees plus humidity), but Washington had to move. He sent General Charles Lee (who had been returned in a prisoner exchange) to attack Clinton's rear, keeping another 8,000 men to attack when he deemed it prudent.

"We Cannot Stand Against Them"

Hearing the initial skirmishing, Clinton immediately ordered Cornwallis to deploy the entire rearguard, and he reversed the march of the main army. Even before the main body of the British army appeared, Lee had lost his nerve, telling Lafayette, who wanted to attack, "Sir, you do not know British soldiers; we cannot stand against them; we shall certainly be driven back at first and we must be cautious." Lee began a cautious withdrawal, and with the numbers on both sides now about equal, he effectively surrendered control of the battle to the British.

At that point Washington, having heard reports that the army was beaten, rode forward. In a famous scene, Washington cursed Lee out in the presence of others, then relieved the general. He immediately halted the retreat, hustled up reinforcements—inspiring the troops by his very presence—and turned the army around to again face the British. The Patriots repelled all British assaults in the great heat, forcing the British to retire at the end of the day. A defeat was avoided, but the great opportunity for a smashing victory had been squandered, once again by poor leadership from one of Washington's subordinates.

Clinton withdrew, reaching Sandy Hook on July 1 and boarding ships for New York City. Washington, barely able to control his temper over Lee's incompetence, took up watching positions at White Plains as the British settled into a comfortable base.

★ ★ ★
Battle of Monmouth Report Card

The British

Sir Henry Clinton: A

He kept his army well in hand, and was able to reach New York with minimal casualties.

The Americans

George Washington: B

He should not have made Lee commander of the attack, but he redeemed himself by saving the army from defeat.

Charles Lee: F

He nearly brought about a disastrous defeat single-handedly, by ordering a retreat at the first opportunity—more evidence that Lee was a traitor, having been turned during his captivity.

Charles Lee was subjected to a court martial on July 2, 1778, on three charges: disobedience of orders; misbehavior before the enemy; and disrespect to the commander-in-chief. He was found guilty and relieved of command. He lobbied Congress to overturn the verdict, but found little sympathy for his position. He then made a series of written and oral attacks on Washington that alienated most of his supporters and caused him to be challenged to a number of duels. In one, Colonel John Laurens, an aide to Washington, wounded Lee, who then withdrew from public life in disgrace.

CHAPTER 12

Mes Amis!
The Treaty of Alliance
with France

It was often said during the Vietnam era that, "no one interfered in our Revolution." In fact, America had a great deal of help. One of George Washington's first acts after being appointed commander-in-chief of the Continental Army was to dispatch emissaries to secure non-aggression treaties with the various Indian tribes. In most cases, they were successful. Holland soon enforced an "armed neutrality" in which Dutch ships would fire at English vessels seeking to board them. Eventually Holland declared war on Great Britain. Spain actively aided the U.S. in the Mississippi Valley, defeating the British at the Battle of St. Louis, and supplying lead for bullets and other munitions.

But of course, the most significant foreign help came from France, England's traditional bitter enemy and the most likely ally the Patriots could hope to find. Still stinging from the loss to England in the Seven Years' War (the French and Indian War in America), France was looking for any opportunity to retaliate. On the other hand, the French had been burned once in North America, and were cautious. And given the early track record of the Patriot armies, the colonists did not appear to be very formidable potential allies. Still, Benjamin Franklin, John Adams, and Thomas Paine all hoped

Did you know?

★ The buckskins and beaver hat Benjamin Franklin wore in France shocked John Adams—but wowed the French

★ Lafayette was only nineteen when he came to America to fight for the Revolution

★ Fighting for America, the French Navy miraculously defeated the British at the Battle of the Chesapeake—then went on a long losing streak against the British Navy

★ ★ ★

Franklin in France

Six months after the signing of the Declaration of Independence, the Continental Congress sent Philadelphia's Benjamin Franklin to Europe as the American commissioner to France. His immediate objective was to win support in the form of French funds and weapons, but the larger goal was to obtain a treaty of alliance and bring the French into the war. Franklin, accompanied by his sixteen-year-old grandson, stayed at a home donated to him by a French supporter of the American Revolution. He hobnobbed with the cream of French society, including intellectuals such as the Comte de Mirabeau, who would later play a central role in France's own revolution. Franklin realized that successful diplomacy would depend on appealing to the French elites' admiration for American values and customs as much as anything. Hence he wore colonial buckskins and a beaver hat, dressing like anything but a diplomat. When John Adams joined him in 1778, the proper diplomat was shocked at Franklin's dress and demeanor, but quickly realized that Franklin was precisely who the French wanted him to be. It is unlikely that any ordinary diplomat would have achieved what Franklin, with his keen insight into human responses, gained: an alliance.

to convince France to help. And some French advisors actually thought a joint Franco-Spanish invasion of England would be possible—an idea that was wisely abandoned.

One thing the young nation might have to offer France and Spain was commerce, and John Adams drafted a model treaty that emphasized trade. The British had just lost over six million pounds of export trade to the United States through the Association; every dime of that and more could now be France's.

But that wasn't the only reason an alliance between France and America made sense. The U.S. had manpower and the commitment to defeat Great Britain, but no military supplies, and most importantly, no navy. By helping the Americans, France could achieve great things against its traditional enemy, Great Britain, at relatively low cost. In the end, the assistance to

America would cost France more than it could pay, but that was not foreseen at the time. And on top of the financial burden, America could and did—quite innocently—export the concept of individual liberty to France, causing a gigantic upheaval.

The initial negotiations were mainly over acquiring a loan from France, and an agreement that neither side would make a separate peace with England. But the French would not loosen the purse strings until they could

★ ★ ★

One of These Revolutions Is Not Like the Other

Edmund Burke, in his great speech in the House of Commons on March 22, 1775, elucidated six aspects of what would come to be called American Exceptionalism: the Americans' descent from freedom-loving English; their popular form of government; their Protestant religion; the influence of slave-holding in the South on the concept of property; the widespread legal education throughout the colonies; and the feeling of separateness from the mother country due to distance. What is striking about these observations is that they were made 240 years ago, yet they are as relevant today as they were then. These unique elements, which formed Americans' understanding of individual liberty, were simply not applicable to France. But the French took no notice. France would fall victim to the siren call of American ideas, lacking the cultural, religious, and political structures to under-stand what they meant. The result was the violent and destructive French Revolution.

When it came time to send a commission to France, Congress wanted Thomas Jefferson. But he refused, citing a sick wife who needed his attention. So in addition to Franklin, Congress named Arthur Lee, already in Europe on business, and Silas Deane (whom no one trusted—Deane was suspected of lining his own pockets with French aid intended for America, and worse, though Franklin did not know that—for good cause, it turned out). Franklin captured the hearts of the French people with his backwoods attire, his homespun humor, his common-sense philosophy, and his womanizing in the best salons in Paris. The joke was that Franklin won over half of France: the female half. Not bad for a widower in his seventies.

★ ★ ★
The Marquis de Lafayette: Epitome of French Support

No one person better exemplifies the French friendship with America than Gilbert du Motier, the Marquis de Lafayette. An aristocrat from southern France, Lafayette became an army officer at an early age. Traveling to America to join the war at age nineteen, he was given the rank of major general but no actual troops to command. He was wounded at the battle of Brandywine, and Washington carefully schooled him in the military arts, until at Valley Forge he was given an expedition to command. Lafayette departed America after the Battle of Rhode Island in August 1778, sailing back to France to help secure more aid to the colonies. His influence in Paris was decisive in gaining loans that kept the Continental Army in the field. Lafayette returned to America and in 1781 Washington gave him a senior command in Virginia. He acquitted himself well and was present at the siege of Yorktown. He not only saw America become a republic, but also witnessed his native country overthrow the shackles of King Louis XVI—although weaknesses in French political culture led to the collapse of the First Republic. In a time when the slightest comment could land a French citizen at the guillotine, Lafayette, the "adopted son" of Washington, survived the Republic, the Empire of Napoleon Bonaparte, the Restoration, and the Second Republic, and died in 1834.

be sure the Revolution had a chance. They were unmoved by Washington's victory at Trenton and disillusioned when Howe took Philadelphia.

But Saratoga turned the tide. Within days of the news of General John Burgoyne's defeat, French Foreign Minister Charles Gravier, Comte de Vergennes, notified the commissioners that he was ready to extend loans to the U.S. in specie; send military aid in the form of muskets, cannons, powder, and critically needed military supplies; and even discuss an alliance. On December 17, 1777, France agreed to recognize the United States and enter into an alliance. The catch was that Spain must also join, and the Spanish balked at a formal alliance. Spain was vulnerable to British sea power in the Western Hemisphere, with a lot to lose. But Vergennes saw the value of going it alone, and by February 1778, a treaty of friendship was signed. American vessels would be allowed into French West Indian ports on a most-favored nation basis, both parties agreed to refrain from making a separate peace, and France promised not to seek any claim to English territory in North America. (Having evicted France once, as British Americans, the Patriots did not want to have to do it again.) In May 1778 Congress approved the treaty, and the next month France joined the war against England.

To France, the American Revolution was merely one front in its war with England. Originally, the French considered landing 40,000 troops in the British Isles; they also debated operations out of the West Indies. The first large-scale landing of French troops was at Savannah in September 1779, to retake the city, which had been lost earlier to the British. Later, the Count de Rochambeau brought in an additional six thousand troops at Newport.

But the most significant battle involving France occurred at sea: the Battle of the Chesapeake in September 1781, which led to the French blockading Cornwallis's army in Yorktown. This French victory was, well, "miraculous." The British would go on to have a long record of defeating the French at sea, most notably at Aboukir Bay, in the 1798 Battle of the Nile, and then at Trafalgar in 1805. It is remarkable that France's greatest naval victory in the eighteenth and nineteenth centuries came…when fighting for the United States.

CHAPTER 13

The Forgotten War

Why do we remember what we remember about the Revolutionary War? Some events—such as Saratoga and Trenton—are memorable for their decisive outcomes. Others? There were many Tea Parties, yet it is the *Boston* Tea Party that is remembered. Patriots and Redcoats fought numerous engagements on land and sea in the pivotal years of the Revolution, and many of them have disappeared into the darkness of history. Probably the best example is George Rogers Clark's stunningly successful expedition to the Mississippi, culminating in the taking of Vincennes. Even though it was arguably the only reason the British gave up the Old Northwest at the Treaty of Paris, Clark's tour de force is not just forgotten—it has been nearly expunged from history. Other than abortive attempts to conquer Canada and Florida, Clark's expedition was the only one mounted by the Patriots to secure additional territory—and the only successful one. But there are many other Revolutionary War battles and even whole campaigns that have faded from history.

Did you know?

★ Until he committed treason, Benedict Arnold was the biggest American hero of the Revolution

★ George Rogers Clark was the only Revolutionary War general who actually conquered new territory for America

★ The original American Navy, under John Paul Jones, had a total of five ships

The Battle of Rhode Island

The Howe brothers would both leave America during 1778—General William Howe after being replaced by General Clinton in May, and Admiral Richard Howe in September after he resigned his command. By that time France had come into the war on the American side, with the result that the Royal Navy was no longer undisputed mistress of the sea. Charles Hector, Comte d'Estaing, was sent to assist the Americans in April 1778, with orders to blockade the British fleet, still believed to be below Philadelphia on the Delaware River. By the time d'Estaing arrived in July, the British had returned from the Philadelphia campaign and were occupying Newport and Aquidneck Island. These looked ripe for an American attack, particularly with the French Navy assisting. Major General John Sullivan was sent to take command of Patriot forces in Rhode Island in March of 1778, and he gathered troops and supplies in fits and starts. Washington reinforced Sullivan with two brigades of Continentals under the command of the French Marquis de Lafayette in July. Large numbers of militia from Rhode Island, Connecticut, Massachusetts, and New Hampshire were gathered by local Association committees, and soon Sullivan's force outnumbered British Major General Sir Robert Pigot's six to seven hundred troops at Newport.

D'Estaing sailed around Long Island and arrived at Point Judith on July 29. There he conferred with generals Lafayette and Sullivan. The resulting plan was to attack the British base at Newport, and by August 9, d'Estaing's fleet had moved up the channel to Newport harbor. Outnumbered, the British ships at Newport were sunk, or set afire by their own crews to avoid capture. Meanwhile the main British fleet under Howe had arrived at Point Judith.

A battle between d'Estaing's and Howe's forces was imminent, but as the two fleets put out to sea and maneuvered to gain an advantage, a violent storm broke out, scattering ships and inflicting major damage on both sides. It took the French until August 20 to regroup and return to Rhode Island, at which point d'Estaing informed Sullivan that he would not be able to assist the Americans in capturing Newport; he sailed for Boston to make repairs two days later.

Without French support, much of the recently raised American militia immediately decamped. Upon receiving intelligence from Washington that Clinton was assembling a relief force for Newport, Sullivan withdrew and took up defensive positions, including at a stone wall over Quaker Hill.

Pigot attacked on August 29. As the British encountered the strength of the American position on their right under John Glover, the attack there stalled. On the left, the Hessians pushed the American forward units up Turkey Hill and back into Nathanael Greene's lines, and then the Royal Navy commenced a cannonade of Greene's positions. But the Americans beat back a second Hessian attack. Sullivan duly became irresolute and withdrew to Tiverton and Bristol the following day. The battle was a British victory in that the Americans withdrew from besieging Newport, but the British had lost 260 men to the Americans' 210. For Rhode Islanders, the battle was a disaster. The British would remain another year in Newport before returning to New York City in October 1779—leaving behind a devastated Rhode Island.

Guerrilla War

Although the French Navy had an inauspicious start in the American conflict, France's entry into the war had another side benefit that generally goes unnoticed. Sir Henry Clinton was ordered to send five thousand of his troops to the West Indies (where England perceived a weakness in its defenses), and the Royal Navy also shifted major units to the Caribbean to confront the French. These redeployments significantly affected the British ability to conduct offensive operations in America. Losing control of the Caribbean would be an economic disaster for England, so battling the Patriots became

★ ★ ★

Never Completely Recovered

Arnold had been wounded twice in his left leg, once at Quebec and once at Saratoga, and he barely fought off the doctors who had wanted to amputate. The leg was saved, but it healed badly. His femur had been shattered, and the wounded leg healed almost two inches shorter than the other. Arnold remained a cripple for life, and in May 1778 when he became the military governor of Philadelphia, he still could not stand without a crutch. Even at West Point he needed a cane to get around.

a secondary mission. For the remainder of the war, Clinton would receive no major reinforcements. Clinton would not risk his troops more than was absolutely necessary, confining himself to raids and subversion. The British may have lost America with this strategy, but the British West Indies remained safe.

Until Washington left the New York area for Yorktown in 1781, Clinton and Washington devoted significant efforts to spying on each other. And the covert war frequently bubbled to the surface in partisan raids by each side, with the Tories referring to themselves as "Cowboys" and calling Patriot bands "Skinners." To be captured by either side usually meant death. This was a war without mercy; these "Cowboys" and "Skinners" weren't much more than hooligans. The battleground was Long Island, southern Connecticut, the lower Hudson Valley, and northern New Jersey. Hundreds, then thousands died in the daily skirmishes, ambushes, and outright guerrilla warfare, and these casualties have never shown up in scholarly treatises of the war's battle deaths. By 1783, Long Island was a barren land, plundered repeatedly by the British and Tories for supplies, regardless of which side the farmers or landowners were on.

Long Island Sound was the site of continual raids by boat, commonly called the "whaleboat wars." Named for the fast thirty-foot-long boats used for hunting whales, the whaleboat wars originated with the 1776 Letters of Marque that the governors of Connecticut, Rhode Island, and New York issued to various captains in Long Island Sound. They were to prey on Tory and British boats as privateers, supposedly taking the heat off of Patriot towns. The whaleboats were crewed by twelve to twenty-four men and were sufficiently light to be carried inland for a considerable distance. Typical of their raids was one in 1777 by Colonel Meigs from Connecticut, who took thirteen boats and 234 men to the British base at Sag Harbor, where he destroyed twelve ships, captured 120 tons of supplies and forage, killed six Tories fighting for the British, and took ninety prisoners. The Tories responded, ambushing Patriots on land and sea, taking hostages, and generally making life within striking distance from Long Island miserable for Patriots. Both sides degenerated into outright piracy, killing, stealing, and burning with a vengeance. The whaleboat wars continued until the British evacuated New York.

Benedict Arnold

Ever since the Valcour Island fight on Lake Champlain in October of 1776, Arnold had been the greatest hero of the Revolution. He certainly had to be ranked among the bravest and best combat leaders in the army. Unfortunately for Arnold, he gathered enemies as horses attract flies. Many other officers, both his seniors and juniors, were outright jealous and looking to disparage Arnold's reputation. They took their venom to Congress, and found a ready hearing among the chair-bound politicians. Washington was Arnold's stalwart defender, but the commander-in-chief also had his own political battles to fight. Arnold did not help his case by personalizing every difference of opinion, exaggerating every perceived

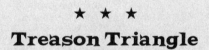

★ ★ ★
Treason Triangle

In May of 1778, Arnold became the military governor of Philadelphia. That summer he fell in love with Peggy Shippen, the daughter of a prominent Tory in Philadelphia—a woman who at the time was in love with a British officer, Major John Andrè. As Arnold's dissatisfaction with Congress festered, Peggy Shippen (at Andrè's urging) offered to provide a conduit to the British. By all accounts the woman was hot, able to handle Andrè as well as Arnold. She married Arnold on April 8, 1779, and Arnold started on his long slide into treason.

slight, and constantly harping on recompense for his expenses at a time when everyone was out of pocket.

Frustration and resentment, in combination with his complicated love life, turned Arnold to treason. Early in May 1779 Arnold offered his services to the British, betraying the Patriot cause and his brothers in arms.

Arnold resigned the military governorship of Philadelphia and in April 1780 was appointed to command West Point, "the key to America" in Washington's opinion, because of its strategic position. Suddenly Arnold's somewhat nebulous value to the British became quite clear. He possessed something of great value, and he began negotiating new terms for his defection and the delivery of West Point. There was even the possibility that Washington and his staff could be captured during a visit at West Point. That was all a matter of timing, and Major John Andrè was sent to work out the details with Arnold.

On September 20, 1780, Andrè set out to meet with Arnold at West Point. Andrè was brought up the Hudson by the HMS *Vulture*, which was then anchored in the middle of the Hudson River. While Arnold and Andrè met, American artillerymen on Teller's Point started firing at the British ship. Against Arnold's specific orders, the cannon fire continued for two hours, and the *Vulture* was heavily damaged. The captain took his ship down river and out of range, forcing Arnold to come up with another plan to get Andrè back to New York City. Arnold rather cavalierly sent Andrè—in civilian clothing—overland with passes to get through American lines.

But Andrè never made it back to British lines. He was stopped by three American militiamen. It is not clear if these men were simply scavengers, or real Patriots, or both. But in removing Andrè's valuable boots, they found the plans to West Point supplied by Arnold and knew these were a matter of importance. In a near comedy of errors, Arnold was notified that a British spy had been arrested minutes before the party sent to arrest Arnold himself arrived, and he escaped down the Hudson. Andrè was brought to Washington and confessed everything. Pressured by his subordinates to make an example (in part as retribution for the hanging of Nathan Hale in 1776), Washington ordered Andrè hanged. Arnold, meanwhile, made good his escape.

The American cause had also had a narrow escape—from the enormous damage Arnold's betrayal could easily have accomplished. The report on Arnold and West Point by British general Henry Clinton emphasized the importance of Arnold's defection: "General Arnold surrendering himself, the forts and garrisons, at this instant, would have given every advantage which could have been desired."

Raids

While Arnold was sinking into treason, Clinton had made several attempts to draw Washington into a position where he might be attacked with a good chance of success, but those efforts failed. Ironically, *both* sides now realized that their central war aim was simply not to lose their armies. Washington knew that the longer his military force stayed viable the more likely the British were to quit, while Clinton understood that one more defeat on the scale of Burgoyne's loss at Saratoga would end the war. Thus the war dwindled into raids on land and sea, at least north of the Carolinas. In July of 1779, former Royal Governor of North Carolina William Tryon raided Connecticut with twenty-six hundred men. He attacked the towns of New Haven, Fairfield, and Norwalk, putting them to the torch after brushing aside the weak resistance by militia units. The port towns of Connecticut were destroyed as havens for the whaleboat raiders, but Washington was untouched. Tryon was criticized for his brutality, and the raids made good recruiting propaganda for the Patriot army.

Washington was not asleep. After Clinton occupied Stony Point on the Hudson and closed King's Ferry, moving in about 750 men, Washington resolved to capture the garrison. He selected "Mad" Anthony Wayne and his newly formed Corps of Light Infantry (armed with muskets featuring bayonets) to do the job. Washington gave Wayne a plan, but also permission to deviate from the plan as Wayne thought necessary. Wayne's men made quick work of the fight, taking the position easily.

As Wayne wrote in his report, "Neither the deep morass, the formidable and double rows of abatis nor the strong works in front or flank could damp the ardor of the troops, who, in the face of the most tremendous and incessant fire of musketry, and from cannon loaded with grapeshot, forced their way at the point of the bayonet through every obstacle, both columns meeting in the center of the enemy's works nearly at the same instant." It was a victory that heartened the Patriots and offset Tryon's raid on Connecticut.

But British raids similar to Tryon's were also conducted by the Royal Navy in Chesapeake Bay. Coastal areas were nearly helpless. The Americans lacked a navy, and the French were busy defending their own vulnerable coasts.

On April 12, 1778, John Paul Jones stood out to sea from France to attack England. Jones's ship, the *Ranger*, a slow sloop of war with only eighteen guns, was inferior to British sloops and frigates. To make matters worse, Jones's crew was all from New England, and highly dissatisfied with having a Virginian as captain. Nonetheless, Jones cruised the Irish Sea taking prizes and landing shore parties to raid ship harbors and other British installations. He couldn't do much damage with his small ship and limited crew, yet he still managed to terrify the coastal areas of western England. Maritime insurance rates went from 1.25 to 5 percent.

★ ★ ★
Privateers in Public Service

When the Revolution broke out there was no such thing as an American Navy. Instead, Congress approved a fleet of privateers—private vessels authorized to seize British shipping. In 1777 there were seventy-three such authorized privateers, but by 1781 there were 449, and they made their presence felt, bringing in some thirty-one hundred merchant vessels. While this hardly put a dent in English trade, American coffers were swelled by the ransoms the privateers demanded and the booty they brought in.

Jones fought a single-ship duel with the twenty-gun British sloop *Drake*, forcing the British ship to strike her colors. Then Jones sent the *Ranger* back to America and worked to obtain a larger ship, and possibly a fleet. The best he could do for a flagship was the old East Indiaman *Duras*, which Jones renamed the *Bon Homme Richard* in honor of Benjamin Franklin. In two months Jones turned the *Richard* into a formidable warship with twenty-eight twelve-pounders on her gun deck and a variety of other guns below deck. The ship was frigate-sized and took a complement of 380 officers and men, only seventy-nine of whom were Americans. Jones had four other ships in his "navy." Three were French ships: the thirty-two-gun *Pallas*, eighteen-gun *Cerf*, and twelve-gun *Vengeance*. There was also one new arrival from America, the thirty-six-gun *Alliance*. The *Alliance* was by far the best ship in the fledgling fleet, but captained by a cashiered French naval officer and self-absorbed adventurer named Pierre Landais. Still, the small fleet, if properly used, could inflict some damage.

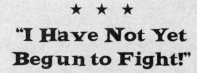

★ ★ ★

"I Have Not Yet Begun to Fight!"

American naval vessels and sailors were on the high seas, but as they were mostly taking prizes from the British merchant marines, their exploits didn't get much publicity. That changed when John Paul Jones was able to acquire first a ship and then a small fleet with which to harass the British on the high seas. Jones's triumphs heartened Americans everywhere, and his courage became part of American military lore.

In September 1779, Jones's little squadron encountered a British supply convoy protected by the forty-four-gun HMS *Serapis* and the twenty-gun HMS *Countess of Scarborough*. Jones immediately headed for the larger ship, while the *Pallas* took on the *Countess*. The *Richard* and the *Serapis* became entangled stern-to-stern, and hand-to-hand combat ensued. After three and a half hours, the *Serapis* finally struck its colors. Early on in the battle, however, the rope flying the American flag had parted and the British captain asked Jones if he was surrendering. Jones's reply—"I have not yet begun to fight," became famous in the annals of naval history. Taking the *Serapis* as his own, Jones

A Book You're Not Supposed to Read

John Paul Jones, A Sailor's Biography by Samuel Eliot Morison (New York: Little, Brown and Company, 1959).

sank the damaged *Richard* after the battle and proudly sailed his prize back to France along with the *Pallas* and the *Countess of Scarborough*. Jones had set the standard for all future American naval officers.

Meanwhile, naval operations nearer home had gone from bad to worse for the Americans. Just as the need for a navy was becoming readily recognized, the Americans squandered the ships they had in a bizarrely mismanaged naval expedition to Penobscot, Maine. In June 1779, an expedition from British Nova Scotia had occupied Castine and declared that Maine, formerly part of Massachusetts, was now New Ireland, a new colony. The British erected a fort, naturally named Fort George, and the community was opened for Tory settlement. The primary motivation for this move was to secure the annual supply of Eastern White Pine ship masts for the Royal Navy, as Maine made the best ship masts in the world. (There was a special fleet of "mast-ships" designed to carry the long, straight, timbers, running regularly between Maine and England.)

Massachusetts was not going to allow a part of its colony to be taken by the king without opposition. A joint expedition was put together by the Continental Congress and Massachusetts to recover Maine and eliminate New Ireland. The naval contingent consisted of forty-four ships with 344 guns under Commodore Dudley Saltonstall, and the land forces numbered slightly less than one thousand militia under Brigadier General Solomon Lovell, including an artillery battalion under Paul Revere.

Fiasco

Upon arriving in Maine, the expedition found itself facing six hundred men in Fort George and three small British vessels in the river mounting thirty guns in total. It should have been a piece of cake. But the expedition rapidly developed into a hopeless debacle. Saltonstall turned out to be a spineless commander, unable to make decisions. Every day a council of war was held to determine what was to happen—including not only the higher-ranking naval officers but also the ground commanders and the captain of each privateer.

After a number of fits and starts, an assault was organized. Some four hundred men—militia and Continental marines—went ashore at Dyce's Head and attacked up the steep bluff toward Fort George. They drove the British outpost at the top of the bluff back into the fort, but then Lovell decided to stop there and entrench. Over a hundred casualties had been incurred in the attack, and no more offensives would follow. Saltonstall, for his part, was appalled by the casualties, which left him shell-shocked and unable to function.

After forty-five days of bickering among Patriot commanders, the Royal Navy put in an appearance. The militia scurried aboard their transports, and Saltonstall led the fleet up the river where the ships were either destroyed by British cannon fire or burned to avoid capture. The naval personnel and militia fled into the woods and attempted to make their way south to New Hampshire through the wilderness with the bare minimum of supplies. Over five hundred Americans perished. Saltonstall was appropriately court-martialed and cashiered. Paul Revere, who had taken no orders from anyone and would not allow his ship to be used to land men since it carried his personal baggage, was also court-martialed and convicted. But in his case there was a second trial, in which he was cleared of all charges.

This was the most embarrassing military operation in the war, and possibly in all of American military history. Maine would remain the colony of New Ireland until it was given back to the Americans in the Treaty of Paris in 1783, and even then its boundaries would remain unsettled until 1842.

Freedom for Service

Other initiatives undertaken by the British also damaged the Patriot cause. Probably the most far-reaching was the Philipsburg Proclamation by Sir Henry Clinton on June 30, 1779. Virginia's Royal Governor Lord Dunmore had issued a similar proclamation in Virginia in 1775, offering freedom to all slaves in return for serving in the British or Tory forces. But Clinton's proclamation went further. It "most strictly forbid any Person to sell or claim Right over any Negro, the property of a Rebel, who may take Refuge with any part" of the British army. Clinton also promised "to every Negro who shall desert the Rebel Standard, full security to follow within these lines, and any occupation which he shall think proper." Once a slave reached the British lines, his status as property ended, and he was free to do whatever he pleased. On the other hand, the Proclamation said that "any Negroes taken in arms or upon any military duty, shall be purchased for a stated price." This implied that any black man fighting for the Patriots could be reduced to slavery and sold in the West Indies, where slavery was much harsher.

The effect of the proclamation was that huge numbers of slaves ran away from their plantations, both Tory and Patriot. In fact, the British returned many to their masters. Over five thousand fled to the British lines at Savannah and in South Carolina, stretching British supplies to the limit.

A few fought for the British—mostly young men without families or other ties to their plantations. Slaves with wives and children were not willing to escape alone, fearing reprisals on their families. Nonetheless, in 1780, when British troops captured Charleston, South Carolina, thousands of slaves joined them. That experience was repeated in Virginia in 1781, with many being freed by Benedict Arnold, who commanded the British expedition. The ex-slaves proved a burden, however, as Cornwallis found it increasingly difficult to feed them or to treat the smallpox that ravaged their ranks. Although the proclamation caused massive dislocation and anguish, in the end, it had a minor impact on who would win the war.

★ ★ ★

Liberty's Daughters

While modern television and movies peddle the Molly Pitcher myth—the idea that average women were fighters, riders, spies, and in Pitcher's case, artillery women—the truth is that "Liberty's Daughters" continued with life pretty much as usual after the war started, only with more chores. With their husbands and sons off in the militia, women had to perform their normal daily work—which could include collecting eggs, milking cows, tending vegetables, taking care of and educating children, cooking, and spinning—but now often added the men's chores as well. These could include cutting wood for fireplaces, tending to the larger livestock, and hunting. (Virtually every household had more than one musket.)

Spinning was a particularly important task. Since the men were gone, women often spun in groups where they had some companionship. The spinning groups became a significant social and informational resource, providing ways that women could obtain news from the front and from other women.

As Mary Beth Norton shows in *Liberty's Daughters*, women's control of the homes and farms increased during the war and sex roles became more equal. For obvious reasons, sex itself became a less frequent activity. Prior to the war, a woman could expect to become pregnant perhaps ten times during her lifetime in order to produce five live children. Mortality rates for babies were very high, and the never-ending pregnancies shortened women's lives. It was not easy to be an American woman in the 1770s.

War against the Red Man

There was constant worry about British seaborne attacks along the coast, but inland the concern centered on Indian raids and atrocities. Though the Indians failed to turn the tide, they did sufficient harm to the Patriots in the western regions that almost all support and sympathy for them was destroyed among colonists. Their bloody atrocities enraged the Patriots—who decided that literally all Indians were beyond any hope of redemption or peaceful coexistence—and permanently seared in the minds of the colonists the notion of the red man as a brutal savage. The atrocities were not isolated instances: incidents of Indian brutality had taken place with alarming frequency and ferocity since the war began. At Cobleskill, New York, a group of Iroquois and Tories under Chief Joseph Brant killed a number of the militia and destroyed most of the settlement. At Cherry Valley, New York, one of the most horrific massacres of the war took place: women and children were specifically targeted, and over one hundred inhabitants were killed or captured. All the houses were destroyed, and Cherry Valley ceased to exist. But the worst was the massacre in Wyoming Valley, Pennsylvania, where Tory John Butler led a mixed group of Tories, Senecas, and Cayugas to clean out the valley. Butler was spectacularly successful, destroying American crops, farms, and settlements, and massacring about 360 civilian defenders—men, women, and children.

In July 1779, Tories and Indians massacred another fifty militiamen at the Battle of Minisink Ford, and were clearly making real progress in depopulating the west. The outrage was so universal that General Sullivan was tasked to punish the Iroquois tribes for their predations in western New York and northern Pennsylvania. Sullivan's army carried out a scorched-earth campaign, methodically eradicating at least forty Iroquois villages. He burned their crops and villages, destroying everything the Indians possessed, breaking their strength and morale. In the only battle of the campaign, over one thousand Iroquois and two hundred of Butler's Rangers were decisively defeated, but the biggest weapon against the Indians was starvation and exposure in the following winter.

Advances and Setbacks

Meanwhile, the Mississippi Valley was being secured for the Patriots. George Rogers Clark led an expedition to Kaskaskia (in present-day Illinois) on the Mississippi, and then took Vincennes (Indiana) in 1779 after an epic march that rivaled Arnold's to Quebec. British hopes to control the area were finally ended at the Battle of St. Louis, fought by Governor Fernando de Leyba and Spanish militia against British fur trappers and their Indian allies. Over a thousand Indians attacked Fort San Carlos on May 26, 1780, but were repulsed by its defenders, including Spanish regulars and militia—of whom half were French. The victory came at great cost to the Spanish, who lost about a hundred killed and captured (to be ritually murdered later), but the defense cemented the alliance between Spain and the Patriots and ensured a steady supply of lead from the nearby mines for the Continental Army.

The French alliance, on the other hand, was not bringing the improvements in the Continental Army's position that many had anticipated. No great numbers of French troops showed up to fight in America. In fact, they spent the first two years after signing the treaty fighting mostly in the West Indies; they seemed concerned mostly about their interests there. Washington's attempts to bring the French, both their navy and army, to New York so he could capture the city and end the war, were met with frustration.

After the Battle of Rhode Island, d'Estaing and the French fleet stayed away from the north. Then, in October of 1779, d'Estaing became involved in the poorly managed siege of Savannah, where he was wounded. His return to France caused Washington to become despondent. Perhaps the French would not tilt the scale to the Americans after all.

Optimism returned when in July 1780 another French fleet under Admiral de Ternay arrived at Newport, bringing General Rochambeau and 6,000 troops—a welcome development solely due to Lafayette's influence on the French king. French naval superiority was short-lived, as British Admiral Graves arrived at New York a few days after de Ternay, and the reinforced British fleet anchored off Point Judith, blockading the French in Rhode Island. As the French army refused to leave the French fleet until France established local naval superiority, French forces remained inactive at Newport for the next eleven months.

At that point the Patriot leadership was becoming fragmented and disillusioned, exhausted by trying to solve unsolvable problems. Congress had run out of credit, and the paper money it had put in circulation had reached almost 250 million dollars. Since there was no provision for its redemption in specie or goods, the notes were "worthless as a Continental." The states were in almost as bad a shape, owing almost 210 million. There was no way to feed or supply the army, and it was only through the French that sufficient powder was obtained to keep the troops able to fight. The situation was desperate, to say the least.

The French alliance had actually become a detriment to recruiting. The average citizen did not understand the importance of sea power, or why the six thousandFrench troops at Newport were doing nothing. Throughout the war, the expiration of one- and three-year enlistments had decimated

★ ★ ★
"Not Worth a Continental"

At the time of the American Revolution, money consisted mainly of gold and silver coins, mostly British or Spanish coins. (The Spanish dollar, in particular, was widely circulated and easy to make change for, as it was divisible by fives, tens, and eights.) Once independence was declared, however, the supply of British gold coins dried up. The Continental Congress in 1775 had already begun issuing Continental currency. It was paper money denominated anywhere from $.12 to $80. Congress ultimately issued $241 million in "Continentals." But since there was no gold with which to back the money, it rapidly depreciated to nothing. To make matters worse, each state was issuing its own unbacked money. And to make matters even worse still, the British proved to be great counterfeiters! Benjamin Franklin expressed admiration for the artists who "performed so well" that immense quantities of fake Continental currency were circulated in New York. By 1780, Continentals were worth only one-fortieth of their par value. Franklin saw the runaway inflation as a tax to pay for the war. Finance would remain a major issue in the new republic until Alexander Hamilton created a viable monetary and financial structure in 1790.

the army at critical times, and the militia came and went as needed to meet threats to their states. The Association kept pumping in new troops by applying local pressure, but by the start of 1781, after the South had been nearly reduced to a British plantation by Cornwallis, the Continental Army's recruitment faced a crisis.

Mutiny

On New Year's Day six Pennsylvania regiments paraded under arms and marched off in the direction of Philadelphia. When Anthony Wayne tried to restrain his men by threatening them with a pistol, several soldiers placed their bayonets against his chest and threatened to kill him if he tried to stop them. It was a mutiny, and one officer was killed and several wounded.

The men's grievances were many: no pay for the last twelve months, insufficient food and clothing, and expiration—as they interpreted it—of their terms of service. They had enlisted for three years or the duration of the war, understood by them to mean whichever was shorter. The army administration interpreted it to mean whichever was longer. Henry Clinton heard of the mutiny and immediately dispatched emissaries to induce the mutineers to come over to the British side. Instead, the insulted mutineers turned Clinton's emissaries over to Wayne, who hanged them after a speedy trial—but that hardly resolved the larger matters.

At Trenton the mutineers were met by representatives of Congress, and their grievances were negotiated. A portion of their back pay would be promptly paid, clothing supplied, and the three-year enlistments honored. Almost all of the mutineers were discharged but then reenlisted, receiving the bounties being paid to new recruits. Later the mutinous regiments were sent to Virginia, where they rendered good service.

Less than two weeks later another mutiny broke out, this time in three New Jersey regiments. Washington had learned from the last mutiny and

★ ★ ★
The Desultory War Report Card

The British

Sir Henry Clinton: B

He made no major mistakes and left open the chance for Great Britain to win the war—if the government wished to make that commitment.

The Americans

George Rogers Clark: A

He did everything that was expected of him and more, winning the only Revolutionary War victories that actually conquered new territory for America.

"Mad" Anthony Wayne: A

His capture of Stony Point was textbook perfect.

Benedict Arnold: F

He may have had cause, but his actions were still treason.

Dudley Saltonstall: F

Nothing can be said in defense of his incompetence.

John Paul Jones: A

Clearly, and rightfully so, the founder of the American Navy.

The American troops: B

They were long-suffering, unpaid, under-fed, poorly housed, and sacrificing when so many civilians were getting on with their lives. To the troops, everyone was doing well except for them. That they stayed in the field was a miracle.

was ready for such disturbances. He surrounded the mutineers' camp at Pompton, disarmed them, selected one ringleader from each regiment, and tried and hanged them on the spot. After that, the mutinies ended, but the underlying problems that had sparked them did not go away. A ray of hope came when Colonel John Laurens, one of Washington's aides, was able to obtain a loan from France for six million francs, some of which was immediately converted into arms, ammunition, and clothing, and the remainder—2.5 million francs—was brought to America as gold coin. This was a temporary life preserver, but even that money would run out. Washington needed to end the war as soon as possible.

CHAPTER 14

The South Laid Waste

The colonies entered the Revolution as three distinct geographical areas, divided by politics, by economic interests, and in some measure by religion. The four New England colonies were Congregationalist or Presbyterian, oriented towards farming, manufacturing, and ocean commerce; they had a population of about seven hundred fifty thousand people. The nearly one million people in the five middle colonies were almost exclusively engaged in agriculture, mostly growing food, and were Quaker, Presbyterian, Anglican, and Dutch Reformed. The four colonies in the South also had a population of about one million (Virginia alone was one-fifth of the colonial population), were almost exclusively agricultural—mostly growing tobacco for export—and Anglican, Presbyterian, Methodist, and other smaller denominations. The Association, with its embargo on the sale of tobacco to England and English dominions, had hit the South hardest.

Most of the South was remote from the two northern regions, and its mostly rural population was beyond the reach of their support. The distances involved were great, with the colonies being spread along the eastern seaboard. It was eleven hundred miles from Boston to Savannah, and letters from New York to South Carolina took thirty days or more. Even when a

Did you know?

★ Andrew Jackson's experiences with the British and the Indians during the Revolutionary War help explain both the Battle of New Orleans and the Trail of Tears

★ By 1780, captivity on a British prison ship was recognized as a death sentence

★ British forces in the South could win battles and hold coastal cities, but not control the backcountry

good road could be found, a coach would typically overturn at least once along the way. Isolating the South was a priority for the British.

To the South!

Henry Clinton had made one attempt to attack the South, at Charleston in 1776, and now a new expedition was formed to conquer the region, relying not just on Redcoats but on an army of Tories that the British military commanders were sure existed below the Mason-Dixon Line. But the whole idea of the campaign was greatly flawed, stressing the capture and submission of territory rather than the defeat of the Patriot armies and the capture of Patriot leaders. But its biggest flaw was that it relied on the fighting prowess of the Tories.

Before leaving Philadelphia in 1778, Clinton had received instructions to send five thousand troops to St. Lucia in the West Indies to counter French moves, and three thousand to Georgia and Florida. He was to abandon major offensive operations in the North, and in the winter of 1779–80 to attack the Southern colonies. Lord Germain's instructions to Clinton said, "Georgia should be first taken, and the passage into South Carolina will then be comparably easy." Lord Germain's statement proved true, but only because of Patriot military incompetence.

In November 1778, British troops were dutifully sent to St. Lucia (they would never return to North America), and the thirty-five hundred-strong expedition to Georgia departed New York on November 27. The soldiers were commanded by Archibald Campbell of the Highlanders; the naval units, by Commodore Hyde Parker. They would have help. For two years a civil war had been raging throughout Georgia and the Carolinas, with the result that a large number of Tories had taken refuge in Florida. Those men were more than ready to assist the British in taking back the Southern colonies.

Washington's spies had found out about the planned attack on Georgia, and Congress sent Benjamin Lincoln to Charleston to be commander of the Southern Department. The governor of Virginia was requested to send a thousand militia to aid Lincoln; North Carolina's quota was three thousand. Near the end of 1778, Campbell dropped anchor off Savannah and disembarked his force of thirty-five hundred. General Augustine Prevost with two thousand Tories moved north from Florida to assist him. Patriot forces consisted of a thousand men under Robert Howe (confusingly, a Patriot general with the same last name as the British Howe brothers) defending Savannah and fifteen hundred troops under Lincoln at Charleston. They were still awaiting the arrival of the promised militia.

The Fall of Georgia

Campbell quickly found a way to flank Howe's defense. While feinting against Howe's left, Campbell sent his light infantry and one New York Tory regiment with a Negro guide who led them on a blind path through a swamp around Howe's right. As Campbell attacked Howe's front, this detachment attacked the Patriot rear. Most of Howe's men fled into South Carolina, but his Georgia regiment fought and took severe casualties. Four hundred fifteen Patriot troops were captured and sent to New York City, where they died aboard the British prison hulks. Howe also lost forty-five cannon, twenty-three mortars, and a large amount of ammunition and supplies. It was a disaster, and Howe's performance was so poor he was later tried by court-martial. (He was acquitted and served in Washington's headquarters until the end of the war, but many believed he had replaced Arnold as Britain's most important spy.)

Prevost added insult to injury. He marched along the Georgia coast plundering and burning, setting an example for depredation and rapine that not even Sherman, eighty-five years later, would equal. He captured

Fort Sunbury and its garrison of two hundred men with negligible losses, and joined Campbell in Savannah. The British then marched north to Augusta, effectively taking possession of all of Georgia. A message was sent to England for the royal governor to return and resume his post, as Georgia was now once again a royal colony.

South Carolina would have been next, but Benjamin Lincoln's determination was formidable—much more so than his military expertise—and he set about retaking Georgia. A series of skirmishes followed, some favorable to the Americans, some not. The first was at Beaufort on February 3, 1779, where a force of four companies of British regulars was met and defeated by General Moultrie and South Carolina militia.

British casualties were nearly double those of the Americans, and Lincoln was emboldened. Ten days later, another large Tory force was all killed, captured, or dispersed. It was typical of battles between Tories and Patriots that the percentage killed was much higher than in battles between Patriots and the British, and the number killed was more than the number wounded. This was the ferocity of neighbors fighting neighbors.

The Cherokee War

Constant guerrilla warfare between Tories and Patriots had been going on in the backcountry of South Carolina for more than four years, with its intensity and brutality steadily growing. In late 1775, Colonel Richard Richardson had raised a militia force of Patriots and rooted out Tories between the area known as Ninety-Six (sixty miles north of Augusta, Georgia) and Savannah. But in other areas the Tories had burnt out Patriot farms and families, and were in the ascendency. The situation had worsened when the Cherokees decided for the crown, raiding Patriot farms and towns in what became known as the "Cherokee War of 1776." The effects were long lasting. Patriots such as Andrew Jackson never forgave the Cherokees for what was considered treachery; his Revolutionary War experience helps explain the Trail of Tears.

The British at Savannah need not have worried: Benjamin Lincoln would soon demonstrate his complete unfitness to be a military commander. He determined to cross the Savannah River and establish a Patriot presence in the upper backcountry of Georgia. Leaving William Moultrie at Purrysburg with only a thousand men to face Prevost moving north from Savannah, Lincoln took 4,000 troops and set out for Augusta, Georgia.

Prevost immediately moved against Moultrie, whose force was too small for effective opposition. Moultrie was pushed back to Charleston and sent repeated messages to Lincoln about the serious situation, but Lincoln refused to believe the threat to Charleston was real. On May 10, Prevost reached Charleston and called upon the city to surrender. The situation was desperate. Every adult male in Charleston was called up as a militiaman and set to work throwing up defenses. Only then did Lincoln begin a return march to rescue the city. Although in a commanding position, Prevost was unsure of the Patriot strength and feared Lincoln's arrival in his rear. He

A Book You're Not Supposed to Read

The American Revolution in Indian Country: Crisis and Diversity in Native American Communities by Colin G. Calloway (New York: Cambridge University Press, 1995).

★ ★ ★
Fighting for Survival

Indian tribes did not see the American Revolution as a fight for "rights"—a concept with which they had no familiarity. Instead, as in any conflict between different European groups, they each independently weighed the value of allying with one group of whites over the other—as a means of survival. Thus Indian alliances were not permanent or even consistent.

★ ★ ★

Andrew Jackson's Revenge

One of the Americans killed in the Stono Ferry battle was Hugh Jackson, one of Andrew Jackson's brothers. Andrew, a boy of thirteen, and his brother Robert were taken prisoner. After his capture, Jackson refused to polish Major John Coffin's boots, and the Tory officer slashed him with his sword. The boys were released, but Robert died soon afterwards and Andrew was permanently scarred from his wound. Because of these experiences—and the death of his mother, who died of cholera while nursing Patriot captives on a British prison ship—he carried a burning hatred for the British his entire life. Jackson would exact his revenge on the British in the War of 1812 at the Battle of New Orleans.

withdrew without attacking, and over the next few days sent the bulk of his force back to Savannah by sea, until only nine hundred men remained at Stono Ferry.

Having wandered about to no good purpose, Lincoln now decided to attack Prevost. He had over six thousand men available to commit, but he moved slowly and sent only 25 percent of his force up to Stono Ferry for the attack. The attack was bungled, and Lincoln retreated back to Charleston with the British pursuing.

Where Are the French?

Meanwhile, the French Admiral d'Estaing was in the West Indies, where he had captured the islands of St. Vincent and Grenada. At Haiti he received letters from Charleston urging him to come to the city's aid. D'Estaing decided to sail to Savannah instead, where he captured a British ship of the line, a frigate, and two supply ships. He had thirty-seven ships with over two thousand guns, and six thousand troops. Lincoln's strength in Charleston had reached a total of a thousand Continentals and five thousand militiamen, and he hurried to invest Savannah. Prevost, with only three thousand men, was outnumbered four to one. Quick action and good leadership on the part of the Patriots and the French could bag Prevost and his entire force.

In one of the saddest operations undertaken by "professional" soldiers in the war, the siege of Savannah was bungled badly. Lincoln arrived bringing only six hundred Continentals and seven hundred fifty militiamen, and d'Estaing landed only thirty-five hundred men. Still, the Patriots and French outnumbered the British by a considerable margin. It was Moultrie's opinion that if an attack had been made when Lincoln first arrived, Savannah would have fallen in a day. Instead, Lincoln and d'Estaing decided on a siege—and they took their time about it. Although Savannah was surrounded on September 12, nearly a full month passed before any assault on the city began, and Prevost used the delay to strengthen his works substantially. When the attack finally started on October 9, the British were well entrenched. D'Estaing was wounded, the Patriot cavalry leader Casimir Pulaski was killed, and the Patriots lost nearly six times as many men as the British defenders.

D'Estaing immediately returned to his ships, personally leading most of his fleet to France while ordering the remainder back to the Caribbean. Lincoln fled back to Charleston to avoid capture. The militia, which had responded so readily to the call for two month's service, went home in disgust.

Charleston, the Prize

The defeat of the French and Americans at Savannah galvanized Henry Clinton into action. Charleston could be his for the taking. From the new British base at Savannah, he could capture Charleston by sending an army overland from Georgia. Clinton put together the necessary force—about eighty-three hundred men under General Charles Cornwallis, not including

★ ★ ★

The Hell Ships

Many Patriot prisoners were trekked from the South to New York City and housed on British prison ships near the Brooklyn Navy Yard. Thousands died of malnutrition and disease on these "hell ships," as they were known, where the crowded men suffered in freezing winters and stifling summers. The most infamous was the HMS *Jersey*. No one knows exactly how many men were imprisoned on these vessels, but about a dozen died each night, and by war's end only fourteen hundred men remained alive. At least eleven thousand died from 1776 to 1783, and at least an equal number were released in such bad health that they expired within a few months. In 1908, President William Howard Taft dedicated the Prison Ship Martyrs Monument to these Patriots.

an escorting Royal Navy fleet consisting of fourteen ships carrying six hundred fifty guns and five thousand men.

Clinton landed to the south of Charleston on February 13, 1780, and within a few days had advanced to the west bank of the Ashley River across from the city. He chased away a detachment of Continental cavalry and a force of militia under Benjamin Huger and sent his own mounted troops north to the Santee River, where they defeated another unit of mounted militia. A small American fleet of nine ships with 248 guns was bottled up in Charleston harbor by British frigates, which had anchored out of range from Fort Moultrie on Sullivan's Island. Not wishing to waste men, Clinton began a traditional siege of the fort according to the tactics of the day. Surrounded, Fort Moultrie surrendered. Clinton received thirty-seven hundred reinforcements in total from New York under Lord Rawdon and Savannah under Prevost, and by May 7, Charleston itself was surrounded. Clinton was ready to make the final assault, but it wasn't necessary. Benjamin Lincoln promptly surrendered the city "to save lives."

Clinton's haul was enormous. The surrender included seven generals and almost 5,400 other officers and men, as well as a massive store of 301 guns,

5,316 muskets, and a great deal of other military supplies. Prisoners were sent to New York City, where most of them died during the next two years. The surrender of Charleston was the greatest disaster for American arms until the Civil War. General Benjamin Lincoln, the author of the fiasco, was immediately set free on parole.

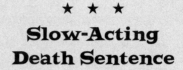

★ ★ ★
Slow-Acting Death Sentence

Most prisoners died in British captivity, and those who didn't were usually released in such poor condition that they didn't survive another year.

Then, in the flush of victory, Clinton made a big mistake. At the beginning of June he disavowed the very terms of surrender that he himself had dictated to Lincoln at Charleston just the month before. He had allowed parolees to remain neutral for the remainder of the war rather than suffer for their past service to the Patriot cause. Now that would be null and void. All citizens, including parolees, would be required to take the oath of loyalty to the king or they would be regarded as "rebels and enemies of their country." Parolees who didn't take the oath could be thrown in prison—which by then was recognized as a virtual death sentence. Clinton's action showed all those with Patriot leanings that British promises and agreements meant nothing. Scotch-Irish militia leaders such as Andrew Pickens who had been captured at Charleston immediately re-entered the fight, declaring their paroles to have been invalidated by Clinton.

Tarleton's (No) Quarter

Well satisfied, Clinton sailed back to New York, leaving Charles Cornwallis in command in the South. Cornwallis immediately set about pacifying the countryside and sent his cavalry leader, Lieutenant Colonel Banastre Tarleton, to terrify the inhabitants into submission. Tarleton—who, as we have already seen, was the model for the "Tavington" character in *The Patriot*, was in command of the British Legion, a mixed force of about 250 cavalry and 200 infantry, accompanied by fast-moving horse artillery. His unit had been raised in New York by Clinton during 1778 specifically to fight Patriot guerrillas operating in New York, New Jersey, and Connecticut. It primarily consisted of New York Tories, stiffened by a number of British Light Dragoons. These New Yorkers had no regard for anyone in the South, Patriot or Tory, man, woman, or child.

Three weeks after Lincoln's surrender, Tarleton was informed that Colonel Abraham Buford, with about 300 men of the Third Virginia Regiment,

★ ★ ★
The Swamp Fox

As a teenager, Francis Marion barely escaped death when a ship on which he was working sank in the West Indies. Marion made it to land after a week on the ocean and returned home to manage his family's plantation. When the French and Indian War broke out, Marion attained the rank of lieutenant during a campaign against the Cherokees. In the Revolution, he was a captain in a South Carolina regiment, fought at Charleston but escaped, and then—hearing about the Waxhaw Massacre—began small-unit guerrilla operations on his own. He briefly joined with General Horatio Gates, but immediately decided (in the words of Benjamin Martin, the hero in Mel Gibson's *The Patriot* who was modeled roughly on Marion) that Gates was "a damned fool." So Marion returned to "scouting"—a cover for guerrilla warfare.

Marion was as effective as any irregular could be. His chief opponent, Lord Charles Cornwallis, observed that, "Colonel Marion had so wrought the minds of the people.... that there was scarcely an inhabitant between the Santee and the Pee Dee that was not in arms against us." Cornwallis specifically ordered Tarleton to dispose of Marion, but after one unsuccessful pursuit, when Marion led Tarleton through twenty-six miles of swamps, Tarleton labeled him "this damned old fox" and said that, "the Devil himself could not catch him." Although Marion fought few major engagements, he did command the right wing under Nathanael Greene at the Battle of Eutaw Springs. Long before *The Patriot*, from 1959 to 1961, Walt Disney's weekly television show featured several episodes called "The Swamp Fox," with Marion played by Leslie Nielsen.

was retreating northward after hearing of the Charleston debacle. Tarleton caught up with Buford at the Waxhaws, just south of the North Carolina border, and annihilated Buford's command. The inexperienced Buford told his men to hold their fire until the British dragoons were nearly upon them to make every shot count, but his equally inexperienced Virginians fired only one wild volley and then took to their heels. Tarleton's horse was killed, and he went down, losing control of his men. They sabered every Patriot in sight while Buford waved a white flag to surrender. The affair became known as the "Waxhaw Massacre," and "Tarleton's Quarter" (meaning no quarter) became a motivator for Patriots to fight to the death.

After Waxhaws, the Patriot position in South Carolina initially went from bad to worse. The only remaining Patriot forces in Georgia and South Carolina were militia units fighting as guerrillas under the command of men such as Francis Marion (the "Swamp Fox"), Andrew Pickens, and Thomas Sumter.

Huck's Defeat

But it soon became clear that Cornwallis and Tarleton had underestimated the South Carolina militia. In July the Patriots turned Huck's Defeat, a relatively minor skirmish, into a major propaganda victory that swung the conflict toward the Patriots in the South. Christian Huck, a captain in Tarleton's Legion, was one of the many German Tories who had been banished from Pennsylvania after the British evacuated Philadelphia. He hated the Scotch-Irish Presbyterians who were in such abundance in the backcountry of North and South Carolina, and he was known for his cruelty toward prisoners. Huck's mission was to find and kill rebel leaders and persuade their followers to swear allegiance to the king in accordance with Clinton's June Proclamation.

But rather than win Patriots over to taking the loyalty oath, Huck mostly violated backcountry women, murdered men and boys, confiscated horses

and supplies, and burned homes and barns. He was the king's darkest avenging angel. And in the backcountry full of Patriots, it was only a matter of time before he would be caught. It happened on July 12.

Huck's force of about thirty-five British dragoons, assisted by eighty Tory militia, savaged the wife of Patriot Colonel William Bratton at his plantation, then moved to the Williamson plantation, where Huck failed to take proper security precautions. Bratton gathered about seventy-five militiamen and attacked the Williamson plantation, killing Huck and most of his men. Huck's defeat rekindled Patriot ardor in the South, because Patriots had been shown that the Tories and marauding British troops did not have and could not gain the upper hand against resolute leadership and fighters, men willing to risk their homes and families to defeat the enemy—men like Francis Marion.

This should have been the turning point for the South. Militia enlistments rose, and all the Patriots in the South needed was a detachment of the Continental Army under a competent commander to handle the regulars under Cornwallis. Sadly, that wasn't forthcoming. Instead, Congress sent "The Hero of Saratoga," General Horatio Gates, to Charlotte, North Carolina to build an army to retake South Carolina.

The Battle of Camden

In early August Gates, with about seven thousand men in his command, moved into South Carolina to confront Lord Rawdon, who had a thousand men at Camden. Lord Cornwallis hurried northward from Charleston with eleven hundred men as reinforcements, arriving on August 13. The day before the battle, Gates fed his men green corn, and a very large number became stricken with diarrhea and dysentery that severely reduced their ability to fight. Gates was only able to put about twenty-five hundred untried and inexperienced militia and about twelve hundred Continentals into the line of battle, and even many of them were sick and weakened.

The Continentals fought well, but the militia simply couldn't face British regulars in an open field. Both Gates and Cornwallis had placed their best troops on their left flanks, so that the militia faced the most experienced British regulars on the field. On Cornwallis's right, the contest was more even, with the Continentals facing light infantry and formations of Tories, who nevertheless had been fighting for a year or more and were well experienced. As the militia fled, Cornwallis ordered Tarleton and his legion to fall on the rear of the Continental line. The result was a rout, with every man attempting to save himself. That number included General Gates, who mounted a fast horse and didn't stop until he reached Charlotte, sixty miles away. Over the following two days, Gates fled another hundred miles, to Hillsborough. This was a man on a mission—to escape. Tarleton pursued for about twenty miles, giving the Patriots "Tarleton's Quarter" as usual. Against Cornwallis's casualties of about 325 killed, wounded, or missing, Gates suffered over 900 killed and wounded and over a thousand taken prisoner. His army had ceased to exist.

Perhaps the biggest casualty of the battle was the reputation of the militia. Once again they had been deployed in a major battle under an incompetent

★ ★ ★
The Gamecock

The sequel to the Battle of Camden involved Thomas Sumter, the prickly and inattentive brigadier general of the South Carolina militia later known as "the Gamecock" for his fighting qualities in battle. On the day of the battle, Sumter's partisans had captured a British supply column coming from Charleston only a few miles away from Camden. Tarleton ended his pursuit of Gates, and went after Sumter, who was retreating toward the Catawba settlements. At Fishing Creek on August 19, Tarleton caught up with Sumter, who had allowed his command to become complacent about security. Tarleton surprised Sumter in his camp and destroyed Sumter's force. Sumter himself escaped—half naked—but 150 of his men were killed or wounded, and 300 taken prisoners.

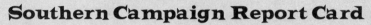

★ ★ ★

Southern Campaign Report Card

The British

Henry Clinton: A

He destroyed a full Patriot army with the absolute minimum of casualties.

Augustine Prevost: A

He put to flight a superior force at Savannah and beat Lincoln at Stono Ferry.

Charles Cornwallis: A

Cornwallis destroyed a second Patriot army with a numerically inferior force.

Banastre Tarleton: C

An expert in multiplying Patriot casualties, he greatly stiffened Patriot resolve.

The British troops: A

They did everything asked of them.

The Americans

Benjamin Lincoln: F

A total failure, without mitigating factors.

Horatio Gates: F

He finally got his comeuppance and demonstrated his combat incompetence to all.

Thomas Sumter: D

His loss of control over his men resulted in the destruction of his force.

Francis Marion: A

Marion's guerrilla activities haunted the British command and had them looking over their shoulders at all times. He was a legend.

The American troops: C

The Continental troops in the South did not perform up to par, but were rarely used in an "apples to apples" situation. The Southern militia was generally only effective as partisans, and even then often failed to take elementary security precautions. Still the guerrilla warfare took its toll on the British psyche and began to erode confidence that Britain could ever control the Americans.

commander—and had been expected to do the impossible. The Continentals had gone toe-to-toe with the Redcoats and acquitted themselves well, until their flank collapsed.

Gates's defeat temporarily eliminated any hopes of defeating Cornwallis, but after Camden, militia and guerrilla operations were still being undertaken almost daily. The Swamp Fox continued to terrorize Tories and isolate detachments of British troops. Leaders like Marion, Lieutenant Colonel Elijah Clarke of Georgia, and others soon made it clear that they, not the British, controlled virtually all of the countryside. Whatever advantages the Royal Navy gave England in coastal cities, the British were prisoners in those cities and could not venture far from them except in large forces. The setback at Camden did little to dampen the desire for revenge. In fact, Camden steeled Patriot resolve.

CHAPTER 15

Neutering Cornwallis

The Battle of Camden and Sumter's defeat two days later was the low-water mark for the revolution in the South. British forces now occupied both Georgia and South Carolina, and only a handful of guerrilla forces under Andrew Pickens and Francis Marion in South Carolina and Elijah Clarke in Georgia remained.

Patriot militias raided Tory towns and farms, and Tories retaliated by burning Patriot farms and hanging Patriots as traitors. Death and destruction were everywhere. Often a family would show up at a neighbor's door absolutely destitute and without a breadwinner. Andrew Jackson, who had become an orphan at fourteen, was the only member of his immediate family to survive the war. If a man left his farm to join either a Patriot or Tory militia, there was a good chance he would be killed, his farm burned down, and the survivors in his family, if any, thrown on the charity of kinfolk. Remaining neutral, on the other hand, was hardly possible—any more than it would be in the Civil War eighty years later. The Association committees took the position that "he who is not with us is against us."

Did you know?

★ Tories recruited in the North could commit atrocities in the South without fear of reprisals on their own families

★ Even before the Revolution, "Overmountain Men" had defied Britain and formed their own government in the future state of Tennessee

★ The Battle of Cowpens—nearly six years into the war— was only the third time the Patriots destroyed a significant British army

Advantage, Tories

There were advantages to being a Tory. If Tories were burned out of their homes, they could always go inside British lines or request assistance from the British army. There was no such assistance for Patriots. There was also some protection for Tory families in the fact that the British raised Tory units in the North and sent them to the South. A soldier's misdeeds in the South could not bring down retribution on his family living in British zones in the North. Thus Tory troops from New York and New Jersey could and did murder Southern Patriots and severely mistreat their wives and children without fear of reprisal. On the other hand, there is no recorded instance of Continental troops from Virginia or Maryland abusing Tory families in South Carolina. Patriot militia in the South summarily executed captured Tories who were well known for brutality to Patriot families, but those instances were few compared to Tory atrocities.

Perhaps one of the best examples of official British cruelty was that dealt out by Lord Cornwallis to militia leader Andrew Pickens and his family. He wrote Colonel John Cruger, in command at Ninety-Six, "If Colonel Pickens has left any Negroes, cattle, or other property that may be useful to. . . . the supply of the troops, I would have it seized accordingly, and I desire that his houses may be burned and his plantations as far as lies in your power totally destroyed and himself if ever taken instantly hanged."

Major James Dunlap, assigned this task, immediately led a detachment to Pickens's plantation, turned his wife and children out of the house into the cold with nothing but the clothes they were wearing, took all the food, cattle, and other useful supplies, and burned the house and all of the other structures. Dunlap departed leaving Rebecca Pickens and her children standing in the middle of the desolation of their lives, braving the January cold without means of survival.

With the Patriot forces routed, there was little to stop British savagery. The only Patriot army south of New Jersey was the remnant of Gates's defeated force of seven hundred that was collecting at Hillsborough, North Carolina—left leaderless by Gates's cowardly flight. Congress, having named three Southern commanders itself—Robert Howe, Benjamin Lincoln, and Horatio Gates (obviously, Congress was not fit to select a military commander)—now threw the problem to Washington. Washington selected Nathanael Greene, less for his military talent, which was unproven at that point, than for his intelligence and loyalty to the commander-in-chief. Within the next three months Greene performed a miracle, assembling a force at Charlotte that numbered over four thousand men, including sixteen hundred Continentals. Few of these new levies had ever been in battle; it was this untried and inexperienced force that Greene would use to oppose Cornwallis. Cornwallis's strength in the Carolinas and Georgia varied between eight and eleven thousand men—two to three times that of the Patriots. About three quarters of Cornwallis's men were regulars; the remainder were Tories, themselves seasoned fighters.

Backcountry War

Meanwhile, war in the Carolina backcountry went on. Some two hundred mounted militiamen under colonels Elijah Clarke and Isaac Shelby clashed with twice that number of Tories at a supply depot near Musgrove Mill in South Carolina. The Patriots—many of them Scotch-Irish "Overmountain Men" from over the Appalachian mountains west of North Carolina in what is now the state of Tennessee—drew the Tories into an ambush and dealt them a stinging defeat. An angry Cornwallis sent Major Patrick Ferguson to seek out and punish the Patriots responsible for Musgrove Mill. Ferguson, knowing that Isaac Shelby had returned to Tennessee to bring in his harvest, sent him a personal message threatening to march into Tennessee, hang all the Overmountain leaders, and scorch the earth.

Ferguson's threat backfired. The Overmountain Men raised an army of nearly five hundred men, who were joined by another four hundred

★ ★ ★

Overmountain Men

While many Americans are familiar with "Mountain Men" such as Jim Bridger, the Overmountain Men who fought in the American Revolution were a different breed entirely.

These frontiersmen, from west of the Appalachian mountains, had been fighting the Cherokee for years. When these settlers, who lived mostly in the Watauga area of North Carolina and around Kingsport in what would be Tennessee, were ordered to leave the Indian land by the British government, they worked out a deal with the Cherokee to formally lease the land. In 1772 they created the "Watauga Association," the first American constitutional government west of the Appalachians.

The crown and Virginia's colonial government saw the Watauga Association as a threat both to their authority and to relations with the Indians, so ordered the settlers off the leased Indian land. The Cherokee, under Dragging Canoe, engaged in attacks on the American settlements, but by 1776 they were defeated. The Overmountain Men were staunch Whigs who planned operations against the British as soon as the Revolution broke out. To honor the exploits of the Overmountain Men, in 1980 Congress established the Overmountain Victory National Historic Trail with the "Overmountain Man Statue" at Elizabethton, Tennessee.

Virginians. More poured in, and soon the Patriot army numbered fourteen hundred men led by William Campbell, who had been voted by the five militia colonels present to be in overall command.

Hearing that Ferguson had made camp about thirty miles west of Charlotte on the top of King's Mountain with about eleven hundred men (mostly of Tory militiamen), the Patriots mounted nine hundred men and rushed east to launch a surprise attack. King's Mountain, just north of the South Carolina line, was a large, flat-topped ridge that made a natural strongpoint. The Patriots arrived at about 4:00 p.m. and quickly surrounded the hill. Ferguson made three bayonet attacks down the hill, but the hunting rifles of the Overmountain Men were devastating.

The heavy wood of the mountain protected the riflemen as they moved up the slopes, picking off Tories as they went. These frontier sharpshooters exacted a bloody toll on Ferguson's men, then on Ferguson himself. A sharpshooter killed him, and the Tories readily surrendered. They had lost 224 killed, 163 wounded, and 716 taken prisoner. Ferguson's entire force had been eliminated, while the Patriots lost fewer than ninety total casualties.

This devastating defeat shook Cornwallis, who was now convinced to retreat from Charlotte back into South Carolina and make camp at Winnsboro in October of 1780. He fell ill and remained idle at Winnsboro for three months while the Patriot partisans ratcheted up their operations. Francis Marion took his force to within a few miles of Georgetown before being driven back. When Cornwallis sent Tarleton to destroy Sumter, it was Sumter who defeated Tarleton, killing or wounding one hundred men at Blackstocks on November 30, 1780.

Still, Greene's army was so inferior to Cornwallis's that Greene split his forces to attack the outlying British posts in the middle of December. He sent Daniel Morgan and Colonel William Washington—a second cousin to George Washington and a fierce fighter—with about six hundred men to join up with Sumter and other guerrilla forces, then move south to threaten Ninety-Six and Augusta. Meanwhile, Greene took eleven hundred men to Cheraw to support Marion.

★ ★ ★

Hessians Become German Americans

The much-hated Hessians were not used in the South except to garrison Charleston since they had become generally unreliable. Desertions occurred nearly every day, and the deserters often joined the Patriot guerrillas. As we have already seen, the desertion rate became so high that Hessians were no longer assigned picket duty—in the South, Scottish regulars and Northern Tories were used on pickets instead. King George didn't have to pay for deserters but did pay for battle deaths, so the Hessian commanders went after them, killing them "in action."

The Battle of Cowpens

Cornwallis remained curiously passive. Instead of taking the field and attempting to defeat Greene, Cornwallis sent Tarleton to attack Daniel Morgan's little army and Major General Alexander Leslie to reinforce Camden in front of Greene. All the while he himself remained at Winnsboro, where he celebrated the arrival of 1781. Perhaps Cornwallis had begun to feel the helplessness of his situation; events soon would make it clear to everyone.

Tarleton found out that Morgan was not at Ninety-Six, as Cornwallis believed, but retreating northward toward North Carolina. Tarleton moved rapidly to intercept Morgan, and soon spies informed him that Morgan had taken up a position at the South Carolina Cowpens, in an open field with the Broad River at his back and his flanks unprotected. Tarleton assumed it would be easy for him to annihilate another Patriot army.

Tarleton was leading a fearsome force of his British Legion, supplemented with veterans of infantry and dragoons, totaling over eleven hundred men. Morgan claimed to have had only about eight hundred men, but more likely his force was closer to Tarleton's numbers when all the stray militiamen coming in and out of camp were counted. Knowing that Tarleton was coming on, Morgan posted most of his men in three lines: 150 expert riflemen were placed in front as skirmishers to slow Tarleton's advance, about 315 militiamen in the center (most of those men had seen combat more than once in the Continental Army, even though they were now militia), then his Maryland Continentals on a slight knoll, supported by more militiamen, about 430 in all. But key to Morgan's strategy was the force he had hidden behind a hill—about 125 cavalry commanded by William Washington. Morgan's troops were well rested, and he had them up and in position before

★ ★ ★
The Numbers Game

Funny when you win a great battle how many people "participated." (Victory, as they say, has a thousand fathers, but defeat is an orphan.) After a battle such as King's Mountain, many more are bound to claim to have been involved than really were. Individual accounts of the battle and pension applications made forty years later have led some historians to believe Morgan's force was as large as ninteen hundred men. Morgan may have underestimated his force at eight hundred, but modern research has failed to take into account the tendency for individuals who were nowhere near the action to claim they fought there. For example, in the 2000 census, 14.85 million Americans claimed to be Vietnam veterans (up from 11.2 million in 1995), although only 8.75 million were on active duty during the war, 2.6 million actually served inside Vietnam, and fewer than 1.6 million either fought in combat or provided support where they were exposed to enemy attack. The real number of Vietnam veterans still alive in 2000 was only slightly above 1 million, making over 13.8 million Americans guilty of being—to judge them generously—highly imaginative. And the general lack of rosters and records in the Southern militia no doubt made it easier—even irresistible—for Revolutionary-era Americans to claim what we call "stolen valor." If people are eager to associate themselves with a "lost" war, how much more enthusiastic would they have been to claim part of a great victory on a pension application that few could refute?

3:00 a.m. on January 17, 1781, awaiting Tarleton. He instructed his skirmishers to pick off the officers, and the militia in the center under Andrew Pickens to fire only two volleys and retire behind the hill. The latter order was crucial: Morgan assumed that he couldn't rely on the militia to stand its ground. They would tend to run, but he wanted an orderly retreat. Knowing they only had to fire two shots and not face the British bayonets would give them the confidence to fire accurately and retreat in good order.

Tarleton had his troops up early and moving as rapidly as possible, and his van arrived at Cowpens in the pre-dawn darkness. They were tired and hungry, but headed straight at Morgan's position. As Morgan hoped, his riflemen took a fearsome toll of the advancing troops, especially the officers. But Tarleton continued to push his men forward relentlessly. Pickens's militia fired its two volleys, then turned to retreat. As dawn was breaking, the British troops assumed the American line was breaking up. They rushed forward, only to be stopped cold by the Maryland regulars in the third line. When a portion of the third line (John Howard's Virginia militia) began to retreat a few steps, Tarleton's Scottish Highlanders charged, believing a rout was at hand. To their shock, the Virginians and the Marylanders turned around, fired a volley at no more than thirty yards, and charged the Highlanders with their bayonets. The Highlanders broke, some fleeing, but many surrendering on the spot. Meanwhile, in a maneuver of exceptional discipline, the militia from the second line, which had fired its two shots, had moved all the way around to the right flank to envelop the remainder of Tarleton's left, while William Washington's hidden cavalry had come around on the left flank to complete the double envelopment. Tarleton's infantry lay down to surrender and were captured, and the vaunted British Legion fled from the field. By the time the sun was fully up, the Americans had won their third annihilation battle over an important British army. Tarleton had lost over 100 men killed and about 830 prisoners—85 percent of his command.

The Race to the Dan

Upon receiving Tarleton's report of the defeat at Cowpens, Cornwallis decided to go all out to capture Morgan's little army. He burned his tents, baggage, and supplies, and even destroyed his substantial store of rum. He mounted as much infantry as he could, and destroyed all his wagons except for those used as ambulances. Cornwallis was risking the welfare of his army in order to capture Morgan before he escaped into Patriot-held

Virginia. Morgan was encumbered by his prisoners and captured equipment and would be slowed accordingly. What ensued was "The Race to the Dan."

Greene, with an aide and three orderlies but no troops, joined Morgan and ordered Pickens to take the prisoners to Charlottesville, Virginia. Morgan set off for the Yadkin River, and General William Davidson's 300 North Carolina militiamen, who had just joined the army, were sent to impede Cornwallis's crossing of the Catawba. Cornwallis had no boats; he was waiting for the river to fall low enough for his men to ford it. The next day Cornwallis crossed at two fords, killed Davidson, but took casualties he could not afford. Meanwhile, Morgan and Greene reached the Yadkin and crossed the swollen river on boats, completing the crossing just as Cornwallis's van reached the river.

Cornwallis was forced to move twenty-five miles up the river to find a passable ford, while Greene continued on to Guilford (modern-day Greensboro.) Cornwallis decided to put himself between Greene and the fords on the upper Dan River, believing the Americans would not be able to cross the wide lower Dan.

At Guilford, Greene ordered Colonel Otho H. Williams and his force to stay in front of Cornwallis and impede his progress. Williams took Colonel Light Horse Harry Lee and his cavalry and became a thorn in Tarleton's side, carrying on a nearly continuous series of skirmishes against the British force. Lee and his cavalry met the British vanguard, killing or capturing all but one man. These were losses—of men and time—that Cornwallis could not make good.

On February 11, a deadly skirmish occurred at Summerfield. A farmer reported to Colonel Williams that Cornwallis's men were nearby. Williams sent Captain James Armstrong and three other men of Lee's legion to investigate. James Gillies, Colonel Henry Lee's fourteen-year-old bugler, had lent his horse to the farmer so he could lead Lee's men to the British, and waited with the farmer's horse for their return. Armstrong and his men bumped into one of Tarleton's detachments and soon came galloping back past young Gillies, pursued by some of Tarleton's dragoons. Seeing the boy holding a horse, Tarleton's Tories hacked him to death with their swords. Lee and the main body of his men, coming up the road at that precise moment, witnessed the scene and attacked in a rage. All the British and Tories were killed or taken prisoner—more losses that Cornwallis could not sustain.

Greene crossed the Dan River two days later, followed by Williams and his exhausted men two days after that. Tired as they were, the Patriots had the river crossing, and the British did not. When Cornwallis finally rode up the following day, there was nothing he could do: he was 230 miles from his base, out of supplies, and his army spent. His ambulances were full of wounded soldiers, and his route was marked with numerous graves.

The Battle of Guilford Courthouse

Now, after so many years, the shoe was on the other foot. The British were no longer the pursuers, but the pursued. Greene immediately sent Williams and Lee after the Redcoats. His men caught a large body of Tory militia who had responded to Cornwallis's call for aid and destroyed them, killing one-third and taking the rest prisoner. Word of the debacle got out, and Cornwallis's North Carolina recruitment dried up.

Greene was not finished. He wanted a battle, and Cornwallis marched westward from Hillsborough to give him one. Greene had selected and occupied a position he felt would be favorable to his army at Guilford Courthouse. He had about forty-five hundred men

★ ★ ★
Hardheaded

Despite the size and destructiveness of musket balls in the Revolutionary War, not everyone found the encounter with one fatal. A doctor in the Revolution recalled treating a soldier who had been shot in the forehead: the ball merely penetrated the skin but flattened out against the soldier's skull, not penetrating it! Talk about a hard head.

★ ★ ★

Cowpens to Guilford Courthouse Report Card

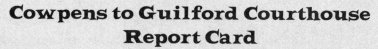

The British

Charles Cornwallis: D

He missed many opportunities—he should, for example, have positioned his army north of Charlotte to trap Morgan after Camden. Instead, Cornwallis stressed garrisoning territory rather than defeating Patriot armies.

Banastre Tarleton: F

He threw away the troops Cornwallis had given him in a rash act of hubris. His name also probably inspired less terror than fury.

The British troops: A

They were unsuccessful only where they were grossly misused.

The Americans

Daniel Morgan: A

At Cowpens, he planned and executed the perfect battle.

Nathanael Greene: B

He was getting better, but not yet ready for prime time.

Andrew Pickens: A

A superb combat commander, he also maintained discipline in his camp.

The American troops: B

The Continental troops (except for the Second Maryland) performed consistently well, and the raw militiamen were sometimes as good as the regulars. At Guilford Courthouse, however, the militia simply ran away from the battle, turning what could have been a great American victory into a defeat.

in his army, of whom more than seventeen hundred were Continentals, but fewer than five hundred had ever been in a major battle. Morgan was now sick and on home leave, but Greene resolved to make good use of his militia following the same tactic Morgan had used at Cowpens. This time the Patriot forces outnumbered the British nearly two to one, but Greene spaced his men too far apart. Nor was there a river at his back, to prevent the militia from running.

It was a seesaw fight. Cornwallis committed his reserve just in time to save a Cowpens-like rout. At that point Greene decided to save his army and ordered a retreat. The result was that by morning Greene again occupied a very good defensive position, behind the Haw River. He had lost seventy-eight killed and 183 wounded, and over 1,000 of the militia members were missing, but soon they began showing up. For Cornwallis, on the other hand, the losses were irreplaceable. He had seen nearly 30 percent of his 1,500 men killed or wounded—and had no supplies, having burned his wagons. A British defeat like Burgoyne's at Saratoga was looking like a real possibility.

Abandoning his wounded, Cornwallis set off for Cross Creek (Fayetteville). When the supplies he ordered failed to show up there, he moved on to Wilmington. He stayed only long enough to re-fit, then headed north to Petersburg, Virginia, to begin what would be his last campaign of the war. Up to this point, Cornwallis had personally lost no battles in the South, but he had put his troops in a position to suffer steady and mounting casualties from skirmishes and raids. Once again, the British had proved they were bound to a handful of coastal enclaves. Very soon the Patriots would again control the South.

CHAPTER 16

The South Rises Again

Long before there was a Confederate States of America, the South rose from defeat to play a decisive role in the War for Independence. Nathanael Greene was at the center of that revival. He began his campaign to reconquer the Carolinas and Georgia after seeing Cornwallis off to the safety of the Royal Navy at Wilmington—but rather than following Cornwallis to Wilmington, a movement of no strategic value, he marched into South Carolina. Greene's army was laughably small for such an endeavor, containing only four infantry regiments, Light Horse Harry Lee's Legion, and William Washington's dragoons, totaling barely fifteen hundred men. (For perspective, recall that George Washington's army that was routed on Long Island had over *ten times* that many combatants!)

For militia and partisan operations, Greene could count on Andrew Pickens in western South Carolina, Francis Marion in the Pee Dee swamps watching Charleston and Georgetown, and to a much lesser extent the very independent Thomas Sumter, who was camped on the Broad River recovering from a wound and recruiting men. Their harassment was impressively effective; no British forces moved freely in the countryside.

Did you know?

★ Francis Marion captured British forts by building towers taller than the forts

★ British and Tory depredations left 1,400 destitute widows in the Ninety-Six District, South Carolina

★ Harsh British military policy in the South contributed to Southerners' hatred of Northerners and Indians and likely to their attachment to slavery

Yet on paper the British were still formidable, maybe even unbeatable. Now under the command of Francis Edward Rawdon-Hastings (Lord Rawdon), over 8,000 regulars remained in South Carolina and Georgia. But these men were spread out over no fewer than eight encampments in various towns and posts, as Rawdon continued Cornwallis's strategy of maintaining a large British presence in important towns to pacify the population, rather than using the troops to defeat Patriot armies.

In fact, without Lord Cornwallis's large roving army, the British were vulnerable. With Tarleton in the field, Cornwallis had been able to terrorize an area into submission, severely punishing a recalcitrant population by burning their crops, farms, and homes, and murdering family members. And there was always the threat of arrest and confinement in one of the prison ships, which meant a miserable death by disease or starvation. Now, Lord Rawdon did not have Tarleton's services, and roving bands of partisans or Patriot militia seemed to have the upper hand. Even worse, the spread-out British posts were not mutually supporting; they could be picked off one by one. Greene set out to capture those posts, but first he had to defeat or neutralize the largest non-coastal detachment, Rawdon and his fourteen hundred men at Camden.

Fool Me Once

While Greene marched on Camden, Marion and Lee attacked Fort Watson on the Santee River, about halfway between Charleston and Camden. Marion built a tower higher than the stockade, rendering the fort untenable. That sent a message that Rawdon heard loud and clear. If he didn't want to be defeated, he was going to have to be aggressive.

Greene had apparently hoped to surprise Rawdon at Camden, but Tories warned the British of his approach. Greene didn't have enough men to assault Rawdon's fortifications or invest Camden for a siege, so he withdrew to a rise called Hobkirk's Hill two miles north of Camden and arrayed his troops in a defensive posture. Rawdon took the bait, even though he only had 900 troops at his disposal. Though he had a superior defensive position, Greene once again tried the "Cowpens maneuver." Unfortunately for Greene, this difficult maneuver depended on solid lines of communications and the enemy playing along.

Rawdon didn't. He extended his line by bringing up his reserves, defeating the flanking attacks, then allowed panic to set in among Greene's militia. Greene retreated, defeated once again. Nonetheless, Hobkirk's Hill turned out to be a strategic victory for the Patriots, as after the battle Rawdon retreated to Monck's Corner, about thirty miles from Charleston.

Picking Them Off

Using essentially the same strategy that would be employed by Ulysses S. Grant in the Civil War and Eisenhower in France and Germany, Greene ordered attacks on all fronts. Pickens moved against Ninety-Six, Marion and Lee were at the Santee Hills, but Sumter had disobeyed orders—not for the first time—and decided to attack Fort Granby (modern-day Columbia). Marion dutifully surrounded Fort Motte and its garrison of 150 men and soon showed his ability to think outside of the box. The post was an old colonial mansion that had been fortified. Marion shot flaming arrows to ignite the dry shingles on the roof of the mansion, and in the resulting conflagration the garrison surrendered.

Meanwhile, the ever-independent Sumter changed his mind and attacked Orangeburg. Rawdon had already given the order to evacuate Orangeburg, and Sumter easily captured its garrison of 350 men. Sumter then retraced his steps to Granby, only to find that Lee had arrived the previous day, and compelled Granby's garrison of 240 men to surrender. Within a month of Hobkirk's Hill, Rawdon had lost three of his outposts and 740 men, forcing him to evacuate Camden. All the interior British bases in South Carolina and Georgia were now in Patriot hands except Ninety-Six and Augusta, and their days were numbered. Greene marched against Ninety-Six, while sending Lee to join with Pickens and Elijah Clarke's Georgia militia to attack Augusta.

In their approach to Augusta on May 21, Lee and Clarke attacked the stockaded post of a royal Indian agent on the Savannah River. The fight did not last long, and the garrison surrendered. There the Patriots found a large amount of supplies intended as inducements to encourage Indians to attack Patriot towns and farms in the west. This evidence of British criminality threw Clarke's men into an unforgiving rage—it would have been their farms the Indians would have attacked. Augusta was doomed.

Augusta was defended by two forts, one in a town called Fort Cornwallis and one about a thousand yards up the Savannah River. The outlying fort was garrisoned by eighty Georgia Tories under Lieutenant Colonel James Grierson; it was left up to Clarke to capture. The Tories lost heart and mounted an escape attempt to the main fort. Nearly half were killed by Clarke's men, and the remainder were captured.

The siege of Fort Cornwallis was undertaken in earnest on May 23. The garrison, comprising over 300 men from the king's Carolina Rangers and other units, was commanded by Colonel Thomas Brown. Brown put up a good defense, but Lee proposed using the same tactic that had proven so successful at Fort Watson. The Patriots built a thirty-foot high tower, mounted a six-pounder cannon at the top, and with the cannon and sharpshooting riflemen, caused havoc in the fort. After unsuccessful British efforts to destroy the tower, the post surrendered.

That left only Ninety-Six remaining of the interior posts manned by British and Tory troops. Greene began his siege with 1,000 men, planning on using the same tactics that had worked elsewhere. But Ninety-Six proved to have more complex and extensive defensive works than those the Patriots had previously encountered, and the tower proved ineffective. The town was set up as a large square; a formidable star-shaped fort covered the approaches to the two sides offering easiest access, and a small redoubt covered another side. Both the British and Patriots sent for reinforcements. Lee and Pickens arrived from their successful siege of Augusta, and Rawdon left Charleston with 2,000 British regulars, pushing Greene's timetable forward. After attack and counterattack, with fierce hand-to-hand fighting, the Patriots were pushed out. Greene retreated northwards two days later, unfairly blaming Marion and Sumter for failing to keep the reinforcements away from Ninety-Six. Greene had had another defeat. It seemed like everyone enjoyed victories but him.

Winning by Losing

Still, the British position at Ninety-Six was obviously exposed, and it could not count on large-scale reinforcements every time it was threatened. Rawdon abandoned Ninety-Six on July 10, leaving the desolated backcountry to the Patriots. Nowhere in America had the countryside been ravaged so completely. There were over 1,400 destitute widows in the Ninety-Six District alone, and the fratricidal war between Patriots and Tories was at its most terrifying. With nothing more to lose, Tories destroyed and murdered in a mad orgy of hopelessness. They had burned their bridges, and safety could be found only inside British lines. Many made the trek to Charleston and established Rawdon Town on its outskirts to await their fate.

Greene had concentrated all the elements of his army at the Santee for the summer. Sumter, however, launched an ill-advised attack near Monck's Corner and was repulsed with heavy losses. Lee and Marion had had enough, and a general revolt took place among the militia. Henry Lee took his men to Greene, Marion returned to the Peyre plantation on the Santee, and the troops in Sumter's brigade became mutinous and unreliable.

A Book You're Not Supposed to Read

The Swamp Fox: How Francis Marion Saved the American Revolution by John Oller (Boston: Da Capo Press, 2016).

Sumter sulked and went home, and—in a change of command that was long overdue—Francis Marion took charge of the South Carolina militia.

Francis Marion, the "Swamp Fox," now became a more traditional commander. Soon he was forced to deal with British perfidy in the case of Isaac Hayne, a colonel in the Colleton County militia. Hayne had surrendered at Charleston and agreed to remain neutral in return for British protection. But when Clinton abrogated the terms of the paroles, Hayne accepted a commission to raise a regiment in Marion's Brigade. When a detachment of British dragoons captured him wearing a Patriot uniform, they tried and hanged him. Patriot rage exploded upon news of the hanging, but Greene forbade any retaliation. Marion nevertheless took his own measures. His men ambushed the dragoons along the Edisto River, dealing them serious losses. The message to the British and Tories had been delivered.

Rawdon, unable to control the Southern backcountry, gave up and returned to England, and was replaced by Alexander Stewart (Scots made up almost 30 percent of the British officers in America and probably the majority of common soldiers in Tory regiments). As a final insult, Rawdon's ship was captured by the Comte de Grasse and he was taken as a prisoner to Yorktown.

Stewart relocated his base to Eutaw Springs, where he was pursued by Greene with a force of twenty-three hundred, the majority of them regulars. Light Horse Harry Lee forced a battle on September 8 by scooping up a foraging party digging potatoes. Stewart formed his men in a single line, and as Greene pushed forward, the fighting grew heavy. The Patriot militia fought well, and the infantry and Lee's cavalry on the right drove the British back through their camp. It seemed for a moment that the day was won. But

Greene lost control of his men: the Virginia and Maryland regiments stopped to plunder the British camp, eating and drinking their fill of rum. Stewart saw the opportunity, counterattacked, and Greene once again had to retreat.

Both sides licked their wounds. This time the Americans had taken a beating, suffering almost five hundred casualties to four hundred British—but Stewart also had more than four hundred men missing (most likely deserters). These were losses England could not replace. Stewart fell back again, then after another skirmish, had to take up a defensive position inside Charleston, his army now down to eight hundred men. After almost two years of constant maneuvering, fighting, and maneuvering again, English troops had been forced inch by inch out of every part of the South except for three coastal cities—despite the fact that Greene had yet to win a battle.

Death by a Thousand Cuts

In fact the Patriots had only won three significant fights in the South other than Moore's Creek Bridge: Fort Moultrie, King's Mountain, and Cowpens. There had been small victories gained by Marion, Pickens, Clarke, Lee, and Sumter, but in every battle where the majority of the British force was comprised of regulars, the British were victorious.

In the end, however, the British lost. They were a great power, but they tried to fight the war on the cheap, using Tory allies—especially Tory units from the North—rather than their own regular forces. The savage war in the South had long-lasting implications. The use of Tory units from the North and of Highlanders fueled a long-standing Southern hatred of Northerners, and of Scots and Irish Catholics. Animosity toward the Cherokee also burned for many years. (When Andrew Jackson had the opportunity to drive them beyond the Mississippi, he took it with relish.)

The British also de facto freed the Negro slaves—a policy that turned out to be more of a problem for the British than the American slave owners.

★ ★ ★

Georgia and the Carolinas Report Card

The British

Lord Rawdon: B

An excellent and prudent commander, he never understood why the Patriots were fighting. Less aggressive than Cornwallis, Rawdon knew that the easiest way England could be defeated was by its commanders taking inadvisable risks.

The British troops: A

The regulars never failed.

The Americans

Nathanael Greene: D

His generalship was uninspired, and he couldn't control his subordinates (notably Sumter).

Francis Marion: A

A winner throughout, he caused the British hundreds upon hundreds of casualties.

Andrew Pickens: A

Consistently one of the best militia commanders in the war.

Elijah Clarke: A

Another highly competent commander like Pickens.

Thomas Sumter: F

Sumter sometimes won skirmishes, but was unreliable and insubordinate. He did only what he wanted to do.

Henry Light Horse Harry Lee: A

Consistently made good decisions and was an outstanding combat leader.

The American troops: C

Sometimes good, sometimes poor. While Cowpens had been pulled off with superb coordination in a time when such battlefield coordination was rare—in large part by militia—the battles of Hobkirk's Hill and Eutaw Springs were both lost by the misbehavior of the troops.

Nonetheless, it may well have played a role in perpetuating the "Peculiar Institution"—steeling South Carolina and Georgia against outside influences that might challenge the institution of slavery. Would Southerners have been more receptive to abolition in the Constitutional debates without British policies in the Revolution? Possibly. But the wounds festered in Georgia and South Carolina all the way to the Civil War and beyond.

As in the North, the Patriots lost the battles, but won the war. They lost, rose, lost, and rose again—over and over. Nathanael Greene lost four major battles, yet he drove the British out of the interior of North Carolina, South Carolina, and Georgia, and into the enclaves of Wilmington, Charleston, and Savannah. The Patriots took horrendous casualties, but so did the English, and Britain found it much more difficult to supply replacements. The population of Tories and neutrals far outnumbered that of Patriots, but the vast majority of them could not be induced to risk their lives and those of their families for the king. It was better to stay neutral and try to play both sides. If England won, you were still a loyal subject; if the Patriots won, you would enjoy self-government. In the South, the Revolutionary War was won by Patriots willing to die for their cause, while Tories could look forward only to continued slights by the king. In the final analysis, however, there was no middle ground of neutrality—the war had become too personal and ugly, and forgiveness was not on the horizon.

CHAPTER 17

Washington Victorious

While Cornwallis was setting the South on fire, Clinton seemed to have developed rigor mortis in New York City. And when Cornwallis reached the temporary haven of Wilmington, the gains from six years of warfare had almost evaporated. On paper, however, things still looked good. In the far north, Canada was secure and Maine had been reconquered and was now the colony of New Ireland; in the South, Savannah and Charleston were unassailable British strongholds, and much of lower New York, upper New Jersey, and Long Island were secure for the crown. Yet the rest of America was in rebel hands, including the territory all the way to the Mississippi.

Clinton wasn't ready to throw in the towel, but his strategy up to the current point had been dead wrong. He, King George, and Lord George Germain—the secretary of state for North America—all mistakenly saw the war in terms of acquiring and securing territory. After all, that was how European wars had been conducted for centuries. Despite the failure of the British plan to split the colonies into sectors that could be defeated in detail, the basic strategy still had not been abandoned.

Did you know?

★ Benedict Arnold captured Richmond for the British and nearly caught Thomas Jefferson

★ An early version of "Yankee Doodle Dandy" threatened John Hancock with tarring and feathering

★ General Henry Clinton won only one major battle as commander-in-chief of the British forces in America

But war-weariness was setting in in England, and it was almost impossible to recruit British troops for service in America. Nor could more troops be recruited from the American Tory population—because of British failures to secure their property and livelihoods from Association attacks. Cornwallis was almost in a fit of depression over developments in the South—he had won battles at every turn, but the rebels bounced back every time and even seemed to grow stronger in defeat.

Benedict Arnold, Redcoat General

Clinton had played one last card before the Battle of Cowpens: Benedict Arnold, now a brigadier general in the British army. His name was worth a thousand troops. Arnold was roundly hated by the Patriots, who would surely flock into the militia hoping to get a chance to kill America's most notorious traitor, and once in the field they could be killed or captured. Clinton would also use Tories to fight—after all, pitting one American against another was the cheapest way to suppress the rebellion.

But the attack by Arnold was just more of the same old strategy that had failed so miserably in Philadelphia, New York, and the South: occupying territory. Through more than five years of war, Virginia had escaped its ravages. Finally in 1781, it was her turn to suffer.

While Cornwallis wintered in Winnsboro, Clinton sent Arnold to Virginia with sixteen hundred Tory troops from the Tory American Legion. Arnold arrived at Hampton Roads on January 1, 1781, after surviving a typical Chesapeake Capes winter storm that had dispersed his forces. In classic Arnold style, he refused to wait for the six hundred men that were yet to arrive, favoring the element of surprise over all else. Ordered by Clinton to establish a base in Portsmouth and avoid unnecessary risks, Arnold took two ships and proceeded up the James River. He knew how to wage war even if Clinton didn't.

Governor Thomas Jefferson, in the classic style of the politician who has never shouldered a rifle, apparently couldn't believe an invasion was in progress, and kept calling for more reports and information. Meanwhile, Arnold captured Hood's Fort and disembarked his troops about twenty-five miles below Richmond on the afternoon of January 4. Finally, Jefferson, whose faith in the militia bordered on insanity, issued a call-up. Only about two hundred responded by the next morning.

During the night Arnold marched overland to Richmond in a pouring rain. The militia, which hadn't had the opportunity to form up, made a stand at the outskirts of the city. It was hopeless. After firing a single wild volley, the militiamen fled for their lives. Arnold's men chased the militia as if they were on a foxhunt, giving no quarter. Jefferson fled from Richmond to Charlottesville, followed by all of his state government officials and their families who could get away. Few, if any, military supplies and stores were destroyed or taken out of the city. Arnold rode in unopposed at the head of a thousand men, proud of his first success as a British general, while Jefferson barely escaped capture.

The Founder vs. the Traitor

The military stores and valuables the Patriots had left behind in Richmond were immense, estimated to be thirty to forty shiploads of tobacco, West Indies goods, wines, sailcloth, precious salt that was in such short supply, and military stores. Arnold offered to spare Richmond if Jefferson allowed the British ships to remove the stores unmolested, and even to pay half price for the non-military items such as tobacco (a substantial portion was owned by merchants and factors still loyal to the crown.) Jefferson sent a scathing letter in reply that infuriated Arnold and probably condemned Richmond to obliteration. By that time Arnold had a fleet of ten captured ships and thirty boats, so was able to empty the city of the most important supplies.

After loading everything he could, Arnold set fire to the public buildings and warehouses, whether empty or still full. The fires rapidly got out of hand, and Richmond went up in flames. The Virginia government papers and records that Jefferson had failed to remove were destroyed in the fire. Whether Richmond was destroyed intentionally or accidentally, it was folly of Jefferson to defy and anger Arnold while Richmond was entirely at his mercy.

Unfortunately, the Patriot losses were not confined to the city of Richmond. Arnold sent Major John Simcoe's Tory Rangers up the James, where they destroyed the largest Patriot foundry in America and more military stores. Another detachment marched to Chesterfield and burned its mills and warehouses before returning to Richmond. Satisfied that he had proven himself to be Britain's most dangerous general, Arnold led his troops back to Portsmouth and constructed defensive positions.

Upon reading reports of the events in Virginia, Washington was livid. There was little he could do, given mutinies among his troops and the total dependence of Congress on French monetary loans that couldn't be repaid. Nonetheless, he ordered Lafayette and Steuben to Virginia with twelve hundred Continental troops from New England and New Jersey. The French promised support, saying they would contribute a similar number of troops and a fleet. Admiral Sochet Destouches would sail from Newport, Rhode Island, and trap Arnold in Portsmouth. Lafayette was to summarily hang Arnold if captured. Jefferson, not to be outdone, offered a five-thousand-guinea reward in gold for Arnold's head. While the Patriots gnashed their teeth and slowly gathered their forces, Arnold remained inactive at Portsmouth. He began to look more like an opportunity than a threat. If the British fleet could be neutralized, Arnold's small army would be isolated and at risk.

Lafayette was slow to move, but the French were even slower. Even the very lethargic British Admiral Mariot Arbuthnot, sailing from New York, was able to catch Destouches off the mouth of the Chesapeake Bay and drive the French fleet away. Destouches hightailed it to Rhode Island, and Lafayette was on his own. Meanwhile, Arnold received reinforcements, bringing his force to about forty-two hundred men. Washington immediately ordered "Mad" Anthony Wayne and his Pennsylvania brigade to Virginia, but Wayne could not get there before late May. For the time being, the British in Virginia outnumbered Steuben's militia almost two to one—Lafayette had still not arrived in Virginia yet—although there were other independent Patriot forces in the region. Virginia had not responded well to the crisis.

A new British general on the scene, William Phillips, replaced Arnold and began shifting the British force inland. In April he moved up the James toward Richmond, where Steuben had managed to concentrate about a thousand militia. Steuben decided to make a stand at Blandford. In the resulting battle, the militia fought like veterans for about two hours, but in the end the disparity in numbers obliged Steuben to retreat.

Finally, Lafayette's troops began to arrive by forced marches from Maryland. But Virginia was a cornucopia of goodies for the British, all ripe for the taking, while Lafayette was slow to concentrate. Phillips marched to Warrick, where he found another undefended bonanza in stores awaiting his arrival. The British troops destroyed five hundred barrels of flour, burned several ships, and set a number of mills and warehouses of tobacco, rope, and hides on fire. At the time the town of Warrick was larger than Richmond, and the losses were catastrophic. Having destroyed or seized everything of value, Phillips retreated down the James to join up with Cornwallis, well satisfied with his work in crippling Virginia. Unexpectedly, however, Phillips took ill and died.

Against Clinton's orders, Cornwallis had abandoned North Carolina and brought the remnant of his once-proud command—now only fifteen hundred men—into Virginia to seek a strategic victory. With Arnold's men, plus reinforcements from New York City, Cornwallis once again had a respectable force of about seventy-two hundred troops. At that point, Cornwallis no longer saw any need for a turncoat like Arnold, so he sent the American traitor back to Clinton in New York City. The result was that the best British general was placed in a location where he could no longer have an impact on the war's outcome.

With the opportunity to capture Virginia and destroy Lafayette and Wayne standing before him, Cornwallis blinked. His forces outnumbered the Americans two to one, but he had never been the same after falling ill at Winnsboro, and the bloodletting at Guilford Courthouse had left him plagued with doubts about operating without the protection of the Royal Navy.

A Narrow Escape

But even while he dithered, Cornwallis loosed his avenging angels, Tarleton and the New York Tory leader—now a British lieutenant colonel—John Graves Simcoe. Tarleton rode hard for Charlottesville to capture the state legislature and its governor, Thomas Jefferson. Jefferson was nearly caught, this time at his home; less than ten minutes after Jefferson left his plantation by a rear gate, Tarleton's Legion arrived at Monticello. It was a long ride, but the raid accomplished little besides spreading terror throughout the countryside and further alienating Americans from the English.

Point of Fork was the location of Steuben's arsenal for the Virginia militia, and may have contained a thousand muskets and three hundred barrels of powder, although the amount of arms and provisions it held is controversial. Steuben abandoned it without a fight at the approach of the raiding party under Simcoe—apparently believing that Simcoe's detachment was the van of Cornwallis's army. Simcoe gathered up the Patriot supplies and leisurely returned down the James River. Cornwallis then took his army to Williamsburg, and the widely separated elements of the American force came together to follow. It was there on June 9 that Lafayette caught up with Cornwallis, and a sharp skirmish resulted—the first actual clash of the armies in over a month.

At that point, Cornwallis received an order from Clinton to send three thousand troops to New York, forcing him to move to Jamestown. Lafayette pressed Cornwallis closely again, but was defeated when Cornwallis laid an elaborate ambush for him. But once again, an American defeat cost the British more than it hurt the Americans. "Mad" Anthony Wayne broke out of the encirclement, inflicting more losses on Cornwallis than he suffered himself. The British situation was becoming precarious.

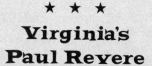

Virginia's Paul Revere

Tarleton's failure to surprise the legislature in session on June 4—he did capture some of its members—was due only to a Virginia "Paul Revere," Captain John Jouett. He spotted Tarleton's force on the roads, found a fast horse, and arrived in Charlottesville ahead of the British to spread the alarm. On June 12, after the British had departed, the legislature voted to present Jouett with an "elegant sword and pair of pistols" for his timely warning.

A Blizzard of Orders

Worse than their manpower situation was the disarray in the British command, with Cornwallis receiving a torrent of letters from Clinton, often several at one time, some of which contradicted earlier letters and left Cornwallis to figure things out as best he could. All of Clinton's conflicting letters contained a caveat—that if Cornwallis had other plans in view, Clinton's instructions were not to be followed—yet when Cornwallis determined that he needed to operate differently, he was subsequently censured for not following Clinton's instructions.

Before Cornwallis placed the three thousand troops Clinton wanted on transports, Clinton changed the orders, this time instructing him to send the men to Philadelphia first, *then* on to New York. Finally Clinton changed his orders yet again, telling Cornwallis to keep the troops in Virginia.

Cornwallis chose Yorktown as his base, going with an early recommendation of Clinton's that Yorktown was superior to Norfolk, and that he needed to be somewhere the Royal Navy could be in support. British troops immediately moved to Yorktown to begin building fortifications and also to occupy Gloucester Point, across the York River. Clinton made no complaint at the time, only later censuring Cornwallis for this choice.

In the north, Washington was still attempting to wring some military benefit out of the French alliance. French loans had kept the Patriots in the war, but as of the beginning of July 1781, French troops had not yet fired a musket ball except during the ill-fated attack on Savannah. Finally, Washington was informed that a new fleet was being sent under the command of Comte de Grasse to cooperate with the French army commander in Rhode Island, the Comte de Rochambeau, under Washington's direction. The two

★ ★ ★

Did the British Ever Have a Chance?

Many historians see the American victory in the Revolutionary War as "almost a miracle," in John Ferling's words. Joseph Ellis, on the other hand, claims that as early as 1776, thanks to poor British military leadership, there was only a slim chance the British could have won. What is the truth of the matter? Despite some advantages, the Americans had the hand of providence on them. Washington's army escaped complete annihilation on several occasions. The failed Canadian invasion alone could have sunk the revolution. One or two crushing defeats at any time would have demoralized the rebellion, empowered the Tories, and changed the perspective of the French. What enabled the Patriots to win was the Association and the unflagging dedication of the American common man to the cause of liberty. It is true that the British made major strategic errors—particularly in their reliance on the Tories and their obsession with controlling cities—but the fact that Patriot militiamen were able to continue to engage the British regulars was remarkable. The war was won by the common soldier and lower-ranking officers, men whose names are unknown today. Often as not, battles were won in spite of the higher-ranking American officers, and certainly in spite of Congress.

armies promptly joined together in July, with the French force numbering over forty-seven hundred and Washington's army about five thousand.

There were only five British armies in the colonies to attack: Clinton's at New York, Cornwallis's at Yorktown, and the smaller detachments at Wilmington, Charleston, and Savannah. The three southern armies were too far away, Clinton's force was too large, and that left only Cornwallis. An attack was inadvisable until de Grasse arrived with the French fleet, but for the first time since Long Island, Washington had a reasonably large and well-trained force of regulars under his command. De Grasse headed for the Chesapeake, but he had a short window: he was required to sail back to France in October. Whatever was going to happen at Yorktown would have to happen fast.

Cornering Corny

Washington moved rapidly to attack Cornwallis. He left a small force to watch Clinton in New York while he took the main body of his army and Rochambeau's to Virginia. This was a very risky move. Clinton had just been reinforced with more Hessians, and with his 16,700 men he had by far the largest force on the continent. Washington was leaving Clinton in New York, making a long flank march to attack Cornwallis, and counting on Clinton's reticence to engage in a major campaign of his own. Defeat or victory, Washington was setting this campaign to be his last throw of the dice: he put all his chips on de Grasse holding off Admiral Graves from rescuing Cornwallis, and Clinton staying put. It was a bold move, typical of Washington.

The French connection finally worked this time. As de Grasse sailed up toward the Chesapeake, the pursuing British Admiral Hood unknowingly passed him. Then when Hood failed to find de Grasse in the Chesapeake, he sailed on to New York rather than maintain a supporting presence for Cornwallis. Once in New York, however, Hood's force was combined with that of

Admiral Graves, and the two British fleets immediately set course back for Virginia. But during the time Hood was in New York, de Grasse had sailed into the Chesapeake and off-loaded his troops near Williamsburg, where they linked up with Lafayette two days later.

When the British fleets finally arrived, de Grasse sailed out to fight and—probably to his surprise—found that his fleet was substantially superior to that of the two combined enemy fleets. When the combatants engaged on September 5, the fight went to the French, although the lines of ships parried for several days. The Battle of the Capes, (or the Chesapeake) as it was called, was decisive. Although France would suffer significant, stinging naval defeats to England in the coming decades, including Trafalgar and Aboukir Bay, at the time America needed France the most, the French Navy delivered.

A cornered Cornwallis faced the very real likelihood of running out of supplies before Graves could return with more men. Washington was that much closer to winning his gamble. In the end Clinton would hesitate so long that he missed the chance to reinforce Cornwallis: Graves assessed that the French fleet was too strong, and Clinton was worried about losing additional men in a vain attempt to save those trapped in Yorktown. All Washington had to do was close the bag.

He began the siege on September 28, 1781, and within two days was already occupying Cornwallis's outer works. The siege progressed rapidly, with the huge guns brought in by the French. Two attacks on outlying redoubts, one American led by Alexander Hamilton, and one French, captured the positions exposing the entire British base. It was only a matter of time as American and French engineers worked their way inward. Cornwallis knew he was doomed. On the night of October 16, he attempted to ferry his army over to Gloucester

Point on the opposite side of the York River to join Tarleton, but his plan miscarried when a storm blew up and swamped his boats—yet another miracle intervention on the side of the Americans. The next day he opened negotiations for surrender.

"The World Turned Upside Down"

Washington made sure he did not repeat Gates's mistakes at Saratoga. The entire British force would be prisoners of war, all public property would belong to the Congress, no provision was made for the exchange of prisoners, and there would be no immunity for American Tories fighting with the British army. On October 19, Cornwallis surrendered 8,077 officers, soldiers, sailors, and camp followers, as well as a massive

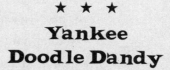

Yankee Doodle Dandy

"The World Turned Upside Down" wasn't the first piece of music to play a role in the war. The famous song "Yankee Doodle" was heard frequently, even though it dated back to the Seven Years' War (and in another form, to medieval times). British officers sang a different version of the song, referring to Thomas Ditson of Massachusetts, who had been tarred and feathered for attempting to purchase a musket. It went, "Yankee Doodle came to town, for to buy a firelock, We will tar and feather him, and so we will John Hancock." The more familiar version came later.

cache of 144 cannon, 6,658 muskets, four frigates, thirty transports, and a large amount of other stores. A British band struck up "The World Turned Upside Down," expressing the British view of what was happening. Cornwallis was supposedly too sick to offer up his sword. (So General Charles O'Hara offered his—first to Rochambeau, but the Frenchman refused and indicated O'Hara should give it to Washington. Then Washington refused it and told O'Hara to give it to Lincoln, who had surrendered at Charleston. Lincoln finally took the sword, but after holding it for a moment, gave it back to O'Hara.) The British rank and file also acted badly, showing the Americans great disrespect. Many smashed their muskets on the ground instead of laying them on a pile in an orderly fashion. The damage was so great that later few authentic and undamaged Brown Bess muskets found their way into the hands of collectors.

Clinton finally sailed from New York accompanied by seven thousand troops and arrived at the Capes while Cornwallis's troops were being marched into captivity in western Virginia (the officers had been paroled.) This was the second time Clinton had stood by looking on while a British army surrendered—the first being Burgoyne's. Upon hearing from fleeing Tories that Cornwallis had already surrendered, Clinton immediately returned to New York. He would still have the largest army on the continent, backed by the world's largest navy, but he had to know that Cornwallis's surrender wrote finis to his own career. Clinton had been in the conflict

★ ★ ★

Virginia and Yorktown Report Card

The British

Charles Cornwallis: C

Hamstrung by Clinton's contradictory and indefinite orders, Cornwallis relied on the Royal Navy, which deserted him in his hour of need.

Sir Henry Clinton: F

He should have reinforced Cornwallis as soon as Washington left New York for Virginia, or gone on the offensive himself. He did nothing, and reaped the result.

Benedict Arnold: A

Proved as good a British general as he had been an American.

The British troops: C

Increasingly embittered and war-weary, they were no longer what they had been.

The Americans

Thomas Jefferson: F

Made a string of decisions in 1781 that were all harmful to the Patriot cause.

George Washington: A

Took great risks and reaped the reward.

The American troops: C

They did well enough for one last winning campaign, but not more. Luckily, that was all they needed to do.

from the battle of Bunker Hill, and other than capturing Charleston, had never won a major battle.

During the conflict, the British had committed thirty-two thousand men, plus twelve Tory regiments that made up another ten thousand. They had sent over one hundred warships and hundreds of transport and supply vessels, and over forty thousand British seamen had seen service in or around America. Yet all Clinton had to show for his service was New York City, won by William Howe; Savannah, won by Augustine Prevost; and Charleston, where he had possessed overwhelming numbers and other advantages. In 1782, Clinton was replaced by Sir Guy Carleton as commander-in-chief in North America.

CHAPTER 18

The War Winds to a Close

As Cornwallis was sinking into his morass at Yorktown, the newly minted British General Benedict Arnold returned to New York to offer multiple proposals for action to win the war. He presented them to Clinton but also sent them to London, going over Clinton's head and earning him Clinton's enmity. Arnold hung around Clinton's headquarters, urging action, requesting that he be put in charge of expeditions like the one he had commanded in Virginia, and in general becoming a pest. Arnold was discovering that no one liked a traitor, especially the stolid British officers who were not only honor-minded but also slow to see the opportunities a traitor offered.

Final Fits of Defeat

A beleaguered Clinton finally approved a raid to destroy the New London, Connecticut, privateering base that was also the source of many of the Patriot raids on Long Island, apparently just to get Arnold off his back. By that point Arnold was practically apoplectic with rage.

Did you know?

★ Benedict Arnold proposed a plan that might have saved Cornwallis at Yorktown

★ Yorktown wasn't the final battle of the Revolutionary War

★ Along with their army, the British evacuated thousands of Tories and former slaves from America

After Washington marched south to Yorktown, only General William Heath—who hadn't been involved in a battle since the retreat from Lexington—remained in the North with a small army of 2,500 Patriots. Clinton's force was six times larger. A quick strike would eliminate Heath, and then the British could fan out, operating freely from Philadelphia to New Hampshire.

Without much support from Clinton, Arnold attacked New London with a force of over 1,700 men, focusing on Fort Griswold. In a stiff fight, the British took the fort but with heavy losses. This victory did not satisfy Arnold; as late as October 2, when Clinton finally decided to take a relief force to Cornwallis's aid, Arnold was still offering proposals to win the war in the North. His most urgent recommendation was for an expedition to Philadelphia. He hoped that the threat to the city would cause Washington to leave the siege lines at Yorktown to save it. Arnold was ignored.

The Plight of the Tories

After Cornwallis's surrender, Tory leaders in New York City became desperate. They had chosen the wrong side, and they knew there would be no place for them in an independent America. Wilmington, North Carolina, was evacuated by the British a month after Cornwallis's surrender, and Patriots took revenge on many Tories that had been left behind. One Tory who had earlier hanged a Patriot was split in half by a sword blow, a warning of the fate that awaited all Tories after the British left.

A Book You're Not Supposed to Read

Tories: Fighting for the King in America's First Civil War by Thomas B. Allen (New York: Harper, 2011).

When Cornwallis and Arnold sailed together to London in January 1782, it was to present proposals for a renewal of the war on a grand scale. Most of the Tory leadership still believed

★ ★ ★

Heated Passions

A handbill had appealed to the inhabitants of Philadelphia in 1779:

> Rouse, America! Your danger is great— great from a quarter where you least expect it. The Tories, the Tories will yet be the ruin of you! 'Tis high time they were separated from you. They are now busy engaged in undermining your liberties. Who were the occasion of this war? The Tories! Who persuaded the tyrant of Britain to prosecute it in a manner before unknown to civilized nations, and shocking even to the barbarians? The Tories! Who prevailed on the savages of the wilderness to join the standard of the enemy? The Tories!...Who advised and who assisted in burning your towns, ravaging your country and violating the chastity of your women? The Tories! Who have always counteracted the endeavors of Congress to secure the liberties of this country? The Tories!...Who take the oaths of allegiance to the States one day and break them the next? The Tories! Who persuade those who have enlisted to desert? The Tories! Who harbor those who do desert? The Tories!...Who wish to see us conquered, to see us slaves?...The Tories!

The Association produced very effective propaganda.

they could win with sufficient British backing, but that was delusional thinking. On March 22, the government of Lord North fell and it was replaced by the Whig government of Lord Rockingham. He and his party demanded an end to all offensive operations in North America and began peace initiatives that would result in American independence.

Meanwhile, the Articles of Confederation had been ratified by all thirteen states—Maryland was the last to do so—and the new nation called the United States of America was a fact on paper as of March 1, 1781. Despite the absence of a peace treaty, the United States now had to operate an effective government in peacetime.

Contrary to what you may have gathered from history books, the combat did not end with Yorktown. Although there were no further major actions between Continental and British armies, the often highly personal conflict between Tory units and guerrillas on the one hand and Patriot militia on the other was still deadly. In South Carolina alone there were fifty-six battles and skirmishes during 1781 and 1782, before the British evacuated Charleston in December of the latter year.

There were also Indians, mostly Cherokee and Creek, still fighting for the British in the South. They weren't ready to quit. The western frontier was ablaze. The 1779 Sullivan expedition had convinced many Indians to throw in their lot with the British—after all, in the Quebec Act the British had reserved all the country west of the Alleghenies as Indian territory. Most of the white settlers crossing the boundary were Scotch-Irish Patriots, and the Indian depredations against them had gone mostly unrecorded and seemingly unnoticed by the inhabitants along the Atlantic seaboard. They had their own problems with Tories.

In June 1782 at Ebenezer, Georgia, outside of Savannah, Creek chief Emistisiguo struck Anthony Wayne's camp. Emistisiguo was killed in the resulting hand-to-hand struggle, and the remaining Indians fled back to Savannah, but the reality of Indian frontier warfare remained, and many of the casualties of these little-known battles were never counted by historians who saw the war as a gentleman's conflict between colonists and their mother country.

The Battles of Sandusky and Blue Licks

In the frontier warfare that raged in the last months of the Revolution, the Battle of Sandusky (or Crawford's Defeat) stands out. In a two-day struggle in northern Ohio in June 1782, William Crawford and five hundred Pennsylvania militiamen attacked a group of three hundred British rangers and Indians. Despite their numerical superiority, the Americans soon found themselves surrounded. That night, the militia-men decided to break out and successfully escaped back to Pennsylvania, but about seventy of them were killed or captured. And the fate of the prisoners was horrific, as the Indians in the Old Northwest commonly tortured their prisoners to death and this time they had extra incentive: a party of Pennsylvania militia had murdered almost a hundred Christian Indians at the town of Gnadenhutten who were innocent of killing settlers, so the motivation for revenge was high.

Another major event was the disastrous defeat of Kentucky militia at the Battle of Blue Licks on August 19, 1782. Tory Captain William Caldwell of Butler's Rangers led a force of about fifty American and Canadian Tories along with three hundred Indians across the Ohio River into Kentucky to surprise and destroy Bryan Station, a Patriot settlement. The settlers took refuge in their stockade, and a relief party of 182 Kentucky militiamen was sent to their aid. The attackers withdrew, and the militia unwisely and recklessly pursued. They were caught in an ambush, and over half were killed, wounded, or captured. Reports of these outrages hardened American frontiersmen against the Indians for decades.

On July 11, 1782 the British force evacuated the city of Savannah, leaving only the British enclave at Charleston, which would mount small unit actions for another five months and give the Tories and Indians hope for as long as it existed. Outside of Charleston, South Carolina continued to see conflicts between detachments of Patriots and Tories, mostly personal encounters settling old scores. But the large force in Charleston remained a problem for the Patriots and their limited resources. When a large foraging force of five hundred British regulars and Tories left Charleston and moved up the Combahee River, Colonel John Laurens set out to harass them. The British were warned of Laurens's approach and set up a successful ambush, killing Laurens at the head of his troops in the first volley. The remaining Americans retreated, but the British didn't obtain the forage they had been after.

From September 11 to 13, 1782, the generally accepted "last battle of the Revolutionary War" took place when a settler's stockade called Fort Henry in Virginia (now West Virginia) was attacked by a force of fifty Tory rangers and more than 250 Indians under the command of a white renegade, Simon Girty. He was a sociopath and a pathological killer with a fearsome reputation for hating whites and torturing his captives. Girty would remain a serious thorn in the side of settlers in the Old Northwest for some time after the war. Even as late as after World War II, mothers in the states bordering the Great Lakes would remind their children to say their prayers at bedtime or "Simon Girty'll get you." The forty men and boys inside the works at Fort Henry withstood the siege until the morning of the third day, when a relief force arrived.

Most likely the last land battle of the war was actually at James Island, South Carolina, on November 14, when an American force attempted to stop the British from cutting firewood for their garrison in Charleston. Captain William Wilmot, who had discovered that British sailors were landing at Dill's Bluff every morning to cut wood, led a force to capture them, but in the interim the British had increased the size of their covering party, and the Americans found themselves outnumbered, facing three hundred regulars with cannons. Wilmot died in the exchange. He was the last Continental soldier killed in the Carolinas and possibly in all of the states, with the exception of a few isolated settlers killed by Indians.

Finally, on December 14, the British withdrew from Charleston, taking 3,380 Tories and five thousand Negro slaves with them. This evacuation completed the British withdrawal of all troops south of northern New Jersey. The destinations of the transports were New York, Nova Scotia, various British holdings in the Caribbean, and England.

On November 30, 1782, the British and U.S. peace commissioners agreed on the Preliminary Articles of Peace, and they were signed in Paris on January 20, 1783, by Great Britain, France, and Spain. This established a military armistice among all the warring nations except Holland. Congress would not ratify the Articles until April 15, 1783, but in the meantime the Continental Army rapidly began to melt away. Washington tried his best to hold it together, but there was no money to pay either the soldiers or the officers, and officers were encouraging individual soldiers to desert. Payment to "catchers"—men who hunted down deserters and returned them to the army for money—was suspended. A few units, such as the commander-in-chief's Guard, received some back pay from private individuals to keep the army from dissolving completely.

★ ★ ★
The Fate of the Slaves

The British had induced many slaves to run away from their masters, but they were not always treated as promised. The British generally honored their promises to those who had fought as soldiers or served the British in some capacity. Others were sent to the Caribbean to be sold back into slavery, along with those taken from Patriot plantations, who were considered prizes of war. Approximately twenty-five thousand slaves fell into that category, and they produced a tidy sum for their new British masters.

American Mutiny

Concern over back pay soon turned into outrage, then grew into the Newburgh Conspiracy, a crisis that threatened the very fabric of the new nation. This time it was not a regiment or two that mutinied, but the entire officer corps. They wanted back pay—something Congress couldn't deliver. Without the power to enforce and actually collect taxes—something it lacked under the Articles of Confederation—Congress couldn't meet its obligations to anyone, including the officers and troops in the army. In 1780 Congress had fecklessly promised Continental officers a lifetime pension on half pay when they were no longer needed. After all, that was the policy of Great Britain. But in early 1782 all army pay was suspended during the hostilities and accrued for payment once the war was over. The army was on the edge of revolting, and a coup could lead to a full-blown military dictatorship.

The army had lost confidence in Congress. In late December of 1782, Brigadier General Alexander McDougall and two colonels presented a "memorial" to Congress concerning the general discontent over the pay arrearages, and doubt among the officers that the half-pay pensions would ever materialize. The officers suggested that a lump sum payment be substituted for the pension—but of course, Congress could not pay that either. Included in the memorial was a vague threat against the United States of "fatal" consequences if Congress didn't act quickly. Military men such as Washington knew exactly what that meant, and by February of 1783 the word "mutiny" was on many lips. Arch-plotter and self-promoter Horatio Gates, reinstated in the army by Congress, was up to his elbows in the conspiracy, as he stood to replace Washington if the commander-in-chief was removed.

In early March, Major John Armstrong of Gates's staff wrote an anonymous letter urging that the army send an ultimatum to Congress. Another anonymous document called for a meeting of all field-grade officers for March 11. Washington squelched that meeting but called one himself for March 15, implying he would not be present. But once the officers gathered, Washington walked in. His entry stunned Gates, who was chairing the meeting, and when Washington asked to speak, Gates was obliged to give him the floor. Washington gave a short speech, then took out a letter he had written to Congress. In a bravura performance, the old general appeared to be unable to read the letter. Taking out a pair of glasses that none of his officers had seen him wear before, he

A Book You're Not Supposed to Read

Swords in Their Hands: George Washington and the Newburgh Conspiracy by Dave Richards (Candler, NC: Pisgah Press, 2014).

said, "Gentlemen, you will permit me to put on my spectacles, for I have not only grown gray but almost blind in the service of my country."

Some of the officers wept openly, others were humiliated and embarrassed at their actions, and all were forced to recognize that Washington had suffered greatly in service to his country. Gates's conspiracy collapsed like wet linguini, and the group that had met to consider marching on Philadelphia instead passed a resolution expressing an "unshaken confidence" in Congress. From that point forward, the United States was never again in danger of falling under a military dictatorship.

On April 19, 1783, Washington announced the end of hostilities against Great Britain. Congress soon ordered Washington to furlough all of the Continental troops that had enlisted for the duration of the war, retaining only a few who had enlisted for a specific period. Each furloughed soldier received three month's pay. Not surprisingly, the money did not come from Congress, but as personal notes from Robert Morris, Washington's premier financier (the man known as the "Banker of the Revolution"). Sadly, many if not most of the soldiers immediately sold the notes to unnamed speculators for enough money to get home, but not a penny more. (All the notes were ultimately paid out in full to the speculators.) Only a skeleton army remained to guard the depots and critical installations in case the British suddenly decided to renew the war.

By November, Congress had ordered the discharge of all furloughed troops. Even though Congress would not ratify the Treaty of Paris until January 14, 1784, and a major British army still occupied New York City, the Continental Army was disbanded. The British government ratified the treaty on April 9, 1784, and the ratified versions were exchanged on May 12. As of that date, the war was finally over. The United States of America had become a fully independent nation.

"New Ireland" reverted to being Maine, under the jurisdiction of the state of Massachusetts; and all of the territory south of Canada from the Atlantic to the Mississippi River except East and West Florida was ceded to the U.S. Many Europeans believed the terms of the treaty were overly generous to the United States, and Great Britain would soon be attempting to recover its lost colonies. British agents continually agitated the Indians in the West against Americans, and many Englishmen fully expected the United States to come to its senses and return (somehow) to British control. Some arrogant delusions are very persistent.

On November 25, 1783, Military Governor and British Commander Guy Carleton evacuated the troops from New York City, also taking about 7,000 Tories and a few freed slaves. Most were sent to Canadian provinces such as Ontario and Nova Scotia, although some went to Great Britain. Before the British left for England, Congress released all the prisoners of war held by the Continental Army—at least all those that could be found. Many had "escaped" captivity and disappeared into the vastness of America. Carleton made no fuss, assuming correctly that such soldiers had simply chosen to stay in America. He particularly made no objections over missing Hessians and simply listed them as deserters, as King George was not obligated to pay the German princes for men that had deserted. All of the American prisoners held in British prisons in the U.S. were also released, but most of them were in such extremely poor condition that they would die within weeks or months.

When, on December 4, 1783, the last British troops from Staten Island and Long Island boarded their transports, officially there remained no more British soldiers on American soil. But the British continued to maintain posts in the Northwest Territory. Their presence in Ohio and Michigan would ultimately prove untenable; they would be driven out in the War of 1812, but the first few presidential administrations ignored their presence.

★ ★ ★

End-of-the-War Report Card

The British

Sir Guy Carleton: A

He handled the last year of the war and the withdrawal of British forces from the U.S. with great tact and diplomacy.

Benedict Arnold: D

The time for him to win the war had passed. All he could do at the end was kill people, spread misery, and add to the infamy of his treason.

The British troops: A

They were professional and, for the most part, restrained in a losing cause.

The Americans

George Washington: A

Having learned from his mistakes throughout the war, Washington understood that his most important job was to keep the army viable. Time alone could win him important victories. Nevertheless, he knew exactly when he needed to fight—and win—and did. By his mere presence, he defeated the Newburgh Conspiracy and saved America from descending into chaos—or military dictatorship.

Horatio Gates: F

Once again, it was all about him, and this time he nearly strangled the newborn American Republic in its cradle.

The American troops: A

Would fight to the end, and did.

CHAPTER 19

Victory in Paris

When news of Yorktown reached Paris and London in late November, the reactions were very different. In Great Britain, Lord North's Tory government days were numbered, and the Whig Lord Rockingham stood by to pick up the pieces and end the war. In Paris, the sole American peace commissioner present was Benjamin Franklin, and he was immediately summoned by the Comte de Vergennes, Louis XVI's foreign minister, to hear the news. Franklin was the first person to whom Vergennes—who had been coming under increasing criticism for his support of the U.S.—told the news, even before his king. The two men shared a victory toast, but Franklin knew the war was not over.

"In Good, I Fear Bad"

On hearing the news of Yorktown, Franklin immediately wrote his very close friend Madame Brillon to explain his attitude in victory and defeat: "I am well aware of the magnitude of our advantage and of its possible consequences, but I do not exult over it. Knowing that war is full of changes and uncertainty, in bad fortune I hope for good, and in good I fear

Did you know?

★ The Americans refused to leave the French out of the peace deal—and then the French tried to give the Mississippi watershed to Spain and England

★ The peace negotiations were complicated by John Adams's visceral hatred of Benjamin Franklin

★ The Tory prime minister who had prosecuted the war against America was returned to office during the peace negotiations

bad. I play this game with almost the same equanimity as when you see me playing chess. You know that I never give up a game before it is finished, always hoping to win, or at least to get a move, and when I have a good game, I guard against presumption."

Madame Brillon offered to put Franklin in contact with a confidential conduit to Lord Shelburne, an Irish-born Whig Member of Parliament currently not in the British government and an old friend of Franklin's. Franklin accepted the offer eagerly, although he did not yet know how valuable the relationship would be. Within a few months, things took a dramatic turn. Lord Rockingham became the prime minister as Lord North's replacement in March of 1782, and Shelburne the first Home Secretary. Even better was that the king put all his trust in Shelburne, thus giving Franklin a back-channel directly into the highest levels of the British government. Franklin would play his connection like a Stradivarius.

Early in April 1782, Henry Laurens, an American peace commissioner on parole in London, was released and sent by Shelburne to John Adams, then sulking in The Hague. Simultaneously, Shelburne sent Scottish merchant Richard Oswald as his go-between to Franklin in Paris.

A Three-Way Negotiation

Franklin told Oswald that the United States would do nothing without the full participation of the French and took him to see Vergennes. When Oswald asked Vergennes to give him specific terms to carry back to London, Vergennes refused, saying that Britain was in a better position to propose terms first since it had no allies to consult. Franklin added that Oswald should be accredited by the British government to enter into direct negotiations for further discussions with himself and Vergennes. He stressed that the peace should be fair and provide reparations for the losses suffered by all parties.

John Adams, who had previously displayed an inclination for the United States to treat with the English without the French, soon came around to Franklin's way of thinking, and he and Laurens kept up a lively correspondence with Franklin. Meanwhile Shelburne tried a back-door approach, writing Sir Guy Carleton, in command of the British troops in North America, to contact Washington and open negotiations for a separate peace that would not include France. Carleton proposed

an armistice only on land in North America, which would leave the Royal Navy in control of American waters and free to continue its sea war against France. Washington refused Carleton's offer and didn't even send the proposal to Congress for consideration.

Carleton then promised that England would give the Americans their independence while negotiations in Paris continued separately. This was a bald-faced attempt to split the American and French; the hope was that once the Americans had independence they would abandon their ally. At this point Washington ended his contacts with Carleton. All negotiations would have to go through Paris. This was one of Washington's finest hours.

Oswald returned to Paris with negotiating credentials and informed Franklin that the British government was willing to give America its independence, but that the terms of Britain's 1763 peace with France and Spain must be reinstated. This proposal was yet another attempt to separate the United States from its allies, which, if it had succeeded, would have made it very difficult for America to attract allies in future wars. Franklin did not accept this offer.

After conferring again in London, Oswald returned to France in May accompanied by Thomas Grenville, the author of the Stamp Act. In

Vergennes's office, the bargaining truly began. The British still insisted that in return for their recognition of American independence, France had to give up the Caribbean Islands she had taken from England in the war. After all, the Revolution had been initiated by France, since she had encouraged the colonies to revolt. Vergennes took offense at Grenville's remarks. In his view, Great Britain had grabbed Canada, Louisiana, Florida, and a number of Caribbean islands in the Seven Years' War (the French and Indian War in America), and was the mean-spirited aggressor nation of the century. The talks were not off to a good start.

Necessary and Advisable

Franklin continued in his role as the sole American peace commissioner in Paris until late in June, when he was joined by John Jay, who had previously been in Madrid. In July, Shelburne replaced Rockingham (who had died) as the new Whig prime minister, and negotiating positions seemed to be hardening. Franklin gave Oswald a list of four necessary and four advisable articles of a peace agreement. They were essentially as follows:

Necessary:

1. Full independence and the withdrawal of all British troops from the United States.
2. A complete settlement on all boundaries.
3. A determination of the limits of Canada.
4. Freedom for American fishermen to fish on the Banks of Newfoundland.

Advisable:

1. Payment of reparations to individuals ruined by the war up to 600,000 pounds.

2. A public statement by Parliament acknowledging Britain's injuries to the United States.

3. No discrimination against American merchants, ships, and trade.

4. Cession of Canada.

★ ★ ★

Peace Negotiations, Fighting Words

During the negotiations, the British continued to refer to the American states as "colonies," enraging Adams and Jay.

Early in August, Shelburne sent word to Franklin that he was ready to accept Franklin's four necessary articles as a basis for a negotiated treaty, but the four advisables must be dropped. Franklin became ill, and Jay took over the negotiations. In September, he received a firm offer of peace on the basis of Franklin's four necessary articles, including full independence.

The Forgotten Ally

Then the almost forgotten Spanish weighed in. They wanted West Florida by right of conquest, and the east bank of the Mississippi north to Ohio. France supported Spain, and drew a boundary along the eastern boundary of the Mississippi watershed to the Ohio River, granting everything south of the Ohio River to Spain and everything to the north to England. Franklin and Jay were appalled.

With the allied negotiators now at odds with each other, and the French and Spanish playing power games as only Europeans can, Jay approached the British to work on a separate peace, leaving out his allies. A great deal was lost, as the British attitudes hardened and new demands were made of the American negotiators. In October, Adams finally arrived in Paris, seeing himself as the shining knight to put everything right. Unfortunately, Adams greatly disliked Franklin, and undercut him at every opportunity.

Finally in late October negotiations began in earnest. By November 5 the negotiators had agreed on a preliminary basis for peace on the terms the Americans had wanted and needed all along—Franklin's necessary articles. On the east, America's boundary would be the Atlantic Ocean and the St. Croix River in Maine. In the north it would be the Canadian line from the St. Lawrence River to the Lake of the Woods in Minnesota, on the west the Mississippi River, and on the south the latitude line of thirty-one degrees from the Mississippi to the Chattahoochee River, then the northern boundary of Florida to the Atlantic.

Unresolved Issues

Issues that remained unsettled would cause a great deal of trouble through the years. For example, Americans would insist on their right to trade freely with any nation in the world, something that was not allowed under the British Navigation Laws. Maine's boundary was still unsettled to the north. And while Great Britain would pay reparations to American Patriots, reparations to American Tories were left up to the states of the United States to pay—which meant in practice that they would not be paid.

Even after the preliminary peace terms were agreed upon, the final peace negotiations dragged on for months. Spain, France, and Holland still had to work out their agreements, and meanwhile Shelburne's government was replaced with another Tory one under Lord North, the man who had pursued war against the colonists for so long. In the end, France acquired a few Caribbean islands, Spain walked away with the Floridas and Minorca, and Holland received back its islands in the Caribbean. The British lost all around, but got to keep Canada, and their trade with America was restored. That in itself was significant.

The world had indeed been turned upside down, and Europe's hegemony had begun its slow slide into oblivion. The world was the better for the

American Revolution, an exceptional event never to be duplicated in any other country. For the first and essentially only time in recorded history, the people had become sovereign, constructing a nation of laws made by the people, answerable only to God, and respecting an individual's right to life, liberty, and property. The glorious, often miraculous revolution would change the world forever. What started as such an unlikely hope had been successful beyond all expectation.

CHAPTER 20

The After Rebellions

The American Revolutionary War was over, but the divisions it had created could not be papered over. In 1775, the American population had stood at 2.5 million, of whom half a million were Negro slaves. The free population was split into three political camps. Despite John Adams's estimate that they were equally divided, there were really about six hundred thousand Patriots, four hundred thousand Tories, and a million neutrals in America at the beginning of the Revolutionary War. By the end of the British evacuation in December 1783, the population of the United States was about 2.7 million, with the slave population unchanged. (The almost 10 percent of the slave population that had died or been shipped out by the British during eight years of war had been replaced, mostly by natural reproduction—the Association having drastically reduced the British slave trade to America.) The remaining Americans at the end of the war comprised nine hundred thousand Patriots, three hundred fifty thousand Tories, and just over one million neutrals.

The conflict had claimed one hundred twenty thousand Patriot men, women, and children, while Tory deaths from all causes were probably about twenty-five thousand. The lower numbers for Tories in 1783 reflect

Did you know?

★ The American Revolution may have been the deadliest war, per capita, in U.S. history

★ An astonishing two-thirds of military-age Patriots fought in the War of Independence

★ Politically correct "social history" has ironically brought recognition to the common Revolutionary War soldier—and the politically *incorrect* ideas for which he fought

★ ★ ★
Mortality Rate

The Revolutionary War may have been the most costly war in American history in terms of per-capita deaths from all war-related causes.

Although official Veterans Affairs numbers for the Revolutionary War are 4,435 killed in battle and 8,188 wounded, these numbers ony reflect official battle reports. Missing are all the actions for which no report was filed, anyone dying of wounds after a report was submitted, soldiers dying of disease at any time, those dying in British captivity, and so forth. There are many actions for which no official report was submitted, such as Indian actions on the frontier, and the total casualties are but a fraction of the actual losses. A better approximation would be nine thousand Patriots killed or mortally wounded in battle (one death for every three wounded), eleven thousand dead of disease or wounds in camp, seven thousand murdered by Tory partisans and Indians, and eighteen thousand who succumbed as prisoners of war in British captivity. To this toll must be added another twelve to twenty thousand who were so enfeebled from wounds or captivity that they expired within a year of leaving the army or being released from the notorious prison ships. A reasonable assessment of Patriot military deaths, therefore, totals fifty-seven to sixty-five thousand men, an astonishing 30 percent of all Patriots who took up arms. This number still understates the total American losses, as it doesn't include civilian deaths caused by privation, exposure, and sickness brought on by wartime conditions. Another sixty thousand would seem to be probable, particularly since the warfare in the South claimed very large numbers of civilian casualties. In President Andrew Jackson's family of a mother and three boys, for example, only one survived the war (the future president), and none was listed as a casualty.

Tory deaths in the war are estimated at eighty-nine hundred, but to that must be added the estimated minimum of twenty thousand Tory civilians who died from privation and sickness, bringing the total carnage on all sides to most likely about one hundred fifty thousand souls. So probably about 6 percent of the American population died from the effects of the Revolutionary War, higher than any other war in American history. The next runner up is the Civil War, which reached about 2 percent military deaths, and less than 1 percent civilian deaths.

their mass exodus at the end of the war (perhaps as many as two hundred thousand left the country by 1795). A natural baby boom occurred in America after hostilities ended.

Some one hundred twenty thousand men had served in the Continental Army, and an additional eighty thousand had joined militia units. Since not all Patriots would have been males of military age, these numbers indicate that a very high percentage of eligible Patriots—certainly over two-thirds—served during the war, even accounting for multiple enlistments and for the fact that some neutral individuals probably served (for the pay, the adventure, or because they were conscripted). The price of freedom was extremely high, but the American Patriots were willing to pay it.

One Revolution Begets Another

The fact that France was the next to fall victim to revolutionary fever was, in part, due to the successful American Revolution. The *ancien regime* in France died partly because of the debts it incurred supporting America. But that's not the whole explanation. France was already ripe for a revolution—but one of a much different sort, lacking all four of the pillars of exceptionalism that, as we have seen, graced America: a free market economy, common law, the sanctity of property rights, and Protestant Christianity.

On the other hand, France was one of the richest and most powerful nations in the world. France enjoyed more political and military power than any other nation on the continent, and its peasants were not any more oppressed than the peasants of neighboring kingdoms. (Only Holland came close to France economically.) Taxes—to support the unsustainable lifestyles of the overly numerous French nobility at the expense of the peasantry were high, but that was common across the continent.

The United States of America, with its novel idea of citizen government, posed a challenge to the *ancien regime*. Even before the American Revolution, ideas of freedom were percolating downward through all European society. But those ideas of freedom, originating in the Enlightenment, entailed an all-out assault on traditional religion, especially Catholicism. Reactionary priests had become part of the problem, or so the enlightened intellectuals claimed. But once the peasants turned their backs on the venerable institution of the papacy, there would be no way to hold them in check. In America, religion had been on the side of the revolutionaries; in France, it was dead set against them.

Freedom in France

In his own inept fashion Louis XVI attempted to head off what was coming by sharing power—first with his nobles and aristocrats, then with the Church, and finally with the merchants and tradespeople. But each concession only whetted the appetites of those who were not included in the power sharing. The American Revolution had shown that power could reside in the people: indeed, it was not the Patriot generals who won the war, it was the common soldiers, inured to all privation, able to suffer any hardship and fight for years for nothing more than an idea, that the French wanted to emulate. But they could not. France had neither common law nor Protestant Christianity, and it scarcely had private property protections and true free market capitalism.

It was inevitable that once the king admitted he needed the Estates General to generate revenue, he discovered (as King Charles I had found out about Parliament in the previous century) that he was now beholden to their will. In short, power sharing was demanded. The situation disintegrated as the king and Estates General could not cooperate, and eventually violence ensued on a scale that dwarfed that of the American

Revolution. The French Revolution is widely compared and contrasted to the American Revolution, but the circumstances that brought the two revolutions about were entirely different (with one exception: debt stemming from the French and Indian War), the course of each revolution was different, and certainly the results were very different. France merely substituted a tyranny of the masses for a tyranny of a monarch because it lacked a common law heritage. The French didn't share the fundamental presupposition that all power emanates from the people after first being given to them by their Protestant God.

★ ★ ★
The Taxing Power

Modern-day critics of the Articles of Confederation sometimes say that it did not give Congress the power to tax. But it clearly did, under Articles VII and IX. The problem was that under the Articles, Congress did not have any enforcement or collection arm because the Articles created no executive. The impetus for a Constitutional Convention came in part from the desire to rectify that weakness.

But even America did not have all the answers. After the Revolution, the United States struggled to establish a sound government. Some aspects of nationhood were lacking under the Articles of Confederation—most notably an executive branch to make treaties and to administer the collection of taxes. And without the ability to collect taxes, the federal government could not meet its obligations.

Many former officers in the Continental Army felt they had been abused by Congress, and that the issues inspiring the Newburgh Conspiracy had not gone away. Almost all of the common soldiers returned from the war with nothing in their pockets, to find their farms run down, their wives and children nearly starving, and their local government in the hands of men who had not served.

The years after the success of the Revolutionary War saw a series of revolts inspired by the very issue that had sparked the Revolution itself: taxation. To many Americans it seemed that politicians of every stripe—American as well as British or French—looked on themselves as a privileged class, and

A Book You're Not Supposed to Read

Shays's Rebellion: The American Revolution's Final Battle by Leonard L. Richards (Philadelphia: University of Pennsylvania Press, 2002).

the tax laws reflected that. Had the war been for nothing? Many had fought for the "rights of Englishmen." Now it appeared that they were being denied those same rights as Americans.

A Rebellious People

Shays' Rebellion, as the Massachusetts revolt was called, was named after Captain Daniel Shays, but the protestors themselves went by the name "Regulators," and Shays was only one of their leaders. Nor was he even the most important. He was tagged by the tabloid newspapers of the times as *the* leader, and exactly why he was chosen—by the opposition to the revolt—to be its representative face is still a mystery. The backbone of the Regulators was large contingents raised from the Western Scotch-Irish (and Presbyterian) towns of Amherst, Colrain, Pelham, and West Springfield, Massachusetts. The Congregationalist Boston elites who controlled the state supported the government against the rebels. This was the first time that the population fractured along this fault line: elite Easterners against agrarian Westerners. But it would not be the last.

Shays' Rebellion was not the only one. Massachusetts was simply, once again, the flash point for protests against the government. But the conditions causing the crisis existed throughout the states. Unrest was endemic, with protests taking place from New Hampshire to Georgia. In fact, even before Shays' Rebellion similar actions by Vermonters against the New York speculators and by settlers on the east bank of the Hudson against the Dutch landholders of millions of acres of prime real estate had already drawn battle lines between rich and poor, the elite and the non-elite. In western North Carolina, John Sevier declared the State of Franklin independent. North Carolina militia showed up and ended the rebellion, but diehards continued to support a "Lesser Franklin" territory carved out from the Cherokees. Only a United States treaty with the Cherokees in 1791 would end the so-called State of Franklin.

Historians usually ascribe the unrest across the West to a lack of specie to pay debts at a time when creditors, merchants, and government tax collectors were no longer willing to work with the debtors. But the lack of gold and silver money was only a small part of the story. Patriot soldiers had been paid in worthless paper currency during the war, and most had sold

★　★　★
Who Were the Speculators?

In modern politics, especially on the Left, "speculators" are faceless evil men who take advantage of the helpless by acquiring their money, debts, or property at a low value, then selling it at a higher price. But by this definition speculation goes on all the time, and everyone engages in it to one degree or another. Merely buying a house involves speculation about its future value. Real speculators usually intend very fast turnaround, rather than acquiring assets they hope will grow in value over time.

The speculators of 1787 had not necessarily all been unscrupulous, at least not in their original purchase of the notes. The farmers, merchants, mechanics, lumbermen, and former soldiers throughout the colonies who owned the debts had taken a genuine risk. At the time they bought them, there was no certainty that the IOUs, debt

certificates, and other instruments of debt that had been issued by states, towns, and even George Washington himself as head of the Continental Army would ever be paid. During the war, men of money would approach debt-holders and offer to acquire the notes for a fraction of their face value. At that point the debt-holder had a decision to make: hang onto the debt and hope the Patriot forces not only won but would eventually have the wherewithal to actually pay, or sell now, "take the money and run." All too often, they chose the latter—and lost out when the notes were eventually redeemed at face value. But at the time the speculation entailed considerable risk for the speculators, who had put their own economic (and often literal) necks on the line by betting on the survival and stability of the United States of America.

their notes for a fraction of their face value, believing they would never be redeemable for good coin. Now the rich speculators who had bought those notes were being paid their full face value—in some cases from taxes that were driving veterans into ruin and debtors' prison. Continental Army veterans were among the hardest hit, although many that had served in the militia were equally badly off.

The 1780 Constitution of Massachusetts had made the state a rich man's paradise, particularly for those who lived in Boston and its environs. Wealthy speculators who held Massachusetts notes controlled the state legislature, and they passed a law specifying the notes were to be redeemed at the value they had when issued. Of the payments made by Massachusetts to holders of its notes that can be traced, about 80 percent was paid to speculators living in Boston or its vicinity. About 40 percent went to just thirty-five individuals—all of whom were or had been state representatives, state senators, or members of the governor's council during the 1780s.

Somewhere in excess of 90 percent of these notes had been purchased from their original owners at a small fraction of their face value, always less than one-fourth, and often less than one-tenth. Because of the new note-holders' political clout, they were able to obtain the legislature's promise of full payment, with interest—raised by a combination of a head tax on males over fifteen years old and a property tax. These taxes were very regressive, benefitting the Boston elites while crushing the average farmer. An entire class of Western farmers—the majority of citizens—felt helpless. Debt collectors were active, gobbling up farms and other property for nonpayment of debts. And Massachusetts still put debtors in jail. Just as before the Revolution, petitions submitted by those hurt most were ignored.

Unrest grew until August 1786, when protestors shut down the Northampton, Massachusetts, court and prevented it from foreclosing or issuing new edicts against farmers. When the county militia was called, it refused to turn out. Shays, who had participated in the Northampton affair, then showed up in Hampshire County, where he was met by three hundred militiamen protecting the court and officials. No violence occurred, but the judges postponed their hearings and adjourned. The elites began depicting the Regulators as evil men of the lowest sort. Still, the unrest as the government sided with the rich against the poor, the townsfolk against the farmers, and the haves against the have-nots continued to grow.

By January 1787, the threat was deemed so serious that Governor James Bowdoin organized a privately funded army commanded by General Benjamin Lincoln, eventually consisting of three thousand men. Funds for the private army were raised by contributions from the Eastern (Boston) speculators, few of whom turned out to face the

★ ★ ★
Not All Bad

The Articles of Confederation had failed to provide for a central government of any strength. Nonetheless, this first attempt to draw the thirteen states together into a nation did have some good points. For example, the Articles provided term limits for congressmen. A representative could not serve more than three years in any six-year period. Unfortunately, this provision of the Articles would be omitted from the Constitution—an omission that Mercy Otis Warren would rail against in her *Observations on the New Constitution, and on the Federal and State Conventions.*

Regulators themselves. Shays and his forces assembled about fifteen hundred men, but they didn't have weapons. Three regiments of Regulators converged on the federal armory at Springfield only to find twelve hundred militiamen under Major General William Shepard waiting for them. As two of the Regulator regiments advanced towards the armory through waist-high snow, Shepard defended it, opening fire with artillery and killing four and wounding twenty Shaysites. Lincoln marched toward the Shays forces with his 3,000 men, and they scattered. The government easily won the propaganda battle. Even former revolutionaries such as Samuel Adams wanted all the rebels to be hanged; John Adams sounded more like the British in 1775 than himself at that time. This affair brought George Washington out of his Mount Vernon retirement and back into public life. He had little regard for the Massachusetts

Regulators. He was a heavy speculator in Western lands (mostly Ohio), and viewed the settlers going west with some disdain.

But Shays' Rebellion highlighted the need for a more powerful national government to handle the nation's financial problems and unrest among the citizenry, ensuring that private armies hired by the wealthy could not simply enforce whatever parts of the law they wanted. It made revising the Articles of Confederation seem more urgent—and so contributed to the creation of the Constitution.

To the Land!

Despite the words of the Declaration of Independence, which was now held as sacred text by Americans, there was a fear that two Americas were developing: the mercantile and trading Easterners east of the Alleghany Mountains, and the agricultural Westerners. The perceptive Thomas Jefferson realized this sooner than most, and early in the 1780s began discussing ways to allow individuals to acquire national land—and to ensure that once they had land they became full citizens, equal to those residing in the existing thirteen states.

In the Land Ordinance of 1785, the so-called "landed states"—those having territory whose grants stretched to the Pacific Ocean—including Pennsylvania, Virginia, and Georgia, ceded their western territories to the United States government for the creation of new territories, which would become states. The ordinance required an orderly U.S. government survey of that land, dividing it into sections of thirty-six square miles and townships of one square mile. Land would be sold in an organized manner, one section at a time, to permit for defense against Indians on the frontier. This survey system would allow access to legal written titles and deeds, buttressing the property rights that made up one of the four pillars of American exceptionalism.

But there was a problem. The settlers wouldn't behave. They raced to unsurveyed land and put down stakes—literally: their claims would be marked by wooden stakes they set out, usually near obvious landmarks such as big rock formations, tree lines, rivers, or mountains. These claims, of course, didn't look anything like the nice neat boxes the government surveys laid out. At that point, the

★ ★ ★
Ahead of Its Time

American land policy established with the Land Ordinance of 1785, based largely on Thomas Jefferson's ideas, was the most advanced and citizen-friendly in human history.

United States government took a critical step. Most governments would have sent the army to root out the squatters and force everyone to wait until the surveys were completed. But in America, with its common law tradition, the law derives from the people and respects what *they* want. And the people were speaking loud and clear: they wanted access to western lands without waiting for the government surveys. So a system called "preemption" or "squatters' rights" was quickly put into law, in which, if a person resided on un-surveyed land for seven years and built either a house or a farm, he gained legal title deed to that land. (This was true even if the land was "owned" by someone else if the "owner" did not ride the fences and inspect his property and evict the squatter.)

These rules were enacted to prevent the appearance of "land barons" such as existed in England and Europe; they rewarded *development* of the land as opposed to just sitting on untended land, hoarding it. Property taxes forced landowners to use their property to make money to pay taxes, rather than hold the land for speculation.

But the Land Ordinance only solved half the problem, namely moving land into the hands of the people as opposed to government. Once people had land in, say, Ohio, were they not colonists all over again? Jefferson saw immediately that a political process for statehood had to follow the land distribution process, and so did Congress, still acting under the Articles of Confederation. It passed the Northwest Ordinance of 1787 to create a system for populations to form states that would have equal representation in the national legislature. Once it had a population of 5,000 inhabitants, an area could apply for "territory" status, in which it received an appointed governor, federal judge, and marshal. And once they reached 60,000, the residents of a territory could apply for statehood and write their own constitution. If it did not conflict with United States laws, the territory would be admitted as a state on equal footing with all the existing states. No nation in human history had ever treated its colonists in this way. Jefferson's genius helped prevent endless frontier rebellions over representation—though revolts would still occur over other matters, such as taxation.

The Whiskey Rebellion

In 1794, the famous "Whiskey Rebellion" broke out in western Pennsylvania, but it was also supported in the western counties of Maryland, Virginia, New York, and all of Kentucky. The federal government had enacted a heavy tax on whiskey, which was the primary source of hard cash for western farmers. The whiskey tax was seen as a punitive measure aimed directly at the western settlers. From their point of view, it seemed to be meant not just to raise revenue, but to demonstrate the power of the national government—and the power of the eastern elites. The result was resistance to the tax—to the current day. The existence of illegal stills has been a constant feature in America's backcountry ever since.

Defiance of the new federal law began almost at its inception in 1791, when it was learned that an internal excise tax on whiskey

A Book You're Not Supposed to Read

The Whiskey Rebellion: Frontier Epilogue to the American Revolution by Thomas P. Slaughter (New York: Oxford University Press, 1986).

production would be the first such tax introduced on a domestic product by Washington's national government. It could have been tobacco, timber, or any other products produced by the rich eastern landowners, but it was a tax on the common man, applied to anyone who planted a few acres of corn and had a still. Backcountry farmers and farm communities erected Liberty Poles, and resistance grew rapidly.

Washington responded to the tax rebellion by raising 12,950 troops from the East: eastern Pennsylvania, Maryland, Virginia, and New Jersey. No one in the army was going to be sympathetic to the resisters. The president reviewed the northern wing of his troops in Carlisle, Pennsylvania, instructing them on the necessity of order. He put Light Horse Harry Lee in command of the southern militia, and Alexander Hamilton, who had originated the tax, was designated by Washington as the unofficial head of the entire expedition. With that, Washington departed for New York. (The reader should ignore inaccurate TV documentaries that depict Washington leading the army to Pittsburgh and suppressing the rebellion.)

Opposition crumbled immediately, and many of the ringleaders fled; only ten were arrested, only two stood trial; and although they were convicted of treason, Washington pardoned them both. More importantly, he sent commissioners to negotiate with the Westerners to arrange for a compromise (which was never reached, but the effort did dampen anger). Eventually, the whiskey tax proved impossible to collect and was repealed by Thomas Jefferson's Congress in 1801.

The Constitution and American Exceptionalism

Weaknesses in the Articles of Confederation had convinced the Founders that they needed to balance the autonomy of the states with a strong national government. For example, under the Articles no single treaty with the entire United States had been possible: a foreign nation had to sign a separate treaty with all thirteen states, *plus* the U.S. government, stifling trade. When the representatives of the states met in Philadelphia in 1787, the Constitution they framed would be one of the two most remarkable political documents in world history (the other was the Declaration of Independence), for seeking to protect the rights of individuals and for establishing a truly federal division of power among communities, states, and the national government.

The Constitutional Convention had not only accepted American exceptionalism, but reinforced it, resting the principles contained in the Constitution firmly on the four great pillars of American exceptionalism. Common law, Protestant Christianity, the sanctity of private property, and later, free market capitalism were thereby entrenched in American law. This combination of factors has never been present *in any other nation, in the past or to the present day*, to the extent it has been in the United States. It was these things for which the common soldier was willing to lay down his life, for all together they comprised individual liberty and sovereignty. It was these things of which Jefferson so eloquently wrote, and for which Washington so devoutly applied himself. It was for these principles the fifty-six signers of the Declaration risked their lives, their money, their families' security and, most important to them, their "sacred honor." And it was for these principles that so many thousands of ordinary Americans signed the Association and backed up their pledges with their lives.

The loss of any of these four—Protestant Christianity, common law, property rights, or the free market economy—would reduce the nation and the common man to hapless subjugation in a political system where individuals are not citizens but subjects, there only to support the lifestyles of the governing elites, be they kings and nobles or adherents to any political philosophy that concentrates power in the hands of the very few.

France found this out. A revolution requires more than guns. Lacking the four pillars of American exceptionalism, the French Revolution gave way to Napoleon's tyranny. Since 1789, the French have repeatedly seen liberty come and go. Most countries have never even gotten that far: other than Switzerland, no country in Europe recognizes the people as sovereign—the government is always supreme. And yet today political correctness threatens to terminate American exceptionalism—and liberty in the American Republic.

The Little People

No one can deny the role the elites played in the Revolution. Their pens and philosophical arguments framed the debate for ordinary citizens. Their money kept the new nation afloat. Their genius in tailoring institutions—particularly in the U.S. Constitution—was indispensable. But it was not the elites that won the Revolutionary War: it was the common citizen soldier, willing to slog through the snow, ice, mud, and water of northern Maine in an attempt to bring liberty to the citizens of Quebec, or the Southern backwoodsman willing to march seemingly endless miles to harass Cornwallis's troops even though he was hundreds of miles from home.

One example will suffice. A soldier volunteered for the Continental Army in June 1775, marched with Arnold to Quebec where he was captured in the assault on Lower Town, was kept in irons for five months and threatened with execution, was paroled in New Jersey, made his way home wearing nothing but a hunting shirt, and within two weeks had reenlisted in another regiment in violation of his parole. From that point onward, he was subject to summary execution if captured by the British for violating his parole. He fought with Washington from Trenton to the end of the war; from Valley Forge to the end as a member of Washington's Lifeguard. From 1775 to 1783 he was home for less than a month, and most of that time was spent fighting Indians on the upper west and east branches of the Susquehanna River. He returned from his long war with nothing in his pockets for his courage and deprivation. History rightly remembers his commander-in-chief. The soldier's name—James Dougherty—is remembered only by his family.

Yet it was forgotten men like that who won the war, and to whom Americans today are so greatly indebted. Ironically, modern "social history"—the politically correct attempt to replace the understanding that ideas and leaders are of primary importance with the notion that only class, gender, and race dictate historical events—has brought some recognition to the significance of those common soldiers. It is doubly ironic that now that their stories are being told we know more clearly than ever that it was precisely ideas—the unalienable rights that came to them from God Himself—for which they fought. The new country followed His design, with sovereignty resting with the people, and all men equal in accordance with divine law. They launched their Great Revolution based on the ideas of "life, liberty, and the pursuit of happiness." It had never happened before, and it has never happened again.

Bibliography

Abbatt, William. *The Crisis of the Revolution*: *Being the Story of Arnold and Andre*. New York: Empire State Society, Sons of the American Revolution, 1899.

Abbot, W. W. et al, eds. *The Papers of George Washington*. Charlottesville, VA: University of Virginia Press, 1983–). Currently being produced in multiple series, of which the important ones for this work are *The Colonial Series, 1744–June 1775, 10 vols.*, and *The Revolutionary War Series, June 1775–December, 1783, 23 vols.*

Adler, Mortimer J. and Charles Van Doren, eds. *The Annals of America, Vols 1–2*. Chicago: Encyclopedia Britannica, 1968.

Alden, John. *A History of the American Revolution*. New York, Knopf, 1969.

Allen, Thomas B. *George Washington, Spymaster*. Washington, DC: National Geographic, 2004.

_____. *Tories*: *Fighting for the King in America's First Civil War*. New York: Harper, 2011.

Anderson, Fred, *The War That Made America* (New York: Penguin Books, 2005).

Anderson, Mark. *The Battle for the Fourteenth Colony*: *America's War of Liberation in Canada, 1774–1776*. Lebanon, NH: University Press of New England, 2013.

_____, ed., and Teresa L. Meadows, trans. *The Invasion of Canada by the Americans, 1775–1776*: *As Told through Jean-Baptiste Badeaux's Three Rivers Journal and New York Captain William Goforth's Letters*. Albany, NY: State University of New York Press, 2016.

Anderson, Troyer Steele. *The Command of the Howe Brothers During the American Revolution*. London: Oxford University Press, 1936.

Babits, Lawrence E. *A Devil of a Whipping*: *The Battle of Cowpen*. Chapel Hill, NC: University of North Carolina Press, 1998.

Bailyn, Bernard. *The New England Merchants in the Seventeenth Century*. Cambridge, Harvard University Press, 1979.

Bass, Robert D. *Ninety Six*: *The Struggle for the South Carolina Back Country*. Orangeburg, SC: Sandlapper Publishing, 1978.

Beeman, Richard R. *Our Lives, Our Fortunes & Our Sacred Honor*. New York: Basic Books, 2013.

Behrens, C. B. A. *The Ancien Régime*. London, Thames and Hudson, 1967.

Belcher, Henry. *The First American Civil War First Period 1775–1778 with Chapters on the Continental or Revolutionary Army and on the Forces of the Crown Vols I & II*. London: Macmillan, 1911.

Berg, Fred Anderson. *Encyclopedia of Continental Army Units, Battalions, Regiments, and Independent Corps*. Harrisburg, PA: Stackpole, 1972.

Bergh, Albert Ellery. *The Writings of Thomas Jefferson, 20 Vols*. Washington, DC: Thomas Jefferson Memorial Association, 1904–1905).

Birnbaum, Louis. *Red Dawn at Lexington*. Boston: Houghton Mifflin, 1986.

Blackmon, Richard D. *Dark and Bloody Ground*: *The American Revolution along the Southern Frontier*. Yardley, PA: Westholme, 2012.

Bonk, David. *Trenton and Princeton 1776–77*. Oxford, GB: Osprey, 2009.

Bonomi, Patricia. *Under the Cope of Heaven*: *Religion, Society, and Politics in Colonial America*. New York, Oxford, 2003.

Botta, Charles. *History of the War of the Independence of the United States of America, Vol I & II*. New Haven, CT: Nathan Whiting, 1834.

Bouton, Terry. *Taming Democracy*: *The People, the Founders, and the Troubled Ending of the American Revolution*. New York: Oxford University Press, 2007.

Bowen, Catherine Drinker. *John Adams and the American Revolution*. Boston: Little, Brown & Co., 1950.

Bowler, Arthur. *Logistics and the Failure of the British Army in America, 1775–1783*. Princeton, NJ: Princeton University Press, 1975.

Braisted, Todd W. *Grand Forage 1778*: *The Battleground around New York City*. Yardley, PA: Westholme, 2016.

Bray Robert and Paul Bushnell, eds. *Diary of a Common Soldier in the American Revolution 1775–1783*: *An Annotated Edition of the Military Journal of Jeremiah Greenman*. DeKalb, IL: Northern Illinois University Press, 1978.

Breen, Timothy H. *Tobacco Culture*: *The Mentality of the Great Tidewater Planters on the Eve of the American Revolution*. Princeton, NJ: Princeton University Press, 1985.

Brinton, Crane. *The Anatomy of Revolution*. Prentice-Hall, 1965.

Brown, Robert. *Kings Mountain and Cowpens*: *Our Victory Was Complete*. Gloucestershire, England: The History Press, 2009.

Brumwell, Stephen. *George Washington*: *Gentleman Warrior*. New York: Quercus, 2013.

Buchanan, John. *The Road to Guilford Courthouse*: *The American Revolution in the Carolinas*. New York: John Wiley & Sons, 1997.

Buel, Richard Jr. *In Irons*: *Britain's Naval Supremacy and the American Revolutionary Economy*. New Haven, CT: Yale University Press, 1998.

Buker, George E. *The Penobscot Expedition*: *Commodore Saltonstall and the Massachusetts Conspiracy of 1779*. Camden ME: Down East Books, 2002.

Burgoyne, Bruce E. *Enemy Views*: *The American Revolutionary Was as Recorded by the Hessian Participants*. Bowie, MD: Heritage Books, 1996.

Burnett, Edmund Cody, ed, *Letters of Members of the Continental Congress, Vols. 1-8*. Washington, DC: Carnegie Institution of Washington, 1921.

Burrows, Edwin G. *Forgotten Patriots*: *The Untold Story of American Prisoners during the Revolutionary War*. New York: Basic Books, 2008.

Callahan, North. *Henry Knox*: *General Washington's General*. South Brunswick, NY: A. S. Barnes & Co., 1958.

Calloway, Colin G. *The American Revolution in Indian Country*: *Crisis and Diversity in Native American Communities*. New York: Cambridge University Press, 1995.

Carbone, Gerald M. *Nathanael Greene*: *A Biography of the American Revolution*. New York: Palgrave Macmillan, 2008.

Carp, Benjamin L. *Rebels Rising*: *Cities and the American Revolution*. London: Oxford University Press, 2007.

Carp, E. Wayne. *To Starve the Army at Pleasure*: *Continental Army Administration and American Political Culture 1775–1783*. Chapel Hill, NC: University of North Carolina Press, 1984.

Castronovo, Russ. *Propaganda 1776*: *Secrets, Leaks, and Revolutionary Communications in Early America*. New York: Oxford, 2014.

Chadwick, Bruce. *The First American Army*. Naperville, IL: Sourcebooks, Inc., 2005.

Clary, David A. *Adopted Son*: *Washington, Lafayette, and the Friendship That Saved the Revolution*. New York: Bantam Books, 2007.

Codman, John II. *Arnold's Expedition to Quebec*. New York: Macmillan, 1901.

Cohen, Eliot A. *Conquered into Liberty*. New York: Free Press, 2011.

Commager, Henry Steele and Richard B. Morris, eds. *The Spirit of 'Seventy-Six*: *The Story of the American Revolution as Told by Participants Vols I & II*. New York: Bobbs-Merrill, 1958.

Cunningham, John T. *The Uncertain Revolution*: *Washington and the Continental Army at Morristown*. West Creek, NJ: Cormorant Publishing, 2007.

Cubbison, Douglas R. *Burgoyne and the Saratoga Campaign*: *His Papers*. Norman, OK: University of Oklahoma Press, 2014.

Curtis, Edward E. *The Organization of the British Army in the American Revolution*. New Haven, CT: Yale University Press, 1926.

Darley, Stephen. *The Battle of Valcour Island*. Middletown, DE: Stephen Darley, 2013.

_____. *Voices From a Wilderness Expedition*: *The Journals and Men of Benedict Arnold's Expedition to Quebec in 1775*. Bloomington, IN: Authorhouse, 2011.

Daughan, George C. *If By Sea*: *The Forging of the American Navy—From the Revolution to the War of 1812*. New York: Basic Books, 2008.

_____. *Revolution on the Hudson*: *New York City and the Hudson River Valley in the American War of Independence*. New York: W. W. Norton & Co., 2016.

Davies, K. G., *Documents of the American Revolution*. 12 vols. Shannon, Ireland: Vallentine Mitchell BPP, 1972–81.

Davis, Kenneth C. *A Nation Rising*. New York: HarperCollins, 2010.

Decker, Michael McMillen. "Baron Von Steuben and the Military Forces in Virginia during the British Invasions of 1780-1781" (1979), University of Richmond Scholarship Repository, *Master's Theses*, Paper 431.

Department of Veterans Affairs."America's Wars."

De Koven, Mrs. Reginald. *The Life and Letters of John Paul Jones, Vols I & II*. Now York: Charles Scribner's Sons, 1913.

Desjardin, Thomas A. *Through a Howling Wilderness*: *Benedict Arnold's March to Quebec 1775*. New York: St. Martin's Press, 2006.

Dorson, Richard M., ed. *American Rebels*: *Personal Narratives of the American Revolution*. New York: Pantheon Books, 1953.

Dupuy, R. Ernest and Trevor N. Dupuy, *Military Heritage of America*. New York: McGraw-Hill Book Co., 1956.

Eckert, Allan W.,*That Dark and Bloody River*: *Chronicles of the Ohio River Valley*. New York: Bantam Books, 1995.

Ellis, Joseph J. *Founding Brothers*: *The Revolutionary Generation*. New York: Vintage Books, 2000.

_____. *Revolutionary Summer*: *The Birth of American Independence*. New York. Random House, 2013.

English, William Hayden. *Conquest of the Country Northwest of the River Ohio 1778–1783 and Life of Gen. George Rogers Clark, Vols I & II*. Indianapolis, IN: Bowen-Merrill Co., 1896.

Everett, Edward, *The Life of George Washington*. New York: Sheldon and Company, 1860.

Faragher, John Mack. *Daniel Boone*: *The Life and Legend of an American Pioneer*. New York: Henry Holt & Co., 1992.

Ferling, John. *A Leap In The Dark*: *The Struggle to Create the American Republic*. New York: Oxford University Press, 2003.

_____. *Almost a Miracle*: *The American Victory in the War of Independence*. New York: Oxford University Press, 2009.

_____. *Independence*: *The Struggle to Set America Free*. New York: Bloomsbury Press, 2011.

_____. *John Adams*: *A Life*. New York: Oxford University Press, 1992.

_____. *The First of Men*: *A Life of George Washington*. New York: University of Tennessee Press, 1988.

_____. *Whirlwind*: *The American Revolution and the War That Won It*. New York: Bloomsbury Press, 2015.

Fischer, David Hackett. *Paul Revere's Ride*. New York, Oxford, 1994.

———. *Washington's Crossing*. New York: Oxford University, 2006.

Fisher, Elijah. *Elijah Fisher's Journal 1775 to 1784*. Augusta, ME: Badger and Manley, 1880.

Fitzpatrick, John C., ed. *The Diaries of George Washington 1748–1799, 4 Vols*. New York: Houghton Mifflin, 1925.

———. *The Writings of Washington from the Original Manuscript Sources, 1745–1799, 39 Vols,*. Washington, DC: US Government Printing Office, 1931–1944.

Flexner, Thomas James, *Washington*: *The Indispensable Man*. New York: Mentor, 1974.

Flood, Charles Bracelen. *Rise, and Fight Again*: *Perilous Times along the Road to Independence*. New York: Dodd, Mead & Co., 1976.

Forbes Esther. *Paul Revere & the World He Lived In*. Cambridge, MA: Riverside Press, 194).

Ford, Worthington C. et al., eds. *The Journals of the Continental Congress, 1774–1789*. 34 vols. Washington, DC: Library of Congress, 1904–37.

Forman, Samuel A. *Dr. Joseph Warren*: *The Boston Tea Party, Bunker Hill, and the Birth of American Liberty*. Gretna, LA: Pelican Publishing, 2012.

Fowler, William M. Jr. *Rebels Under Sail*: *The American Navy during the Revolution*. New York: Charles Scribner's Sons, 1976.

Freeman, Douglas Southall. *George Washington A Biography, 7 Vols*. New York: Charles Scribner's Sons, 1948–57.

Frothingham, Richard. *The Rise of the Republic of the United States*. Boston: Little, Brown & Co., 1872.

Gallagher, John J. *The Battle of Brooklyn, 1776*. Edison, NJ: Castle Books, 2002.

Galloway, Colin G. *The American Revolution in Indian Country*. New York: Cambridge University Press, 1995.

Galvin, John R. *Three Men of Boston*. New York: Thomas Crowell, 1967).

Gingrich, Newt and William B. Forstchen. *Valley Forge*: *George Washington and the Crucible of Victory.* New York: St. Martin's, 2011.

Gipson, Lawrence Henry. *The British Empire before the American Revolution, 14 Vols.* New York: Alfred A. Knopf, 1958–68.

_____. *The Coming of the Revolution 1763–1775.* New York: Harper & Row, 1954.

Glickstein, Don, *After Yorktown*: *The Final Struggle for American Independence.* Yardley, PA: Westholme, 2015.

Godfrey, Carlos E. *The Commander-In-Chief's Guard, Revolutionary War.* Baltimore, MD: Genealogical Publishing, 1972 (reprint of 1904 edition).

Gragg, Rod. *By the Hand of Providence.* New York: Howard Books, 2011.

Greene, George Washington. *Historical View of The American Revolution.* Port Washington, NY: Kennikat Press, 1970 (reprint of 1865 edition).

Gross, Robert A. *The Minutemen and Their World.* New York: Hill & Wang, 1976.

Gruber, Ira D. *The Howe Brothers and the American Revolution.* Boston: W. W. Norton, 1975.

Hammond, George P. *New Spain and the Anglo-American West Historical*: *Contributions Presented to Herbert Eugene Bolton.* Unknown: Privately Printed, 1932.

Harris, Michael C. *Brandywine*: *A Military History of the Battle That Lost Philadelphia but Saved America, September 11, 1777.* El Dorado Hills, CA: Savas Beatie, 2014.

Harvey, Robert. *A Few Bloody Noses*: *The Realities and Mythologies of the American Revolution.* Woodstock, NY: The Overlook, 2001.

Hattendorf, John B., ed. *The Oxford Encyclopedia of Maritime History, 4 Vols.* New York: Oxford University Press, 2007.

Heitman, Frances B. *Historical Register of Officers of the Continental Army during the War of the Revolution: April, 1775, to December, 1783 Revised Ed.* Washington, DC: Rare Book Shop Publishing, 1914.

Henderson, Donald. *Smallpox: The Death of a Disease*. Amherst, NY: Prometheus, 2009.

Henriques, Peter R. *Realistic Visionary: A Portrait of George Washington* (Charlottesville, VA: University of Virginia Press, 2006.

Henry, John Joseph, *Account of Arnold's Campaign Against Quebec, and the Hardships and Sufferings of that Band of Heroes Who Traversed the Wilderness of Maine from Cambridge to the St. Lawrence in the Autumn of 1775*. Albany, NY: Joel Munsell, 1877.

Hibbert, Christopher. *Redcoats and Rebels: The American Revolution through British Eyes*. New York: Avon Books, 1991.

Horry, Colonel Peter. *The Life of Francis Marion the Most Celebrated Partisan Officer in the Revolutionary War, Against the British and Tories, in South Carolina and Georgia*. New York: P. M. Davis, 1835.

Howe, Archibald. *Colonel John Brown, of Pittsfield, Massachusetts, the Brave Accuser of Benedict Arnold*. Boston: W. B. Clark, 1908.

Hutson, James H. and Jaroslav Pelikan. *Religion and the Founding of the American Republic*. Washington, DC: Library of Congress, 1998.

Jefferson, Thomas, *The Life and Morals of Jesus of Nazareth Extracted Textually from the Gospels in Greek, Latin, French & English*. Reprint edition. Washington, DC: Smithsonian Books, 2011.

Johnson, William J., *George Washington the Christian*. Milford, MI: Mott Media, 1976.

Johnston, Henry P., *The Battle of Harlem Heights, September 16, 1776 with a Review of the Events of the Campaign*. London: The Macmillan Company, 1897.

_____. *The Yorktown Campaign and the Surrender of Cornwallis, 1781*. New York: Harper & Brothers, 1881.

Kennedy, Francis H., ed. *The American Revolution: A Historical Guidebook*. New York: Oxford University Press, 2014.

Ketchum, Richard M. *Decisive Day*: *The Battle of Bunker Hill*. Garden City, NY: Doubleday & Co., 1974.

_____. Ketchum, Richard M. *Victory at Yorktown*: *The Campaign that Won the Revolution*. New York: Henry Holt, 2004.

Kilmeade, Brian and Don Yaeger. *George Washington's Secret Six*: *The Spy Ring That Saved the American Revolution*. New York: Sentinel, 2013.

Langguth A. J. *Patriots*: *The Men Who Started the American Revolution*. New York: Simon & Schuster, 1988.

Leake, Isaac Q. *Memoir of the Life and Times of General John Lamb*: *An Officer of the Revolution, Who Commanded the Post at West Point at the Time of Arnold's Defection*. Albany, NY: Joel Munsell, 1850.

Lear, Mrs. Tobias. *Letters and Recollections of George Washington*. Garden City, NY: Doubleday, Doran & Co., 1932.

Leckie, Robert. *George Washington's War:The Saga of the American Revolution*. New York: HarperCollins, 1992.

Lecky, William E. Hartpole and James A. Woodburn. *The American Revolution, 1763–1783*: *Being the Chapters and Passages Relating to America from the Authors' History Of England in the 18th Century*. New York: D. Appleton & Co., 1898.

Lee, Henry. *Memoirs of the War in the Southern Department of the United States*. New York: University Publishing Co., 1869.

Lefkowitz, Arthur S. *Benedict Arnold in the Company of Heroes*. El Dorado Hills, CA: Savas Beatie, 2012.

_____. *Benedict Arnold's Army*: *The 1775 American Invasion of Canada during the Revolutionary War*. El Dorado Hills, CA: Savas Beatie, 2008.

_____. *George Washington's Indispensable Men*: *The 32 Aides-de-Camp Who Helped Win American Independence*. Mechanicsburg, PA: Stackpole, 2003.

_____. *The Long Retreat*: *The Calamitous American Defense of New Jersey, 1776*. New Brunswick, NJ: Rutgers University Press, 1998.

Lesser, Charles H. ed. *The Sinews of Independence: Monthly Strength Reports of the Continental Army.* Chicago: University of Chicago Press, 1976.

Lilleback, Peter A. *George Washington's Sacred Fire.* Bryn Mawr, PA: Providence Forum Press, 2006.

Lincoln, Charles H. *The Revolutionary Movement in Pennsylvania 1760–1776.* Philadelphia, PA: University of Pennsylvania Press, 1901.

Lipscomb, Andrew A. and Albert Ellery Bergh, eds. *The Writing of Thomas Jefferson, Monticello Ed., 20 Vols.* Washington DC: The Thomas Jefferson Memorial Association, 1904.

Lockhart, Paul. *The Drillmaster of Valley Forge: The Baron de Steuben and the Making of the American Army.* New York: HarperCollins, 2008.

Lunt, James *John Burgoyne of Saratoga.* New York: Harcourt Brace Jovanovich, 1975.

Luzader, John F. *Saratoga: A Military History of the Decisive Campaign of the American Revolution.* El Dorado Hills, CA: Savas Beatie, 2008.

Mahan, A. T. *The Influence of Sea Power Upon History, 1660–1783.* 12th Ed. Boston: Little, Brown & Co., 1918.

Maier, Pauline. *American Scripture: Making the Declaration of Independence.* New York: Vintage, 1998.

Marshall, John. *The Life of George Washington, 2nd Edition, 2 Vols.* Philadelphia: James Crissy, 1832.

Marshall, William. *Ulster Sails West.* Baltimore: Genealogical Publishing, 1979.

Marson, Philip. *Yankee Voices.* Cambridge, MA: Schenkman Publishing Co., 1967.

Martin, James Kirby and Mark Edward Lender. *"A Respectable Army": The Military Origins of the Republic, 1763–1789.* New York: John Wiley & Sons, 2015.

Martin, Joseph Plumb. *A Narrative of a Revolutionary Soldier*. New York, Signet Classic, 2001.

McClelland, Peter. "The New Economic History and the Burdens of the Navigation Acts: A Comment," *Economic History Review* 26 (1973), 679–86.

McConkey, Rebecca. *The Hero of Cowpens: A Revolutionary Sketch*. New York: Funk & Wagnalls, 188).

McCullough, David, *1776*. New York: Simon & Schuster, 2005.

McGuire, Thomas J. *Battle of Paoli*. Mechanicsburg, PA: Stackpole, 2000.

_____. *The Philadelphia Campaign, Vols I & II*. Mechanicsburg, PA: Stackpole, 2006, 2007.

Meacham, Jon. *American Gospel: God, the Founding Fathers, and the Making of a Nation*. New York: Random House, 2006.

Middlekauf, Robert. *The Glorious Cause: The American Revolution, 1763–1789*. New York, Oxford University Press, 1982.

Millar, A. *A Plan for Establishing and Disciplining a National Militia in Great Britain, Ireland, and in all the British Dominions of America*. London: A. Millar, 1745. New edition contains *Washington's Lost Plan Revived: National Guard Today the Proposal of 150 Years Ago*, by General Roy D. Keehn, written 1935.

Miller, John C. *Origins of the American Revolution,*. Boston: Little, Brown and Company, 1943.

Mintz, Max M. *The Generals of Saratoga*. Yale University Press, 1990.

Moore, George H. *The Treason of Charles Lee, Major General Second in Command in the American Army of the Revolution*. New York: Charles Scribner, 1860.

Morison, Samuel Eliot. *John Paul Jones: A Sailor's Biography*. Boston: Little, Brown & Co. 1959.

Morrill, Dan L. *Southern Campaigns of the American Revolution*. Baltimore, MD: Nautical & Aviation Publishing, 1993.

Moultrie William. *Memoirs of the American Revolution So Far as it Related to the States of North and South Carolina, and Georgia, Vols 1 & 2*. New York: David Longsworth, 1802.

Mowday, Bruce E, *September 11, 1777*: *Washington's Defeat at Brandywine Dooms Philadelphia*. Shippensburg, PA: White Mane, 2002.

Namier, Lewis. *England in the Age of the American Revolution*. London: Palgrave, 1961.

Nash, Gilbert. *The Original Journal of General Solomon Lovell Kept During the Penobscot Expedition 1779, with a Sketch of his Life*. Weymouth, MA: Weymouth Historical Society, 188).

North, Douglas. *Growth and Welfare in the American Past*. Upper Saddle River, New Jersey. Prentice-Hall, 1974.

Norton, Mary Beth. *Liberty's Daughters*: *The Revolutionary Experience of American Women*: *1750–1800*. Ithaca, NY: Cornell University Press, 1996.

Novak, Michael and Jana Novak, *Washington's God*: *Religion, Liberty, and the Father of Our Country*. New York: Basic Books, 2006.

Oller, John. *The Swamp Fox*: *How Francis Marion Saved the American Revolution*. Boston: Da Capo Press, 2016.

Perkins, James Breck. *France in the American Revolution*. New York, Houghton Mifflin, 1911.

Peterson, John. "Class Struggle and the American Revolution," https://www.marxist.com/class-struggle-and-the-american-revolution.htm.

Philbrick, Nathanael. *Bunker Hill*: *A City, a Siege, a Revolution*. New York: Penguin, 2014.

_____. *Valiant Ambition*: *George Washington, Benedict Arnold, and the Fate of the American Revolution*. New York: Viking, 2016.

Phillips, Kevin. *1775*: *A Good Year for Revolution*. New York: Viking, 2012.

_____. *The Cousins' Wars*. New York: Basis Books, 1999.

Preston, John Hyde, *Revolution 1776*. New York: Harcourt, Brace & Co., 1933.

"Q&A: Douglas Cubbis on on British General Burgoyne," in The New York History Blog: Historical News and Views from the Empire State, June 27, 2012.

Raab, James W., *Spain, Britain and the American Revolution in Florida, 1763–1783*. Jefferson, NC: McFarland & Co., 2008.

Raphael, Raphael. *A People's History of the American Revolution*: *How the Common People Shaped the Fight for Independence*. New York: Harper Perennial, 2002.

Randall, Willard Sterne. *Ethan Allen*: *His life and Times*. New York: W. W. Norton, 2011.

_____. *Benedict Arnold*: *Patriot and Traitor*. New York: William Morrow & Co., 1990.

Rankin, Hugh F., *Narratives of the American Revolution*. Chicago, IL: R. R. Donnelley & Sons, 1976.

_____. *North Carolina in the American Revolution*. Raleigh, NC: North Carolina Division of Archives and History, 1996.

Raphael, Ray. *A People's History of the American Revolution*: *How the Common People Shaped the Fight for Independence*. New York: Harper Perennial, 2002.

_____. *Founders*: *The People Who Brought You a Nation*. New York: The New Press, 2009.

Richards, Dave. *Swords in Their Hands*: *George Washington and the Newburgh Conspiracy*. Candler, NC: Pisgah Press, 2014.

Richards, Jeffery H. *Mercy Otis Warren*. New York: Twayne Publishers, 1995.

_____. and Sharon M. Harris, eds. *Mercy Otis Warren*: *Selected Letters*. Athens, GA: University of Georgia Press, 2009.

Richards, Leonard L. *Shays's Rebellion*: *The American Revolution's Final Battle*. University of Pennsylvania Press, 2002.

Ridpath, John Clark, *James Otis*: *The Pre-Revolutionist*. Chicago: Union School Furnishing Company, 1898.

Riordan, Liam. *Many Identities, One Nation*. Philadelphia, PA: University of Pennsylvania Press, 2007.

Ritz, Wilfred J. "The Authentication of the Engrossed Declaration of Independence on July 4, 1776," *Law and History Review* 4:1 (April 1986), 179–204.

Roberts, Kenneth. *March to Quebec*: *Journals of the Members of Arnold's Expedition*. Garden City, NY: Doubleday & Co., 1946.

Rose, Alexander. *Washington's Spies*: *The Story of America's First Spy Ring*. New York: Random House, 2006.

Russell, David Lee. *Victory on Sullivan's Island*: *The British Cape Fear/ Charles Town Expedition of 1776*. Haverford, PA: Infinity Publishing, 2002.

Sanders, Jennings B. *The Presidency of the Continental Congress 1774–89*: *A Study in American Institutional History*. Gloucester, MA: Peter Smith, 1971.

Schecter, Barnet. *The Battle for New York*. New York: Penguin, 2002.

Scheer, George F. and Hugh F. Rankin. *Rebels & Redcoats*. New York: World Publishing, 1957.

Schenck, David– *North Carolina 1780–'81*: *Being a History of the Invasion of the Carolinas by the British Army Under Lord Cornwallis in 1780–'81*. Raleigh, NC: Edwards & Broughton, Publishers, 1889.

Schoenbrun, David. *Triumph in Paris*: *The Exploits of Benjamin Franklin*. New York: Harper & Row, 1976.

Schweikart, Larry. *America's Victories*: *Why the U.S. Wins Wars and Will Win the War on Terror*. Point Pleasant, NJ, 2015.

_____. *What Would The Founders Say?* New York: Sentinel, 2011.

Schweikart, Larry and Michael Allen. *A Patriot's History of the United States*: *From Columbus's Great Discovery to America's Age of Entitlement, 10th Anniversary Edition*. New York, Sentinel, 2014.

Schweikart, Larry and Dave Dougherty. *A Patriot's History of the Modern World, vol. 1, From America's Exceptional Ascent to the Atomic Bomb, 1898-1945*. New York: Sentinel, 2012.

_____. *A Patriot's History of the Modern World, vol. 2, From the Cold War to the Age of Entitlement, 1945–2012*. New York, Sentinel, 2013.

Schweikart, Larry, Dave Dougherty, and Michael Allen. *The Patriot's History Reader*. New York: Sentinel, 2011.

Schweikart, Larry, and Lynne Pierson Doti. American Entrepeneur. New York: AMACOM, 2009.

Scot, Kenneth. *Countefeiting in Colonial America*. Philadelphia: University of Pennsylvania Press, 2000, 259–60.

Searcy, Martha Condray. *The Georgia-Florida Contest in the American Revolution, 1776-1778*. University, AL: University of Alabama Press, 1985.

Shea, John Gilmary. *Life and Times of the Most Rev. John Carroll, Bishop and First Archbishop of Baltimore: Embracing the History of the Catholic Church in the United States, 1763-1815*. New York, Edward Jenkins' Sons, 1888.

Shy, John, *A People Numerous and Armed: Reflections on the Military Struggle for American Independence, Revised Ed*. Ann Arbor, MI: University of Michigan Press, 1990.

Simms, William Gilmore. *The Life of Francis Marion: The True Story of South Carolina's Swamp Fox*. New York: Henry Langley, 1844.

Slaughter, Thomas P. *The Whiskey Rebellion: Frontier Epilogue to the American Revolution*. New York: Oxford University Press, 1986.

Smith, Justin H. *Arnold's March from Cambridge to Quebec*. New York: G. P. Putnam's Sons, 1903.

_____. *Our Struggle for the Fourteenth Colony: Canada and the American Revolution Vols I & II*. New York: G. P. Putnam's Sons, 1907.

Smith, Page. *John Adams, Vols I & II*. Garden City, NY: Doubleday & Co., 1962.

Smith, Paul H. et al., eds. *Letters of Delegates to Congress, 1774–1789*. 29 vols. Washington, DC: Library of Congress, 1976–2000.

Snowden, Richard. *The American Revolution*. Canton, OH: Smith and Mardle, 1815.

Sparks, Jared, ed. *The Writings of George Washington*; *Being his Correspondence, Addresses, Messages, and Other Papers, Official and Private, Selected and Published from the Original Manuscripts*; *With a Life of the Author, Notes and Illustrations, Vols 1-12,*. Boston: Various publishers, 1833–1838.

Stephenson, Michael. *Patriot Battles*: *How the Way for Independence Was Fought*. New York: HarperCollins, 2007.

Stoll, Ira. *Samuel Adam: A Life*. New York: Free Press, 2008.

Stryker, William S. and William Starr Meyers. *The Battle of Monmouth*. Princeton, NJ: Princeton University Press, 1927.

Steuben, Baron Frederick Wilhelm de. *Regulations for the Order and Discipline of the Troops of the United States to Which is Added, an Appendix, Containing the United States Militia Act, passed by Congress May, 1781*. Boston: Thomas & Andrews, 1794.

Sullivan, Edward Dean. *Benedict Arnold*: *Military Racketeer*. New York: Vanguard Press, 1932.

Syfert, Scott. *The First American Declaration of Independence? The Disputed History of the Mecklenburg Declaration of May 20, 1775*. Jefferson, NC: MacFarland & Co., 2014.

Taylor, Robert J. et al., eds. *Papers of John Adams*. 16 vols to date. Cambridge, MA: Harvard University Press, 1977.

Thomas, Peter D. G. *Tea Party to Independence*: *The Third Phase of the American Revolution, 1773–1776*. Oxford, England: Oxford University Press, 1991.

Thomas, Robert. "A Quantitative Approach to the Study of the Effects of British Imperial Policy of Colonial Welfare: Some Preliminary Findings," *The Journal of Economic History* 25 (1964): 615–638.

Thornton, John Wingate. *The Pulpit of the American Revolution, or the Political Sermons of the Period of 1776, with a Historical Introduction, Notes, and Illustrations.* Boston: D. Lothrop & Co., 1876.

Tower, Charlemagne Jr. *The Marquis de La Fayette in the American Revolution with Some Account of the Attitude of France toward the War of Independence Vols I & II.* Philadelphia, PA: J. B. Lippincott Co., 1895.

Trevelyan, Sir George Otto. *The American Revolution.* New York: David McKay Company, 1964.

Truxes, Thomas M. *Defying Empire: Trading with the Enemy in Colonial New York.* New Haven, CT: Yale University Press, 2008.

Tucker Glenn. *Mad Anthony Wayne and the New Nation.* Harrisburg, PA: Stackpole, 1973.

Van Doren, Carl. *Mutiny in January.* New York: Viking Press, 1943.

_____. *Secret History of the American Revolution: An Account of the Conspiracies of Benedict Arnold and Numerous Others, Drawn from the Secret Service Papers of the British Headquarters in North America.* New York: Viking Press, 1941.

Ward, Harry M., *George Washington's Enforcers: Policing the Continental Army.* Carbondale, IL: Southern Illinois University Press, 2006.

Warren, Mrs. Mercy Otis. *History of the Rise, Progress and Termination of the American Revolution Interspersed with Biographical, Political and Moral Observations 3 Vols.* Boston: Manning & Loring, 1805.

Weintraub, Stanley. *Iron Tears: America's Battle for Freedom, Britain's Quagmire: 1775–1783.* New York: Free Press, 2005.

Wellenreuther, Hermann, ed. *The Revolution of the People: Thoughts and Documents on the Revolutionary Process in North America 1774–1776.* Göttingen, Germany: Universitätsverlag Göttingen, 2006.

Williams, Gomer, *History of the Liverpool Privateers and Letters of Marque 1722–1812*. London: Liverpool University Press, 2004.

Willis, Sam. *The Struggle for Sea Power*: *A Naval History of the American Revolution*. Boston: W. W. Norton, 2016.

Wilson, William E. *Big Knife*: *The Story of George Rogers Clark*. New York: Farrar & Rinehart, 1940.

Wood, Gordon S. *The Radicalism of the American Revolution*. New York: Alfred A. Knopf, 1992.

Wright, Robert K. Jr. *The Continental Army*. Washington, DC: Center of Military History United States Army, 1983.

Zagarri, Rosemarie. *A Woman's Dilemma*: *Mercy Otis Warren and the American Revolution*. Wheeling, IL: Harland Davidson, 1995.

Zinn, Howard. *A People's History of the United States*. New York: Harper Perennial, 2015.

Index

Index

NB

Wilmot, William, 266
Winnsboro, SC, 229–30, 248, 252
Woodhull, Abraham (Samuel Culper Sr.),
   125, 176
Wooster, David, 111–12, 115
Wright, Robert K., 80
writs of assistance, 35
Wyoming Valley, PA, 204

Y
"Yankee Doodle Dandy," 247, 257
Yeardley, George, 16
Yorktown, VA, 7–8, 12, 63, 188–89, 194,
   242, 254–56, 258, 261–62, 264, 273

Z
Zinn, Howard, 1